W9-APW-233

True Enough

Learning to Live in a Post-Fact Society

FARHAD MANJOO

WILEY

John Wiley & Sons, Inc.

Copyright © 2008 by Farhad Manjoo. All rights reserved

Published by John Wiley & Sons, Inc., Hoboken, New Jersey
Published simultaneously in Canada

No part of this publication may be reproduced, stored in a retrieval system, or transmitted in any form or by any means, electronic, mechanical, photocopying, recording, scanning, or otherwise, except as permitted under Section 107 or 108 of the 1976 United States Copyright Act, without either the prior written permission of the Publisher, or authorization through payment of the appropriate per-copy fee to the Copyright Clearance Center, 222 Rosewood Drive, Danvers, MA 01923, (978) 750-8400, fax (978) 646-8600, or on the web at www.copyright.com. Requests to the Publisher for permission should be addressed to the Permissions Department, John Wiley & Sons, Inc., 111 River Street, Hoboken, NJ 07030, (201) 748-6011, fax (201) 748-6008, or online at http://www.wiley.com/go/permissions.

Limit of Liability/Disclaimer of Warranty: While the publisher and the author have used their best efforts in preparing this book, they make no representations or warranties with respect to the accuracy or completeness of the contents of this book and specifically disclaim any implied warranties of merchantability or fitness for a particular purpose. No warranty may be created or extended by sales representatives or written sales materials. The advice and strategies contained herein may not be suitable for your situation. You should consult with a professional where appropriate. Neither the publisher nor the author shall be liable for any loss of profit or any other commercial damages, including but not limited to special, incidental, consequential, or other damages.

For general information about our other products and services, please contact our Customer Care Department within the United States at (800) 762-2974, outside the United States at (317) 572-3993, or fax (317) 572-4002.

Wiley also publishes its books in a variety of electronic formats. Some content that appears in print may not be available in electronic books. For more information about Wiley products, visit our web site at www.wiley.com.

Library of Congress Cataloging-in-Publication Data:

Manjoo, Farhad, date.
    True enough : learning to live in a post-fact society / Farhad Manjoo.
        p.   cm.
    Includes index.
    ISBN 978-0-470-05010-1 (cloth)
    1.   Truthfulness and falsehood—United States. 2.   Deception—United States.
3.   Communication in politics—United States.   I. Title.
    BJ1421.M299 2008
    177′.3—dc22

                                                                2007044573

Printed in the United States of America

10 9 8 7 6 5 4 3 2 1

To Mom and Dad

Contents

INTRODUCTION

Why Facts No Longer Matter

This book dances upon a paradox: at the same time that technology and globalization has pushed the world together, it is driving our minds apart. From above, the three hundred million citizens of the United States look like clones, or *Matrix*-like drones, each of us plugged snugly into a common consumerist grid. A single corporation, Wal-Mart, serves 90 percent of the American population. A ubiquitous national brand of coffee keeps us buzzing. Happy-looking strip malls of similar architecture dot our suburbs, our cities growing nearly indistinguishable from one another. Parachute into suburban Atlanta and you'll find yourself looking for the freeways you remember from Los Angeles or Houston or Phoenix.

Yet for all our shared shopping experiences, we are not morphing into a common people—not as a nation and not as a planet. *True Enough* chronicles a society's splintering. I am not describing the oversimplified cable-news trope of the red-blue electoral divide. What I address is more drastic, and more acute. The story has its roots in the digital revolution, which has given us more information, and more power over that information, than seems believable. On the Web, television, radio, and all manner of new devices, today you can watch, listen to, and read what you want, whenever you want; seek out and discuss, in exhaustive and insular detail, the kind of news that pleases you; and indulge your political, social, or scientific theories, whether sophisticated or naive, extremist or banal, grounded in reality or so far out you're floating in an asteroid belt, among people who feel exactly the same way.

In the last few years, pollsters and political researchers have begun to document a fundamental shift in the way Americans are thinking about the news. No longer are we merely holding opinions different from one another; we're also holding different facts. Increasingly, our arguments aren't over what we *should* be doing—in the Iraq War, in the war on terrorism, on global warming, or about any number of controversial subjects—but, instead, over what *is happening*. Political scientists have characterized our epoch as one of heightened polarization; now, as I'll document, the creeping partisanship has begun to distort our very perceptions about what is "real" and what isn't. Indeed, you can go so far as to say we're now fighting over competing versions of reality. And it is more convenient than ever before for some of us to live in a world built out of our own facts.

Late in April 2005, Eliza Jane Scovill, a three-and-a-half-year-old girl who lived with her parents in the Los Angeles suburb of Van Nuys, came down with the sniffles. Within a few days, her breathing became shallow and she developed a phlegmy cough. Her mother, Christine Maggiore, took the girl to a pediatrician, who found nothing serious and prescribed no medication. The next week, Maggiore asked a second pediatrician to examine Eliza Jane. He suspected an ear infection but felt it would clear up without antibiotics. Soon Eliza Jane's cough subsided, but when Maggiore sought the advice of a third doctor, he found fluid in the girl's right eardrum, and, also suspecting an ear infection, prescribed a simple antibiotic, amoxicillin. On Sunday, May 15, Eliza Jane grew pale, her fever shot up to 101 degrees, and she vomited several times. Late that night, Maggiore called a doctor. While she was on the phone, Eliza Jane suddenly collapsed. She stopped breathing. Maggiore would later tell the county coroner that her daughter had "crumpled like a paper doll."

The doctors who examined Eliza Jane in the days before she died had proceeded as if she were a normal little girl. In fact, they all should have suspected that she might be ill with something far more grave than a pediatric ear infection. In 1992, Eliza Jane's mother had tested positive for HIV. In the years since her diagnosis, Maggiore, unlike most HIV patients, had declined the antiretroviral medications that have been hailed for staving off death from AIDS. Instead, Maggiore had come to accept the unconventional views of a set of activists who argue that HIV does not cause AIDS. Indeed, during the 1990s, Maggiore became one of the nation's leading proponents of this idea. She founded Alive & Well AIDS Alternatives, a nonprofit organization devoted to questioning the "validity of most common assumptions about HIV and AIDS," and has attracted enormous attention. The rock band the Foo Fighters once held a benefit concert for Maggiore's group. Her self-published book, *What If Everything You Thought You Knew About AIDS Was Wrong?* has sold 50,000 copies.

Maggiore advises HIV-positive pregnant women to avoid taking drugs that doctors say reduce the risk of transmitting the virus to a developing fetus. She is also a proponent of breast-feeding, which researchers have found is a major vehicle of transmission of the virus from an infected mother to her child. Maggiore breastfed both her children—Charles, who was born in 1997, and Eliza, born in 2001, both of whom Maggiore conceived naturally with her husband, Robin Scovill, a filmmaker who shares her beliefs about AIDS. Neither child was tested for HIV, and Maggiore maintains that Eliza Jane was killed by an acute allergic reaction to the amoxicillin she began taking the day before she died. AIDS, that is, was not a factor. "I am a devastated, broken, grieving mother," she told one reporter, "but I am not second-guessing or questioning my understanding of the issue."

Two days after Eliza Jane died, a medical examiner at the Los Angeles County coroner's office performed an autopsy on the girl's body. Eliza Jane was just under 3 feet tall and weighed 29 pounds, underweight and short for her age. Her thymus gland was markedly atrophied, a suggestion of HIV infection; the suggestion was confirmed by a neuropathologist, who saw protein markers of the virus while examining cells from Eliza Jane's brain. White patches were found on the lobes of each of her lungs. When the lung tissue was examined under a microscope, doctors saw an opportunistic fungal infection known as *Pneumocystis carinii pneumonia*. PCP is a leading cause of death in patients with advanced HIV. The medical examiner concluded that Eliza Jane Scovill had died of AIDS.

The death of a little girl in Los Angeles may not look immediately germane to the thesis of this book: that the limitless choice we now enjoy over the information we get about our world has loosened our grip on what is—and isn't—true. But consider this: according to AIDS specialists, Eliza Jane Scovill's condition was highly treatable. Thanks to antiretroviral medication and aggressive therapies for infections, middle-class toddlers in postmillennial America simply do not die any longer of AIDS. What killed Eliza Jane, then, was not only a disease but more precisely the lack of notice and care for a disease—a denial, even, that her condition existed. What killed her was disregard for scientific fact. It was the certainty with which her parents jettisoned the views of experts in favor of another idea, their own idea, far removed from observable reality. It was a willingness to trade in what was true for what was merely true enough.

The "controversy" over HIV's role in AIDS will seem, to most readers, no controversy at all—those who espouse such ideas can look as loony as folks who wonder whether Americans really did land on the moon. But we are all just a mouse and a modem away from a world that sees the disease very differently. HIV doubts, on the Web, carry the vestments of science—there are AIDS-questioning journals that ape traditional academic publications, apparently well-credentialed experts who say they're actively researching the disease, and reports of legitimate-sounding successful experiments becoming novel treatments. Denial reaches beyond the Web, too. Anti-AIDS activists routinely cross the globe to give lectures and hold symposia, and several have published books pushing their ideas. In the spring of 2006, Harper's magazine published a lengthy article by Celia Farber, a journalist who has long been skeptical of the HIV thesis, in which she put forward Peter Duesberg's claims on the disease.

In 2004, researchers at the Centers for Disease Control staked out gay pride events in Baltimore, Detroit, Oakland, and San Francisco. They asked more than a thousand men their thoughts about AIDS and HIV. What did the men believe was the cause of AIDS? How dangerous did they think the disease was? What the researchers found is almost hard to stomach:

Among minorities, conspiracy beliefs were ascendant. More than half of the African American men surveyed did not believe HIV causes AIDS. Forty-eight percent of the Hispanic men and more than a quarter of the white men also questioned the link. Another survey conducted that year by the RAND Corporation and researchers at Oregon State University found that black men who espoused such theories were far less likely than people who did subscribe to the HIV theory to regularly use condoms.

The high rates of denial point to what's so remarkable about how HIV skepticism has spread through the culture. Though AIDS doubters rarely break through to the mainstream, and though their ideas are dismissed by established scientists, they have created a lasting underground culture. Think of it as a parallel universe of fact: a place at once a part of the mainland but profoundly distant from it, a place where another truth—a truth pocked with holes, but one just *true enough* to do damage—hold sway. It's a place where a lot of people are taking up residence.

Some important points before we begin: books about lies dominate the shelves, but this one is very different. Although I will discuss some of the most controversial news stories of our time, this is not a partisan endeavor. In the following chapters, I'll cover deception by groups on the right—the Swift Boat Veterans for Truth, for instance—as well as those on the left, such as the folks who claim that Republicans rigged the 2004 presidential election. I'll also dig into examples that don't fit neatly into either dominant ideology—the people who believe the government carried out the September 11 attacks, the memoirists who stretch the truth, and the adherents of Lou Dobbs, the fire-breathing anti-immigrant populist CNN anchor.

But this story is less about ideology than it is about psychology, economics, and technology. It is a story about a media *system* rather than any particular players in that system. The system is us. To understand why America is splitting into niches, I will look at how humans process information in the face of many choices; how we interpret documentary proof in a world now glutted with videos, photos, and audio recordings; how we decide whom to believe in an era in which "experts" of unknown quality dominate every news discussion; and how news media outlets react to all these changes, how they're driven to pander to our preconceived ideas about society. I've tried to answer a key question: How can so many people who live in the same place see the world so differently?

1

"Reality" Is Splitting

I n April 2004, a dozen men traveled from cities across the country to attend a clandestine meeting in a quaint, tucked-away corner of Dallas. The men were in their late fifties and early sixties, and they had about them a similar look: weathered yet tough. For more than thirty years, they had led divergent lives, but they were here to revisit their shared past—the crucible of Vietnam. John Kerry, the Massachusetts senator and decorated Vietnam veteran, had recently emerged as leader in the contest for the Democratic Party's presidential nomination. Like Kerry, the men in Dallas had once served on navy Swift boats, the shallow-water craft used in dangerous counterinsurgency missions around the Mekong Delta, in southeastern Vietnam, between 1968 and 1970. These men couldn't stand the thought of their fellow vet becoming president. When they considered the manner in which Kerry, as a young man, had protested the war, words like *traitor* and *criminal* came to mind. Now they hatched an audacious plan to undo Kerry's reputation as a hero. Here's the amazing thing: it worked.

The men gathered in a grand two-story mansion that functions as the headquarters of Spaeth Communications, a public relations firm founded by a brilliant PR expert named Merrie Spaeth. Spaeth had agreed to host the meeting at the request of her old friend John O'Neill, the Swift boat veteran who rose to prominence in 1971, when he and Kerry debated the war in an appearance on *The Dick Cavett Show*. O'Neill and the others who'd assembled here all agreed on one thing about Kerry: he was "unfit for command," a phrase they would later fashion into a slogan for their campaign. But now, as they planned their effort, there emerged among the men a disagreement concerning the fundamental nature and scope of Kerry's Vietnam-era sins.

In 1971, shortly after Kerry returned from Vietnam, he declared his opposition to the war in an unforgettable speech to the Senate Foreign Relations Committee. For decades, veterans have simmered over his suggestion, during that testimony, that American troops had committed atrocities against Vietnamese civilians. The best course of action now, some at the Dallas meeting suggested, would be to remind voters about Kerry's speech and to explain why many who served in Vietnam resented the senator for it. The United States was again embroiled in war, and questions of patriotism dominated politics. If the men could show that Kerry had once betrayed our troops, some argued, they could prompt voters to think twice before giving the senator ultimate command of the military now.

But most here wanted to go further. Early in 2004, the historian Douglas Brinkley published *Tour of Duty: John Kerry and the Vietnam War*, a best-selling account of Kerry's service based largely on the journals Kerry kept during the war. But Kerry's version of what had occurred in Vietnam, as reported by Brinkley, did not square with what some Swift boat veterans recalled. "They all brought along the Brinkley book," Spaeth remembers of the meeting in her office that spring day. "They had annotated it, tabbed it. There were a million sticky notes." Again and again during the course of the afternoon, the men referred back to their copies, pointing out passages they considered suspect. "They would say, 'Look what it says here. And look what it says here. That's not the way it was.'"

To these veterans, the Brinkley book represented an ambitious politician's attempt to repackage a scurrilous period in his life into a time of high-flying heroism. The John Kerry they remembered was no hero—he'd behaved dishonorably after the war, but, more important, they believed he'd acted badly *during* the war. The Kerry they remembered had engaged the enemy recklessly, endangering other men; he had lied to win his medals; and he might even have committed war crimes. To these veterans, it would not do to indict Kerry only for his *post*war actions. They pressed for an expansive case against the candidate—a case that posited, *Everything you think you know about John Kerry in Vietnam is wrong.*

Merrie Spaeth was skeptical. Spaeth is a gregarious, middle-aged woman who has attempted to influence the public mind all her life. As a teenage actress in the 1960s, she landed walk-on roles in a couple of long-forgotten TV shows and a big spot alongside Peter Sellers in *The World of Henry Orient*. Spaeth later worked as a newspaper reporter, then produced local and network television news shows. In the eighties she went to Washington, D.C., where Ronald Reagan spotted her easy conversational

manner and installed her as head of the White House Office of
Media Relations. Today, Spaeth works on ways to inspire word-
of-mouth praise for corporate clients. She describes herself,
with characteristic confidence, as "the world's expert in what
makes people remember certain things and pass them along."
Telling the nation that Kerry lied about his time in Vietnam
did not look to Spaeth like an immediately winning strategy.
She sided with the minority—better to stick to criticizing what
Kerry did after the war, not during it.

Spaeth's instinct rested on a commonsensical axiom of advocacy: when you're taking your case to the American public,
you've got to marshal your best evidence. Spaeth believed there
was plenty of audio and video documentation to support the
case that Kerry had maligned his fellow vets when he returned
from war and that such footage could have made for a damaging campaign against the senator. Video of Kerry testifying
to the Senate had him pointing to soldiers who'd "personally
raped, cut off ears, cut off heads, taped wires from portable
telephones to human genitals and turned up the power, cut off
limbs, blown up bodies, randomly shot at civilians." There were
images of Kerry at sit-ins and protests, and there he was again
and again on TV, alleging that the United States had lost its soul
in Vietnam. To be sure, many voters saw nothing amiss with
this history; Kerry's supporters weaved these documents into a
narrative of bravery and political strength. But any skilled opponent could turn the pictures and the sounds into something
less flattering, easily painting Kerry as anti-American, a pacifist,
a hippie, or the many other epithets critics hurled his way.

Arguing that Kerry had displayed little courage while *in Vietnam*, however, would call for manipulation of a wholly different
order. Every bit of important evidence—from Kerry's wartime
journals to the navy's official papers—suggested that Kerry had

been an uncommonly brave fighter. In fact, some of the very men who'd come to Dallas had long praised Kerry's service, even signing his commendation letters. Their sudden turnabout was bound to appear suspiciously partisan. Moreover, only one of the Swift Boat veterans who eventually turned on Kerry, Steve Gardner, had actually served on the same boat as the future senator. Many hadn't even been in Vietnam at the same time as Kerry.

That day in Dallas, the men who would later label themselves the Swift Boat Veterans for Truth made an intriguing—and underreported—decision about how they might derail Kerry's bid for the White House. The two roads before them could not have been more divergent: Would the veterans choose to focus on a point of the past that really was not in doubt—that Kerry had protested the war, and that many veterans reviled him for it? Or would they instead claim that Kerry had been disloyal during the war, a point about which nothing could be verified? Would they stick with well-documented facts, or would they ask the public to dismiss the record, overlook the evidence, and accept something far murkier? Would they work from the accepted truth—or would they choose to market a truth all their own?

Several years have passed since that meeting. Everyone who follows politics is familiar with the path that the Swift Boat Veterans for Truth chose that day: they decided to make the expansive case, charging Kerry not only with betraying the troops after Vietnam, but also with lying about his behavior during the war.

Of course, they made the right call.

It's true that when journalists later looked at the vets' case against Kerry, they unearthed virtually nothing to disqualify the senator's claims to heroism. But that didn't matter. Indeed, this is exactly what's so remarkable about the Swift Boat campaign, and the reason I mention it here, at the inception of a book about truth in the digital age. During the summer of 2004, the historical record played a very small part in the debate concerning Kerry's service in Vietnam. The veterans lacked any compelling evidence to support their claims, yet they managed, anyway, to plant a competing narrative, a kind of alternate version of reality, into the minds of a small but important slice of the electorate. As a result of their efforts, a war hero became, to many Americans, a liar, a traitor, unfit for command. George W. Bush won reelection by a hair more than 2 percentage points. The vets might well have swung the whole thing. But how?

Years later, the question lingers: why did the Swift Boat Veterans' completely fact-free campaign work? Contrary to widespread assumptions, at the start of their campaign the men had relatively little money and little access to the news media. How did they ever convince Americans to accept a new, unprovable theory about John Kerry?

Because they designed it that way. As we'll see, in the early months of their effort, the Swift Boat Veterans for Truth, with Spaeth at the helm, put forward something distinctly new. The campaign was nearly magically effective because it took advantage of the defining media force of the day. Scholars call this force "media fragmentation." The phrase simply refers to the way that information—broadly, everything that you know about the world—was once disseminated by a handful of organizations but has lately been cracking up. Today, people can get the news from all directions. It's a revolution we're all familiar with: the revolution of the Web, cable TV, talk radio, iPods, digital cameras, and every other buzzing, beeping mainstay of modern life.

But the Swift Boat campaign points to a critical danger of what you might call the modern *infosphere*. People who skillfully manipulate today's fragmented media landscape can dissemble, distort, exaggerate, fake—essentially, they can lie—to more people, more effectively, than ever before. In this environment, as the Swift Boat Veterans proved, evidence doesn't matter. What they managed to do in 2004 wasn't a fluke. It was a sign of things to come.

Like many on the right—and, increasingly, on the left—Merrie Spaeth is suspicious of the national journalistic organs known in the zeitgeist by the collective label "the MSM," or mainstream media. The largest metro newspapers and national wire services, in addition to the broadcast TV networks, have long enjoyed unrivaled power in shaping national perceptions. That these outlets exist mainly to push a liberal point of view has been a mainstay of right-wing punditry for at least four decades, and Spaeth takes unmistakable glee in the MSM's recent troubles. "You know what my favorite statistic is these days?" she asked me one afternoon. "You may have heard this. So the *Washington Star* goes out of business in 1981, and the *Post* becomes a monopoly. In the last two decades the population in Metro D.C. has doubled, and income has doubled. But what's happened to the circulation at the *Washington Post*? Down 5 percent."

For more than forty years, ABC, CBS, NBC, the Associated Press, and a half dozen large newspapers, including the *Post*, working in loose concordance, have collectively set the American news agenda. You could picture the old-time network news anchors—men like Walter Cronkite, Dan Rather, Peter Jennings, Tom Brokaw—as particularly attentive and imposing hosts of a national dinner party. For decades, they guided their guests, the American people, to whichever topics they considered worthy of our attention, and we hung on their every word. Their power was legendary. Early in 1968, CBS's Cronkite, a man Americans would have trusted with their checkbooks, ended a Tuesday evening telecast with his view that the United States was "mired in stalemate" in Vietnam. "If I've lost Cronkite," President Lyndon Johnson remarked to an aide, "I've lost Middle America." Johnson soon announced that he wouldn't stand for reelection.

But the MSM is now an institution in winter, with the largest media outlets serving ever-narrower slices of the public. The mainstream is drying up. In some ways, we are returning to the freewheeling days before radio and television launched the very idea of mass media—the era of partisan newspapers and pamphleteers. But our niches, now, are more niche than ever before. We are entering what you might call the trillion-channel universe: over the last two decades, advances in technology— the digital recording and distribution of text, images, and sound over information networks, aka, the modern world—have helped to turn each of us into producers, distributors, and ed- itors of our own media diet. Now we collect the news firsthand through digital cameras, we send our accounts and opinions to the world over blogs, and we use Google, TiVo, the iPod, and a raft of other tools to carefully screen what we consume.

This trend toward niches, which began decades ago but has recently been accelerating at a blinding pace, has itself become a topic of national conversation, feted for its capacity to return power to the people. You need look no further than your favorite political blog to understand the thrill of these people-powered movements—now, finally, ordinary folks can propel outré po- litical candidates to the big time and turn forgotten events into the biggest news events of the day.

A peculiarly utopian sensibility colors much of the discussion about how these new tools will affect politics and society; the tone is surprising, given the magnitude of the shift we're talking about. It's probably unrealistic to think that we'll undergo these changes without any pain or that, indeed, we're not undergoing any pain now.

To continue the analogy: We, the guests at Cronkite's dinner party, have all jumped up from the table and turned the event into a stand-up cocktail affair, open bar. Now we're free to talk amongst ourselves. We mingle, flitting from group to group, or we stay put in our own circle of friends. This party is democratic and egalitarian; information no longer flows from a furrowed-brow host at the top, and now we all get to talk and listen to whomever we want, about whatever we want. The shindig is undeniably messier than in the past. There's a guy in the corner yelling about how NASA didn't really land on the moon, and he's attracting a crowd. A woman in a lab coat claiming to be the surgeon general of the United States is dispensing medical advice. You're suspicious of her credentials, but all your friends seem to believe her. On a table somewhere, people find a stash of photos of Britney Spears mistreating her baby. They make a million copies. Within minutes, a fellow is comparing Spears to Adolf Hitler. Rumors spread, cliques form. The prettiest girl in the room attracts all the attention. The people dressed in blue hold a secret meeting on the left side of the room. Everyone is wary.

The analogy may sound simplistic, but I mean only to highlight, in brief, some of the dangers I'll examine in this book. Studies of the media and of human psychology, some conducted recently but many long before the digital revolution, provide compelling insight into the consequences of a fragmented media. Although information now flows more freely than it did in the past—and this is certainly a salutary development—today's news landscape will also, inevitably, help us to indulge our biases and preexisting beliefs.

While new technology eases connections between people, it also, paradoxically, facilitates a closeted view of the world, keeping us coiled tightly with those who share our ideas. In a world that lacks real gatekeepers and authority figures, and in which digital manipulation is so effortless, spin, conspiracy theories, myths, and outright lies may get the better of many of us. All these factors contributed to the success of the Swift Boat campaign. New media, patchworks of niches, were at the scene of that crime.

To understand what I mean when I talk about how niche media cultivate bias, consider a study by Shanto Iyengar, a professor of communications at Stanford, and Richard Morin, the *Washington Post*'s director of polling. In 2006, the pair set out to discover how the source of a particular news story affects readers' attraction to that story. For instance, is a Republican reader more likely to read a piece of news because it comes from Fox News rather than from NPR?

To do this, the researchers obtained a list of news headlines spanning six broad categories—there were headlines about U.S. politics, the war in Iraq, race relations, crime, travel, and sports. Without disclosing which news outlet the headlines had come from, Iyengar and Morin asked some of the participants in the study to rate their interest in the headlines. This gave the researchers a baseline measure of the intrinsic attractiveness of each headline. Then, with another group of participants, Iyengar and Morin slightly tweaked how they presented the news stories. They added one of four randomly picked news logos alongside the headlines—from either Fox News, NPR, CNN, or the BBC. How would the logos affect people's interest in the headlines?

As they expected, people were biased toward certain news sources—Republicans preferred stories with the Fox News logo, and Democrats converged on CNN and NPR. But the nature and the intensity of the bias that Iyengar and Morin found are intriguing. For starters, they discovered that Republicans were far friendlier to Fox than were Democrats to either CNN or NPR; Republicans showed, in other words, a much greater propensity toward giving in to their bias. Adding the Fox label to a story about Iraq or national politics tripled its attractiveness to Republicans. No label prompted so great a shift in people on the left. The greater Republican bias is in keeping with numerous psychological studies that show conservatives to be much more willing to consume media that toe the ideological line. This phenomenon, which I'll explore in some detail in forthcoming chapters, helps explain, in no small degree, the amazingly successful right-wing pundit factory.

The team's most surprising finding, though, didn't have to do with politics. Rather, it concerned "soft" news—people showed bias even when looking at news stories about travel and sports. "It's one thing when people prefer sources that they agree with when the news is talking about Iraq or President Bush—that's perfectly understandable," Iyengar says. "But what we show is that it even applies for issues on which the boundaries between Democrats and Republicans are not as clear-cut. If you're looking for a Caribbean getaway, why would it make any difference whether it's coming from Fox or NPR?" But it did make a difference—adding a Fox label to travel stories made them more attractive to Republicans and less attractive to Democrats. People "have generalized their preference for politically consonant news to nonpolitical domains," Iyengar says—in other words, they've become addicted to their own preferred spin. "They've gotten into the habit of saying, 'Whatever the news is talking about, I'm just going to go to Fox.'"

Think back to the height of the 2004 presidential campaign. Try to recall how you felt every time an advertisement for the Swift

Boat Veterans for Truth popped up on your television screen. If you are a Democrat, it's likely that the ads provoked in you the sort of anger whose intensity can only properly be rendered here in a string of typewriter expletive symbols (#%&@!). What the Swift Boat Veterans for Truth were saying about John Kerry was plainly false. Everything you'd learned about Kerry, and everything you'd learned about the Swift Boat Veterans, corroborated this idea: Web sites, newspapers, and books teemed with evidence to support your view, and anyone who believed otherwise was willfully ignoring reality. If, on the other hand, you supported George W. Bush, you felt something like pure joy on seeing the same Swift Boat ads. To you, what the Swift Boat Veterans for Truth were saying about John Kerry was plainly true. Everything you'd learned about Kerry, and everything you'd learned about the Swift Boat Veterans, corroborated this idea: Web sites, newspapers, and books teemed with evidence to support your view, and anyone who believed otherwise was willfully ignoring reality.

My guess about how you might have reacted to the Swift Boat campaign is informed by opinion surveys taken at the time, which show that Democrats and Republicans experienced the ads in diametrically opposite ways. When Democrats saw the group's first TV spot—which alleged that Kerry lied about the medals he'd earned in Vietnam—they immediately recognized it as false, and the vast majority felt no need to change their belief that Kerry had been a hero at war. Republicans, meanwhile, saw the commercial as pretty much on the mark; it confirmed what they'd suspected of Kerry all along, that his claims to heroism weren't true. In a survey by the Annenberg Public Policy Center of the University of Pennsylvania, 68 percent of Republicans who saw the ad reported finding it believable, while 73 percent of Democrats found it *un*believable. At first blush, such survey results might not sound too surprising. Of course people of different political parties had different reactions to this heated political campaign—isn't that what you'd expect in politics?

But there is something remarkable about the contrary ways that Republicans and Democrats reacted to the Swift Boat ad; it has to do with the chief question that the Swift Boat campaign raised in the public mind: did John Kerry legitimately earn his medals in Vietnam? Now, unless you subscribe to a fuzzy, postmodern view of the world (more on that later), it's clear that there can be only one correct answer to this question. Either John Kerry earned his medals, or he did not.

There is, in other words, a definite, inarguable truth to what happened in the Mekong more than thirty years ago. This truth has been documented, and it can be verified through investigation. Moreover, the truth is universal—it ought to be consistent across party lines, whether the person who's answering the question is a Republican or a Democrat. The Swift Boat controversy over whether Kerry truly did earn his medals, then, can be seen as a fight over two competing *versions of reality*. In essence, the ads were asking us to look at history—the history of Kerry's time in Vietnam—and to decide which reality *actually occurred*.

This may sound obvious, but most debates in modern politics simply aren't like this. When we fight over important issues, we're not usually arguing over the fundamental state of the world but instead over what to do about it. Your stance on health-care policy in the United States, for instance, hinges on your specific economic, ethical, religious, legal, and civic views: What would constitute a fair distribution of health care to the public? Do you believe health care falls under the list of services a government should provide to its citizens? How much should anyone spend to save a single life? And so on.

People harbor profound disagreements about all these questions, and yet, at the same time, there clearly are facts about health care in the United States with which everyone agrees. Tens of millions of Americans currently lack health insurance. Heart disease and cancer are, by far, the nation's most deadly ailments. Prescription drug use is on the rise. These are examples of a shared political reality—empirical, verifiable measures of the world about which there are, and really can be, no argument. For any issue, we find a set of such basic shared truths, a view of the world that is largely consistent regardless of partisanship.

At least, it has been this way until now. But there were few shared truths in the story of John Kerry's service in Vietnam. Shared truths are absent in other areas, too—in many issues surrounding national security policy, for instance. Whether or not Saddam Hussein was "personally involved" in the September 11, 2001, attacks on the World Trade Center and the Pentagon is, like the question of Kerry's medals, an issue for which there is a definitive, correct answer. Either he was, or he was not. Although the Bush administration at one time suggested (loudly) otherwise, the White House now admits Saddam didn't do it. More important, every major investigation of the issue—including by the nonpartisan 9/11 Commission—determined that Saddam had no role in 9/11, while other government reports have proved that Iraq was not tied to al-Qaeda. A stunningly large number of Americans, however, blame Saddam. In the fall of 2003, a poll commissioned by the *Washington Post* showed that almost 70 percent of the nation thought the Iraqi dictator had been personally involved in the attack. A *New York Times* survey taken four years later, at the six-year anniversary of the attacks, marked a huge improvement—but it's still amazing. A third of Americans said they saw Saddam's hand in 9/11, despite a complete lack of evidence to support the position.

Did Iraq possess weapons of mass destruction at the time of the U.S. invasion? The most comprehensive investigations into Iraq's WMD programs prove that Saddam had no banned weapons. Even President Bush and Vice President Dick Cheney now acknowledge this point. But a Harris survey conducted in July 2006 showed that half of Americans reject this idea. They believe instead that the weapons were there.

It's not only in expectedly partisan national security issues that we see Americans disagreeing about what's happening in the world. Look, for instance, at global warming. Every major American scientific body that has studied the world's climate has concluded that the planet is heating up due to human activity. In 2004, Naomi Oreskes, a researcher at the University of California, San Diego, surveyed the 928 studies concerned with climate change that were published in peer-reviewed scientific journals between 1993 and 2003. Not a single one, she found, disagreed with the consensus view about global warming. But the American public is not nearly so united. Polls show that, first, few Americans believe the science. A survey conducted by the Pew Research Center in 2006 revealed that only 41 percent of respondents think that there's solid evidence that humans are changing the Earth's climate. Democrats, though, are twice as likely as Republicans to accept the evidence. Even scientific fact isn't safe from politically motivated perception.

Perhaps the most striking example of Americans' partisan divisions over what's really happening in the world involves the economy. For several years, says Andrew Kohut, the director of the Pew Research Center, Democrats and Republicans have largely agreed with one another when asked about the current state of the economy. This, he points out, isn't very surprising, because economic questions "are not as directly associated in the public mind with political parties or political figures." If someone asked you how well the nation's economy was doing, you'd probably think about your job and the jobs of people around you, rather than, say, about President Bush. Indeed, this was the case during the 1990s. We remember the Clinton years as extremely politically volatile, with Republicans and Democrats at odds on just about every issue of the day, but Americans were largely united in their view of the nation's prospects. When unemployment declined, satisfaction rose across the board, the blue lines and the red lines commingling on graphs of national opinion.

But that's no longer the case, Kohut has found. Just before President Bush's State of the Union Address in 2006, surveyors at the Pew Center called up 1,500 Americans and asked, "How would you rate economic conditions in this country today—as excellent, good, only fair, or poor?" The results were vastly divergent. Fifty-six percent of Republicans believed that the economy was in either excellent or good shape, while only 23 percent of Democrats thought this was the case. Sixty-two percent of Democrats said it was difficult to find a job in their communities, but only 38 percent of Republicans thought so. You might wonder whether this was because Republicans actually *were* facing better job prospects than Democrats were—could Republicans have been reporting better economic conditions because their lives were economically better off than Democrats'? Actually, no.

The Pew study found that the partisan bias held even when controlling for the respondents' incomes. Two-thirds of Republicans who made more than $75,000 a year thought the economy was in great shape, but only one-third of Democrats who earned as much had the same idea. Similarly, Democrats who made less than $50,000 annually were far more gloomy about economic conditions than were Republicans in the same bracket.

Think about this for a minute. Here were people living in the same economy as one another, folks with a roughly equal likelihood of finding a job or seeing wealth in the housing market or hitting on hard times. They were swimming in the same pool—but half of them thought the water was lovely, while the other half were dying of chill. They were, Kohut says, "living different realities."

It was in this tide of divergent, parallel realities that the Swift Boat Veterans for Truth launched their ship. For thirty years, there had been a shared national truth regarding John Kerry— whatever his behavior after the war, the evidence showed that he'd fought honorably in Vietnam. To many partisans, though, this was an unwelcome truth. And the new truth offered by the Swift Boat campaign, the version of reality they sought to propagate, was much friendlier to the right-wing cause.

Welcome to the Rashomon world, where the very idea of objective reality is under attack.

2

The New Tribalism: Swift Boats and the Power of Choosing

I n 1967, Timothy Brock and Joe Balloun, two researchers looking into the psychological underpinnings of advertising, set out to determine what happens when people are presented with information that contradicts their core beliefs. The core belief, in this case, was a topic on which our personal views tend to be pretty well fixed: cigarettes. Imagine that you are a smoker. If you were tuning your radio one day and you heard a faint, static-filled broadcast describing the link between smoking and lung cancer, what would you do? Would you try to hone in for a better signal so that you could learn more about your dangerous habit, or would you instead tune out?

To test this question, Brock and Balloun asked undergraduate students to listen to a series of prerecorded speeches on a range of topics, most of which had nothing to do with smoking's link to cancer. The test subjects were under the impression that they were there to rate the speakers' persuasiveness and sincerity. They were also told that each of the speeches had been recorded on a cheap portable tape recorder, creating a great deal of static interference in the audio—but they could reduce the interference for a few seconds by pressing a button mounted in the room. Finally, after listening to all the speeches, the subjects were asked several questions about their lifestyles, including how frequently, if ever, they smoked.

Of course, it was the static-eliminating button that was the true object of Brock and Balloun's inquiry. The button acted as a measure of each subject's free will: every time a student pressed it, she was trying to get a better signal, expressing interest in the topic on the tape. Brock and Balloun conducted the test four times with different sets of students, slightly varying the parameters in each phase (they changed the volume of the audio, the number of seconds of clear speech you heard each time you pressed the button, or the order in which the different tapes were played). In each round, they found the same thing: both smokers and nonsmokers tuned out information that conflicted with their beliefs, while tuning in to what they thought to be true. When people who smoke were played the speech arguing that cigarettes cause cancer, they pressed the button far fewer times, on average, than did the nonsmokers. Conversely, when the subjects listened to a recording that *challenged* the connection between smoking and cancer, it was the nonsmokers who preferred static, while smokers hit the button to get a better listen. Both sides were choosing what comforted them.

It wasn't just the charged subject of smoking that prompted people to contemplate pressing the button. Religious beliefs did it, too, Brock and Balloun found. Another of the speeches they played for test subjects was one they called "Christianity

Is Evil," in which a speaker read an excerpt from the anarchist thinker Alexander Berkman's 1920 book *Now and After*. When people who frequently attended church listened to this speech, they hardly tapped on the button—sometimes they pressed it only a handful of times and then let static take over, so uninterested were they in this rant against organized religion. Those who reported hardly ever going to church, though, found more pleasure in Berkman's writing; they jammed on the button to listen to the speech. As with the tapes on cigarettes and cancer, both the churched and the unchurched paid attention only when the tape supported their ideas about the world.

Brock and Balloun's experiment became one of the first to confirm the existence of a psychological coping mechanism known as selective exposure—an idea that goes far in explaining why narratives with so little basis in fact, such as that proposed by the Swift Boat Veterans for Truth, can now so effortlessly enter our political discourse. Selective exposure arises out of the more famous theory of cognitive dissonance, which the psychologist Leon Festinger first proposed in 1957 to explain the mental acrobatics people engage in when they're confronted with two or more "dissonant" thoughts.

Festinger had studied a doomsday cult whose members believed the Earth was going to end in a great flood at midnight on December 21, 1954. When the promised flood didn't come, *dissonance* ensued—the cult members' psychological discomfort at the all-too-clear gulf between their cherished prophesy and the reality of the still-dry, quite-alive planet. But Festinger saw that the condition did not worry the cult for long. Just after the expected apocalypse, their leader, Marion Keech, a Minneapolis housewife who claimed to receive supernatural messages through vibrations that entered her body and caused her to write, received a new communication—that the cult, by believing, had prompted God to spare the planet. It was a coping mechanism: to mitigate the pain of dissonance, the cult had adapted its beliefs to fit the new circumstances.

But changing your beliefs isn't easy, and it isn't fun. Sometimes you have no choice. If you thought that Earth should have ended a few hours ago, yet here you are, occupying a planet in obvious want of apocalypse, you've got to adjust your view somehow. But Festinger proposed another, easier way for us to deal with the unpleasant sensation of having our beliefs tested: we simply steer clear of information that contradicts what we think we know. This is selective exposure. It says, simply, that in an effort to avoid the cognitive dissonance that comes out of receiving news that challenges our beliefs, we cunningly select the messages we consume.

For the smokers in Brock and Balloun's experiment, this meant tuning out a speech about cigarettes' link to cancer. For the Christians, it meant choosing not to listen to "Christianity Is Evil." And if you are a partisan living in digital America, a land of endless information and endless choice, the selective-exposure reflex means availing yourself—even if not consciously—of unprecedented technological opportunities, from the Web to the iPod to TiVo to the satellite radio in the car, for fashioning your own personal media environment: reading or watching or listening only to ideas that confirm what you already feel, deep down, must be true.

If you want to understand why our perceptions of reality are diverging, selective exposure is a good place to start your investigation. The phenomenon explains why truth doesn't always prevail: giving people information that runs contrary to their core beliefs doesn't necessarily prompt them to reconsider their ideas. Sometimes it prompts a deaf ear. The true believers simply lift their finger off the button, letting static fill the room.

The John Peter Zenger Room is one of three studio apartment–sized conference spaces available for rent at the National Press Club's headquarters in the National Press Building, just down the street from the White House in the Northwest section of Washington. Named for an early defender of American press freedoms, the Zenger Room sits at the end of a long corridor honoring paragons of journalism—the Peter Lisagor Room, the Margaret Bourke-White Room, the Edward R. Murrow Room. But the routine business of newsmaking occurs here at a clear remove from anything so exalted. On any given weekday, organizations of trifling news value pay for space in the Zenger ($450 per three-hour slot) in the hopes of marshaling the capital's prodigious journalistic hordes to their cause. When the American Society of Microbiology wanted to remind us about National Clean Hands Week or the Consumer Federation of America sought to speculate about the nation's holiday spending plans or the Grocery Manufacturers of America aimed to make clear their views on national sugar-subsidy policy, it was to the Zenger Room they came.

And it was on this inauspicious stage that on May 4, 2004, eighteen Vietnam veterans announced the creation of a national campaign questioning the wartime service record of Senator John Kerry. This is the forgotten story of the Swift Boat Veterans for Truth—a tale of humble origins, of months spent languishing in venues just like this one, on the margins of mainstream political debate. But it's also the story of an unconventional—and, in hindsight, astonishingly successful—plan for grabbing national attention, a plan built out of the raw material of selective exposure.

The veterans' failure to quickly gain the news media's attention was a predictable thing. If I had asked you at the beginning
of the 2004 presidential run to sketch out the perfect political
weapon with which to defeat presidential candidate Kerry, I
bet you wouldn't have come up with this band of veterans. As
any political analyst might have then pointed out, the group's
problem was its message—it was, to say the least, impolitic. Asking whether a man whom the nation considers a hero has truly
earned his medals is the sort of question that causes people to re-
coil. The Swift Boat Vets weren't ideal spokesmen, either. Many
weren't particularly photogenic or eloquent, and they lacked
natural credibility.

At the podium that morning in the Zenger Room, you couldn't
miss the veterans' shortcomings as media stars. They scowled,
they snarled. "Thirty-five years ago," said Andrew Horne, a former Swift boat commander, "many of us fell silent when we
came back to the stain of sewage that Mr. Kerry had thrown
on us and all of our colleagues who served over there. I don't
intend to be silent today or ever again."

The room swelled with reporters, but the veterans might as
well have been talking to the walls. Of the three broadcast TV
networks, only CBS mentioned the press conference on the
evening news. Big-city newspapers also devoted scant, skeptical coverage. The Associated Press, the wire service that pro-
vides national news to more than a thousand papers across the
country, sent a junior reporter to the event but later decided
that it didn't merit a story. The AP published its first article on
the Swift Boat Veterans on August 5—three months after their
press conference. If you search the *New York Times*'s archives,
you'll find only two Swift Boat Veterans stories from that period. It was the same pretty much everywhere. Between May
and August 2004, the months in which the Swift Boat Veterans
built a following among people on the right, leading political

reporters and just about every mainstream political institution were oblivious to the group. It was if they didn't exist.

Conservatives would later see a liberal bias in the media's oversight, but the true cause of journalists' early inattention was likely much simpler—what "The Note," ABC News's popular online political newsletter, labeled the "he said/he said" nature of the Swift Boat story. Both the Swift Vets and Kerry loyalists offered conflicting narratives of events that had taken place thirty years in the past; their recollections were subject, as such things are, to the fog of war and the haze of memory. But Kerry's version had the clear advantage. Not only was it bolstered by stacks of documents and eyewitnesses, it was also, more important, widely accepted as true—and had been so for decades. The Swift Boat Veterans were offering an uncorroborated story that conflicted with the well-established history of Kerry's experiences in Vietnam. Under the normal rules of journalism, they didn't stand a chance.

But the normal rules were hardly the only way to play the game. The mainstream news establishment—morning and evening TV shows, mass-market newspapers, the national wire services—lands conveniently at the front door of the typical American home. If you want people to know about your thing, whatever your thing might be, the front door is a nice way to come to them. But there are also back doors and side doors, windows in out-of-the-way places, skylights letting information stream in from above. The Swift Boat Veterans may not have had evidence on their side, but what they lacked in proof they could make up for in nimbleness. All that they needed, they figured, was a new path to the American voter, one unencumbered by the whims of reporters. "We learned from some former POWs that when they were held captive in Vietnam, they developed a 'tap code' to communicate with each other without the guards' knowing," John O'Neill, one of the group's founders, once told an interviewer. "We realized we needed our own tap code to talk to the public."

Early in February 2004, Merrie Spaeth picked up the phone to find a frantic John O'Neill on the other end. "He says, 'Kerry's a war criminal! I'm going to have him put in jail!'" Spaeth later recalled. C-SPAN and other networks had been asking O'Neill for his thoughts on the senator's success in the Democratic presidential primary. Thirty-three years earlier, the pair had debated the war on *The Dick Cavett Show*, a meeting in which O'Neill, a Swift Boat Veteran who supported the effort in Vietnam, had accused Kerry of dishonorable conduct. Yet it was Kerry who had emerged with the public's esteem. And here he was, now, with a pretty good shot at the presidency. What O'Neill wanted from Spaeth was advice on how to take on Kerry once again. He had, he told her, a lot that could damage his old foe. "He just let loose with this string of all these things," Spaeth told me. "And I'm thinking, *What are you talking about*? I was shocked."

It was no surprise that when he needed help, O'Neill called on Merrie Spaeth. Although she now works primarily for corporate clients, in the two decades since she left the White House, Spaeth has cemented a reputation as a trusted *consigliore* for Republicans with media needs. Her firm has helped candidates, cabinet secretaries, and a slew of aides and assistants present their ideas to the public; during the impeachment trial against Bill Clinton, she coached Independent Counsel Kenneth Starr on how to sell his charges to a weary Congress.

Not long ago, I paid Spaeth a visit in Dallas. A life spent in four high-profile fields—the movies, journalism, national politics, and corporate PR—has left her with an admirable collection of friends. The walls of her office are plastered with photographs and handwritten letters from the famous and the mighty, advertising a privileged proximity to the world's levers of power. Yet Spaeth is remarkably accessible and is proud to discuss the intricacies of the Swift Boat Veterans' effort. She points out that unlike the men in the group, she did not join the campaign to renew a wartime fraternity or even, she insists, to further any great political end (although she supported Bush in 2004, she calls herself a Reagan Republican, which she contrasts, pointedly, with George W. Bush's ideology). Instead, Spaeth says she signed up only because she thought very highly of O'Neill, an old friend of her late husband's. Plus, she had some good ideas.

To understand how the Swift Boat Veterans got from nowhere to everywhere, you've got to understand how Merrie Spaeth sees the world. She's a believer in social networks and "people power." These are jargony techno-neologisms, but they describe ideas that she picked up in the early 1980s, while she was working in the press office at the Federal Trade Commission. The FTC regulates direct-marketing companies—firms like Tupperware and Mary Kay that use people, rather than advertisements, to spread the word about their products.

Although the biggest direct-marketing firms are household names, Spaeth recognized that their success often passes below our collective notice. You may occasionally see a trademark Mary Kay pink Cadillac flying down the freeway, but the fact that the company employs more than a million and a half women who sell $2 billion in cosmetics to tens of millions of exceedingly loyal customers each year comes as something of a shock. "I was fascinated by them," she says. "How do they get that many people to carry a message?" If you could assemble an army to sell cosmetics, Spaeth wondered, why couldn't you cultivate groups to talk about other things—hospital services, say, or express shipping, or the grievances of a group of veterans from

a thirty-year-old war? Getting people to pass your message—
what she called "person-to-person marketing"—would, Spaeth
realized, dominate the future of advertising.

Spaeth had a second epiphany soon afterward. In 1984,
Reagan appointed her to direct the White House Office of
Media Relations. It was an election year, and Reagan had a problem. This wasn't really a novel problem, and considering how
well Reagan would do against Walter Mondale that November,
you couldn't even say it was especially grave. But Reagan was
famously sensitive to how he was portrayed in the media, and he
simply didn't like the way the press was covering him. Like many
politicians, especially those on the right, Reagan believed that
the reporters conspired against his policies and that they frequently misinterpreted and distorted his ideas. CBS News and
its evening anchor Dan Rather bore the brunt of the criticism;
White House officials sometimes called the network to complain or to request that changes be made before certain stories
were to be broadcast. It was in this environment that, one day,
Spaeth wondered about taking a completely different course:
Instead of asking the networks to alter their broadcasts, why not
simply go around them? Why not go straight to the people?

This wasn't something you could really have considered before 1984. Indeed, even then, when almost fifty million people—
a fifth of the nation—tuned in to ABC, CBS, and NBC each
evening for the news, presidents had little choice but to go
along with the networks. But Spaeth saw that technology was
slowly eroding this power. Advances in the tools used to create and broadcast information were beginning to allow for alternative television channels, radio programs, and newspapers.
Upstart reporters in out-of-the-way places now had access to
satellite feeds, desktop PCs, and electronic databases to boost
their coverage. For the national TV shows and the biggest newspapers, the trend lines weren't encouraging: every year, fewer

Americans were turning to these outlets for their news. Inside the White House, Spaeth became, she says, "an apostle of local media"; she advocated focusing the warm glow of the president's attention on smaller newspapers, regional TV shows, and radio programs that serve just a small slice of the nation. If the elite media were losing a grip on the news, a clever strategist, Spaeth saw, could do well by mining their downfall.

One of the technologies she considered worthy was a new electronic service called ITT Dialcom. Dialcom allowed anyone with a desktop computer to send e-mail or read the news through ordinary phone lines. It was intended mainly for businesspeople—computers weren't cheap, and customers paid more than $12 an hour to access the service—but Spaeth was taken by Dialcom's potential. She thought it could liberate the president's words; if Reagan's speeches could be found on a computer, why would folks need to look for them in the *New York Times*?

Spaeth convinced the White House to push out all of its press materials—text of Reagan's speeches, his policy announcements, and a host of other documents that had heretofore been reserved for the handful of reporters who covered the president—on to Dialcom. The system was small; in the first six months of operation, about thirteen thousand Dialcom users downloaded Reagan's words, nothing that would prompt fear in TV networks or the *New York Times*. But it was the beginning of something important. "It's no big whoopee now," Spaeth says, "but when you could dial in from Oakland and get any press release, any speech, any document from the White House, all of a sudden the press corps was obsolete."

By the spring of 2004, the trends that Spaeth spotted in the early 1980s were beginning to consume politics. Outmaneuvering the national reporters who covered the White House was no longer an outré strategy; George W. Bush's aides had turned the technique into an intricate ballet, making local and cable news shows and partisan radio programs the pride of their affectations. The president often granted exclusive interviews to regional broadcasters, and the vice president and the cabinet secretaries frequently made policy pronouncements on Fox News and Rush Limbaugh's radio show.

Meanwhile, person-to-person marketing had seen a tech-age reinvention; in the Democrat presidential primary, Vermont governor Howard Dean used blogs and e-mail to tickle the hopes and dreams of millions of voters on the left, not to mention raise astronomical campaign sums. The Deaniacs called their fuel "people power"—and even if, in the end, Dean himself seemed to explode in a too-rich mixture of the stuff, nobody in politics missed its potential. Merrie Spaeth had seen her ideas come around. Now, in the Swift Boat Veterans for Truth, she had a vehicle to make something big of them.

Spaeth's strategy was one of overwhelming force: she decided that if reporters wouldn't cover what the Swift Boat Veterans had to say, the men would just keep saying it anyway. "It's like the Girl Scouts," she says. "You go to talk to anybody you can, and you keep trying to sell cookies." So the plan was to talk—or, more precisely, to talk and talk and talk, to anyone, from any outlet, in any medium, who cared to listen. There were more than a dozen veterans, and each could discuss Kerry with passion and venom for hours on end. So why not take the show on the road? But there was hidden precision in the plan, too. Their strategy hinged on an expectation that the only media that would care to feature the Swift Boat Veterans were those that attracted an audience that was predisposed to believe what the veterans had to say. In other words, right-wing talk radio, whose alternating currents of invective and mock self-pity had long powered the conservative movement, would be their target. Here the veterans would be talking to their natural allies, in a setting where these allies congregated regularly in the manner of devout parishioners. They would be leveraging the power of selective exposure; they'd be talking to those who understood the code.

In the same way that Mary Kay needed an army to sell cosmetics, Spaeth's first goal was to collect people to sell the Swift Boat message. Spaeth devised a simple script: Taking to the airwaves in those early months, the Swift Boat Vets would urge people in the audience, especially fellow veterans, to visit their campaign's Web site. There, they'd posted an open letter asking Kerry to release his full military records, as well as a set of short video clips showing each Swift Boat Veteran speaking at the group's initial press conference. Visitors were asked to sign the letter and to pass the videos on to their friends. In this way, the message traveled underground—a press conference that the networks and the newspapers had ignored began to seep into the conservative conversation. "That's how we started the snowball rolling," Spaeth says. "The Dean campaign showed us that person-to-person marketing had gone electronic. So we designed this to say to whoever was interested—the Swift Boat Veterans and their families would be the first ones—'Come here.' And it worked fabulously."

They left no corner of talk radio untouched. When I asked Spaeth how many radio interviews the veterans did in their early days, she answered, "hundreds and hundreds and hundreds." The true figure is probably slightly more than one hundred, but any count lacks precision for the simple fact that the interviews were occurring too fast for people to keep up.

Spaeth handed me a document that her firm drew up in July 2004 listing the programs that the veterans had appeared on until that point. It begins with the admonition that the list is "incomplete because of the sheer volume." Every day for months, each man spoke on two or three shows, including some of the biggest acts in talk radio, but also many of the smallest. They granted fifteen interviews alone to the Salem Radio Network, a Christian outfit in Texas whose programs go out to fifteen hundred stations across the country. *Hot Talk with Scott Hennen* reaches a few thousand listeners every day in the tiny radio market of Fargo, North Dakota; the veterans landed on the show three times. The men also made four appearances on the *Steve Kane Show*, which airs during morning drive time in south Florida. Twice in Seattle. Twice in San Francisco. Twice in Pittsburgh, Denver, and San Antonio. Four times on *NRANews*, a show produced by the National Rifle Association that runs on the Internet and on satellite radio networks. Charley Jones, who hosts a program called *Texas Overnight* that broadcasts from midnight to four in the morning in Dallas, featured the veterans four times. Baltimore. Erie. Montpelier. Sacramento. All of Connecticut. Boston. Washington. New York. Los Angeles. And all of Mississippi. Twice.

For conservatives living through John Kerry's rise in the campaign for the Democratic presidential nomination, cognitive dissonance would have been a chronic condition. It was the dissonance of right-wing perception grinding against historical fact. Republicans were perceived to be the party of the military. It was the Republicans who advocated a muscular, martial foreign policy. It was the Republicans who'd been winning the military vote for years and who claimed to represent the views of soldiers and generals. But the facts were different, dissonant. The Republican Party's nominee for the presidency—and the vice presidency, for that matter—had not served in the war that had consumed a generation. The Democratic Party was zooming in on a man who'd not only served but had done so with distinction, despite an unhidden disgust with the endeavor. For Republicans, there was the dissonance between expectation and actuality: the difference between believing the world is going to end at midnight and the reality of the globe spinning past the appointed hour without incident.

You can see how, in this atmosphere, the surprising anti-Kerry charges put forward by a couple dozen veterans would have found an audience with the right. Peddling their alternative history on the radio and on the Web, the Swift Boat Veterans offered a balm for cognitive dissonance. If you were a Bush supporter, selectively exposing yourself to the Swift Boat Vets' ideas relieved you of the burden of having to alter your perceptions. Saying the other guy was not who he claimed he was, that his heroism was merely a front for dishonor and disgrace, let you keep your head high. It was the standard model of selective exposure, the one that has kept conservative talk radio buzzing for a couple of decades.

But there was something else going on here as well, another mechanism whirring in the brains of the right-wing hordes that Merrie Spaeth was trying to recruit to the Swift Boat camp. You can think of it as the mystery of selective exposure, and over the last generation, its effects have shaped the American media diet into the archly partisan plate that sits before us today. When it comes to how we choose media, there is, it turns out, a difference between liberals and conservatives: people on the right are a lot more choosy.

To understand this difference, it is helpful to look into the work of a psychologist named Aaron Lowin and the clever experiment he once devised to see how people use selective exposure in a real-world setting—that is, outside of a psychology lab. The setting was the 1964 presidential election, which pitted a moderate Democrat, Lyndon Johnson, against Barry Goldwater, who had become the standard-bearer for the conservative wing of the Republican Party. Johnson assumed the mantle of the slain John F. Kennedy and won in a landslide. Given the profound difference between the candidates, the race proved to be an ideal environment to examine how partisans on each side acted under the assault of propaganda.

Lowin was interested in how the "strength" of a political message—the relative ease with which you could refute it—affects a voter's desire to consume it. Imagine, for instance, that it's a few weeks before the 1964 race, and you are Democrat. One day, you receive a letter in the mail from an anticommunist group. The letter warns that Johnson is secretly in bed with the communists, and it offers to give you more information if you send back a postage-paid postcard expressing your interest. What do you do?

On the one hand, the mailing produces some dissonance. You don't want to think that your party's candidate has ties to the Commies; like the smokers listening to the speech about cigarettes and lung cancer, you might prefer to avoid this negative message. Yet the mailing is also, you note, rather absurd: Johnson may not share Goldwater's anticommunist zeal, but he has just sent thousands of Americans to fight in South Vietnam, so anyone claiming that he's got something to do with the Reds would need pretty strong proof. And this leads you to think about sending in the postcard. After all, if this group mails you back something that's laughably false about Johnson, a bit of propaganda that you can easily knock down, you might find the thing sort of funny. The ostensibly dissonant message could actually *strengthen* your hold on your own views.

Telling a Democrat that Lyndon Johnson might harbor communistic sympathies is what Lowin would have called a *weak dissonant* message—it's negative, but because it's so clearly spurious, it lacks any real punch. Lowin contrasted these with *strong dissonant* messages, arguments that contradict your views and are difficult to refute. To smokers, news about the dangers of cigarettes would be strong dissonant information— it's hard to argue that smoking *isn't* bad for you. As Lowin saw it, the strength of each message has to be a key factor in how we decide to selectively expose ourselves to information. If we're given a message that's strong and dissonant, we avoid it. And if we're given a message that we find strong and *consonant*—one that supports our views, and that is easy to prove—we consume it. These two are obvious.

But Lowin also theorized that a weak dissonant message— telling a Johnson supporter that his candidate likes communists, say—would attract us because we'd take pleasure in refuting it. This isn't especially surprising when you consider how people argue about politics. Putting forward the other guy's dumbest ideas is a surefire true tactic. When the Fox News anchor Bill O'Reilly invites someone he identifies as a far-left, out-of-touch liberal on his program and then makes a show of berating him, what O'Reilly is doing is rejoicing in weak dissonance. Sure, the liberal is offering a negative message, one that could provoke some discomfort in the conservative audience—but because the dissonance is so quickly erased by O'Reilly's smack-down, the audience's belief system is bolstered, not damaged, by the exchange. Weak dissonance is the engine of cable talk.

Lowin thought that weak dissonance was so attractive that most people, if given a choice, might actually prefer to listen to such messages over those he called *weak consonant*—messages that seem to jibe with our views but that we consider factually unsteady. When you think about it, this seems logical. We'd rather listen to the other side's flimsy attacks on our side than our side's flimsy attacks on theirs.

Lowin conducted two experiments to test his assumptions about how people might respond to variously strong and weak consonant and dissonant messages, and the results of his first experiment, at least, fit his expectations perfectly. Using a telephone survey and the registration lists of the Republican and Democratic clubs at Ivy League colleges, he found more than six hundred partisan supporters of either Johnson or Goldwater. He mailed each of these people a letter that offered a short message about either of the candidates, and then asked people to mail back a postcard for more information. Each letter was designed to look as if it had come from a third-party political interest group, and it focused on one of many topics pertinent to the race. Some people received a message that was consonant with their views, while others received one that was dissonant; some arguments were obviously weak, while others were strong. (Lowin ran the messages by a panel of judges, who were also students of the Ivy League, to determine what he called each message's "ease of refutation.") To see how each side employed selective exposure, all that Lowin had to do was count the postcards that came back.

Lowin's assumptions panned out. The people who mailed back the most postcards were those who'd been sent strong messages consonant with their beliefs. People who had received weak dissonant messages—messages that criticized a respondent's favored candidate but that were easy to dispute—were also quick to mail back their forms. Only a few people responded to the strong dissonant messages—messages that credibly took on their favorite candidate, which makes sense. And a similar small number responded to the weak consonant arguments, which fit Lowin's hypothesis that we reject messages that support our side but that we think may be false.

The results, Lowin noted, were consistent across party lines; supporters of Johnson and of Goldwater all responded to the same kinds of arguments in the same way. Thus Lowin thought he'd hit upon a clear algorithm to determine whether people would be attracted to or repulsed by certain messages: we like strong consonance and weak dissonance, and we hate strong dissonance and weak consonance.

But then, in a very similar second experiment using another group of Republicans and Democrats, Lowin's hypothesis came unglued. The main difference this time was that Lowin mailed all respondents the same letter. The mailing was designed to look as if it had come from a nonpartisan election group, and it asked people to select four out of eight available campaign brochures that they'd like to be sent free of charge. Whereas people in the first study were each sent only one message that they could choose to either accept or reject, here they were shown all the possible messages and were free to choose which ones to indulge.

Something about the expanded choice seemed to jumble people's minds, because now Republicans and Democrats behaved very differently from each other. People on the left, remarkably, showed no bias. Democrats chose brochures that bore no relation to their views—they were all over the place, picking arguments that were consonant, dissonant, weak, and strong. The pattern seemed to reflect nothing more than their pure interest. Republicans, though, were extremely biased. Not only did they prefer strong consonant messages over strong dissonant ones, they even liked weak consonant messages over weak dissonant ones. Republicans, that is, preferred to hear messages that supported their ideas even though the arguments were flimsy; they even preferred to hear their own side's weak arguments over the other side's weak arguments.

Are people on the left really immune to bias when they select their news? Are people on the right, meanwhile, so biased that they'll indulge arguments that are plainly false? Which of

Lowin's experiments about selective exposure applies to how we really consume political messages—the first one, which showed everyone to be selective, or the second, which paints only the Republicans as biased?

Lowin himself was puzzled by these findings, and he could only come up with a guess at why the two experiments yielded different results. The second study involved letters sent by an ostensibly neutral source, and it offered recipients a choice among arguments they'd like to see. These factors, he thought, must have subtly cued people on the left to act in a rational—that is, nonbiased—manner. But Lowin couldn't say why the same factors didn't also prompt Republicans to behave in an unbiased way. In fact, the very changes that reduced selectivity in Democrats seemed to make people on the right *more* prone to choosing their side's arguments.

But Lowin's study is not the only one to suggest that conservatives exhibit greater partisan selectivity in their news choices; this has actually been a consistent finding over a range of research areas. I've already told you about the experiment by Shanto Iyengar involving news logos. When you attach the Fox News label to any news article, Republicans find it immensely more attractive than the same article that carries no such logo. In the 2000 election, Iyengar monitored supporters of both Bush and Al Gore to see how they would examine speeches and policy documents that the candidates put out on their Web sites. Here, too, he found Republicans looking more closely at the pro-Bush pages, while "moderates and liberals tended to pursue an 'equal opportunity' strategy, examining both candidates more or less equally."

Iyengar and other scholars believe that such results point to a landmark feature of right-wing ideology. "Republicans and conservatives are more ideological in their political posture,"

Iyengar explains. "Their opinions tend to be derived from political principles or political values, and the rest of us tend to be
more—for want of a better term—'wishy-washy.'" Think about
the people in Lowin's study. They were supporters of Barry
Goldwater, a politician who is remembered mainly for the stub-
bornness with which he held on to his far-right positions. (Goldwater famously proclaimed that "extremism in the defense of
liberty is no vice," and "moderation in the pursuit of justice is no
virtue.") Is it any wonder that the people he attracted were similarly single-minded in the way they collected information—that
they were simply too biased to select news in a rational manner,
even when it was offered by a nonpartisan source?

This does not mean that people on the left aren't biased in
how they consume the news. As Lowin's first experiment proves,
Democrats, in some circumstances, can exhibit strong partisan
selectivity. When Iyengar added the NPR label to news stories,
liberals did respond more favorably—just not as favorably as
conservatives did to the Fox label. In 2005, Lada Adamic and
Natalie Glance, researchers at HP Labs and Intelliseek, studied
the patterns in which both conservative and liberal bloggers
posted links to other Web sites. They found that liberal blogs
tend to favor other left-wing sources. A link from a lefty blog
is more likely to point to either another liberal blog or a liberal
news site such as *Salon* than to a conservative site. If you're
looking for a wide-ranging, cross-party conversation, the liberal
blogosphere isn't the place to look, their research suggests. It's
an echo chamber.

But the echo is even louder on the right. Adamic and Glance's
study shows that right-leaning blogs exhibit a greater tendency
to link to one another; their network, the researchers found,
is even more densely connected than that of the lefty bloggers. Right-wing blogs also have a strong propensity to link to

right-wing news sources, and many of these—like Fox News—
are far more influential than the sites on the left.*

Thus blogs, too, point to greater partisan bias and greater
ideological purity on the right than on the left. As occurred first
on the radio and then on cable TV, conservatives are building
a cloud of partisan thought on the Web, a group of sites that
work in loose confederation to allow for even greater selective
consumption by their partisan audiences. The right-wing network on the Web hooks into the greater network spanning other
platforms, from TV to radio to book publishing to an army of
direct marketers. On the left you find an echo chamber, but on
the right you find an echo planet.

In the spring of 2004, the Swift Boat Veterans for Truth dug
themselves deep into this rich soil. In Lowin's taxonomy, you
would say that the group's message fit all the characteristics
of weak consonance—it jibed with right-wing philosophy but
lacked proof. Lowin predicted that such stories should repel
partisans. But, of course, his own experiment showed otherwise.
Give some people on the right a choice of political messages,
and they'll choose the ones that support their views. They may
do so even if the story is transparently false.

At the height of World War II, as the United States began to
ship much of its food supply to troops in the field, the federal

---

* Note that I'm not saying that blogs of opposing ideologies never link to one
another. Indeed, links to the other side show up all the time. But if you look
closely at the rhythm of blog postings, you notice here, too, proof of Lowin's
theories about strong and weak consonance and dissonance. Bloggers frequently
link to weak dissonant messages—sites that are oppositional but that are easy to
knock down; far less often do you see liberal blogs point out a well-reasoned argument by a conservative writer, or a conservative site pointing to a left-wing
blogger's brilliant plan to end the Iraq war. It's the same thing as when Bill
O'Reilly invites liberals on his show to shoot them down: political bloggers, like
all partisans, love shooting fish in a barrel.

government imposed tight rations on staple foods for citizens at home. Sugar, butter, coffee, and meat were limited. The measures, born out of emergency and bolstered by overflowing patriotism, worked surprisingly well; Americans were only too glad to scrimp in an effort to help the boys at war. But military planners worried that if the war dragged on for many years, the domestic population might become malnourished for want of protein. This posed a logistical threat—a starved nation could never hold up the industrial demands of war.

Some people in the government proposed an unusual solution to the problem: that people turn to organ meat as a source of nutrition during the war years. Hearts, kidneys, brains, stomachs, and other protein-rich animal parts were in large supply but had rarely come near the American table. How could Americans be persuaded to eat offal? Even upsurging patriotism, after all, wouldn't make a hog's head palatable on the plate. To look into the question, the War Department set up a research group, the Committee on Food Habits, composed of several influential social scientists, including the cultural anthropologist Margaret Mead and the psychologist Kurt Lewin, who was renowned for his work on how groups of people interact with one another.

In an attempt to change what Americans ate, the Committee on Food Habits conducted surveys and interviews to find out, first, how Americans thought about food. Their work, though, illustrates an idea that is quite a bit more intriguing than the vagaries of mid-century American menu-planning: it shows that even for something as fundamental as eating, people look to others to determine the "reality" around them.

You eat to live, but *what* you eat is more a cultural choice than a mere act of biological survival. When the Committee on Food Habits asked Americans about their diets, it found that people's

feelings about food were tied up with their social identities—
with what they thought was appropriate for "us" to eat. Middle-
class white people considered some foods—like lutefisk or col-
lard greens—to be inappropriate for their tables; it was food for
other people. Organ meat wasn't acceptable either; only poor
people ate offal. But the committee's research suggested a way
for the government to go about altering these tastes.

During interviews with women in a small midwestern city,
Lewin and his assistants hit upon a characteristic of wartime
America. Housewives, they found, were the nation's "gatekeepers" of food. Husbands and children often ate whatever wives
and mothers brought to the table. The best way to change
what the nation ate, then, would be to change what housewives
served.

But how could the government do that? Working with housewives who were volunteers for the Red Cross, Lewin and his
assistants tried two different strategies to convince women to
cook organ meats for their families. The first was straightforward: they had an expert on nutrition talk to housewives about
how and why they ought to serve the new meats (the nutritionist handed out recipe ideas for "delicious dishes" that had
been a great success with her own family). But Lewin, who
had long been captivated by group dynamics—how interacting
with others changes human behavior—was also curious about
another method; he wanted to let groups of women talk about
organ meats for themselves, in the absence of a nutritionist's
lecture.

In these sessions, a researcher usually started the discussion
by going over why America needed to change its diet, and then
she asked the women for their own opinions on the problem.
This often prompted a wide-ranging discussion. The housewives
wondered about the nutritional benefits of switching to organ

meat, brought up their worries that offal was what lower-class people ate, or expressed their ignorance about how to cook the new meats. The researcher interjected nutrition information or handed out recipes and answered questions about cooking techniques. Then, after about ten or fifteen minutes, the researcher asked the women to reflect on their discussion and to come to a decision, as a group, about whether they should begin serving organ meats to their families. Together, then, the women would take a vow to change their menus.

A week after these sessions, Lewin and his staff checked back with all the women to see whether they had cooked up any heart, kidney, or brain dishes for their families. Of the forty-one housewives who had seen the nutritionist's lecture, only four had prepared organ meat. The women who'd discussed the decision with one another, though, had acted quite differently; twenty-three of the forty-four in those groups had made good on their pledge to cook a new meat recipe (most of them served hearts, not kidneys or brains). A group discussion, then, was five times more effective at changing housewives' menus than was a lecture by a nutritionist.

Several researchers investigating Americans' food habits later replicated Lewin's findings with other groups. It seems clear why the discussion method worked so well. If people's beliefs about food were really social values rather than nutritional values—if, for instance, middle-class whites avoided collards out of their prejudice toward blacks—then a presentation by a nutritionist would seem to miss the main lever of persuasion. The discussion groups, Lewin believed, worked by altering the women's social calculus; because each housewife had seen the others acknowledging the importance of serving offal for dinner, she'd decided to cook hearts in order to fit in with what had become a new cultural norm. In describing these women's actions

today, we might invoke that well-known after-school-special so-
briquet: the housewives had given in to "peer pressure."

The government never put the Committee on Food Habits'
findings to wide use. The war lasted half as long as military
planners had feared and thus did not seriously threaten nutrition
at home. Lewin's work with the housewives, though, still has
resonance today. It wasn't only remarkable that the women had
decided to cook differently after talking to their peers; it's that
they'd been persuaded to *feel* differently, too. Fourteen women
who had taken part in the organ-meat discussion groups told
Lewin and his staff that they had never before cooked kidneys,
hearts, or brains. They were intensely put off by these foods;
they went into the study thinking of organ meat as not even
falling within the realm of food. Yet after they talked to other
women about the meat, and after they decided with the group
to change their habits, a cow heart was transformed, for them,
into a perfectly edible thing.

Numerous experiments with small groups have documented
a similar idea: that what we understand to be acceptable for us—
and in a sense what we understand to be the "truth" around us—
is defined through our interactions with other people. In interviews with soldiers during World War II, the sociologist Samuel
Stouffer discovered that when "green" soldiers—men who'd
never seen combat—were placed in divisions of other green
men, few reported feeling ready for the fight. But when green
soldiers were sent as replacements to divisions of veterans,
more than twice as many considered themselves well prepared.
Their sense of readiness wasn't a product of simple conformity;
rather, their feeling had to do with the context in which they
were living. The green soldiers who came into daily contact
with veterans took on the sensibility of their more experienced
brothers in arms, and thus they, too, felt ready.

Lewin had a name for this idea: "social reality." When many people around us feel that a certain thing is right or true—whether it concerns the combat-readiness of a division, the propriety of eating cow hearts, or even, indeed, whether John Kerry acted heroically during war—that group belief becomes, for each of us, an idea that we, too, take as fact. "To the South Sea Islanders the world may be flat," Lewin summed the story up. "To the European it is round. 'Reality' . . . is not absolute. It differs with the group to which the individual belongs."

Social reality, a phenomenon that Kurt Lewin described in the middle of the last century, becomes important today if you consider how technology is changing the ways we form our social groups. The groups that Lewin studied—Red Cross–volunteering housewives in a midwestern town, for instance—came together as a result of propinquity, the members' geographical proximity to one another. Propinquity plays a surprisingly large role in most human relationships. In 1950, Leon Festinger, Stanley Schachter, and Kurt Back, who were protégés of Lewin, studied the interactions between residents of the Westgate apartment complex, near the MIT campus. They found that most people's friends were others who lived nearby; 90 percent of the friendships were between people in the same apartment building, and 42 percent were between next-door neighbors. The propinquity effect has been demonstrated in a host of other settings: in offices, college dorms, classrooms, army barracks, and other physical spaces, we become friendly—and even more than friendly, as propinquity is a key factor in marriage—with those we're closest to spatially.

There is something stultifying, to be sure, about propinquity's hold over life; the idea that our friends, romances, business partnerships, and consequently our very conceptions of "reality" are in some way predetermined by physical space seems unfair, a denial of the full range of the life's possibilities. Freedom from propinquity is part of what makes new communications technology so exhilarating. The Web, talk radio, cable news—they connect us to others who are like us but are far away. They provide a haven from the oppressiveness of the nearby. Instead of getting together with people who are close to us physically, now we can get together with people who are close to us ideologically, psychically, emotionally, aesthetically. In other words, rather than through propinquity, we find our social groups nowadays through selective exposure.

And it's in this fact that the world splits apart: it's here that you see why new possibilities to choose what you read, what you watch, and what you listen to can fracture the culture's sense of what's real and what's not. Selective exposure is not important only because it lets you choose the information that suits you; it's important because it lets you choose *people* who suit you. And it's the people who matter. Whether the question involves organ meat or an officer's medals, it's through our connections with others, as Kurt Lewin discovered, that we choose our social reality. To the South Sea Islanders the world is flat. To the Europeans it is round. And for the tribe that had sprung up around the Swift Boat Veterans for Truth, the world was plainly wrong about John Kerry: his unfitness was, to them, reality.

The Kerry campaign has frequently been criticized for the clumsy way it handled the Swift Boat attacks. Through the spring and for much of the summer of 2004, Kerry's operatives and the candidate himself were publicly cool to the story, choosing to ignore the veterans' arguments rather than responding in any strong way. Yet it's easy to appreciate the campaign's dilemma. The Kerry people were keenly monitoring the veterans' growing strength, but many in the campaign believed that responding to the group would inevitably draw greater attention to their effort. The difficulty stemmed from the novel design of the Swift Boat marketing plan—because the chatter was confined to right-wing channels, Bob Shrum and Mary Beth Cahill, the two operatives who ran the Kerry shop, saw the veterans' charges as nothing more than a bit of extremist silliness. Sure, they were all over the radio and the Web, but that didn't mean their message would ever filter into the vast middle. And the middle was what Kerry was fighting for.

Some people in the campaign counseled otherwise. Mark Mellman, Kerry's pollster, told me that he was an advocate of strong action. "While it may not have been getting high coverage, this is the kind of story people talk about at the water cooler," he said. Mellman saw the Swift Boat story as having the potential to go supernova—once the blog and radio buzz crossed the line into TV, things would just explode. "I thought there would be a lot of people talking about this even if they're not watching it on the national networks."

His advice was prophetic. In June and July, the Swift Boat story began to develop in just the way that Mellman had worried. Cable television began to notice. Twenty-four-hour news networks function like baleen whales of the media world, trolling the currents to pick up every bit of warm life floating about. TV producers began to swim toward the Swift Vets. It wasn't a swarm; between April and the start of August, the cable networks ran only a couple dozen segments mentioning the Swift Boat campaign, a relatively small number considering the huge blocks of time they're responsible for filling. A typical cable news viewer would have had a slim chance of learning about the campaign in those months. Still, the attention suggested to the Swift Boat Veterans that they were in possession of a story that, given the right kind of stoking, could be turned into something hot—something big enough to dominate cable news.

The second measure of the Swift Boat campaign's growing success involved money. The veterans had begun their effort well near broke. O'Neill himself was one of their largest early donors, putting $25,000 into the effort; Harlan Crow, a Dallas developer and Republican contributor, added a similar amount in the early weeks. And after that, for a while, this was about the only cash they had—a sum that in politics isn't especially great, considering all that it costs to set up something big (Spaeth's services alone cost the group more than $27,000 during their first month). But now, as they began to land on the beaches of talk radio, Republican money men, particularly the handful of Texas millionaires and billionaires who had long supported many conservative Southern politicians (including, notably, George W. Bush), took notice.

Late in June, Bob Perry, a homebuilding tycoon in Houston, contributed $100,000 to the Swift Boat Veterans, and then in the middle of July, he did it again (over the course of the campaign, Perry would donate more than $4 million). On August 2, T. Boone Pickens, a Texas oilman, sent the group a check for $400,000. Now they finally had enough to light the match that would spark a nationwide fire.

Their match was television advertising. August 4, 2004, was the day the group announced its advertising plan, and it's at this point that the Swift Boat story crossed the line from something analyzable—something discrete, something you could see flaring up in a few hundred places over a period of a few months, on the radio and a handful of Web sites—into the conflagration that then consumed America. Rick Reed, a political advertising consultant who designed the group's TV spots, told me that everyone in the campaign was caught off-guard by what happened after they put out the ads. They had purchased a tiny ad run—just a half-million dollars of TV time in some of the smallest markets in Ohio and a couple other swing states. "We couldn't afford Columbus, Cleveland, and Cincinnati," Reed said. "It was more like Dayton and Charleston, West Virginia."

But the ferocious attack—the ad accused Kerry of lying to win his medals—immediately became the main topic on right-wing radio. "My first indication that this thing was going to get major coverage was when Rush and Gordon Liddy and Laura Ingraham mentioned it," Reed said, referring to the biggest acts in talk radio.

Soon the ad was plastered all over cable news and then was even aired on broadcast TV. The Swift Boat Veterans' Web site got so much traffic—you could watch the ad there and mail it to your friends—that it briefly went down. The group quickly got it back up again, which was fortunate, because it soon became a major point in their fund-raising effort. Conservatives from all over, encouraged by this one ad, began to open up their pocketbooks.

After the ads began running, Mark Mellman noticed an immediate impact in Kerry's polling, but others in the campaign still counseled against attacking. "They took the view that it was impossible for ads in a small number of markets covered mainly on Fox and other right-wing places to be doing something big," Mellman said. It would be two weeks before Kerry made a statement against the veterans. By then, the boat had sailed.

If you look back at coverage in the national newspapers and other news outlets from that time, you can find some excellent reporting that pointed to the flaws in nearly every Swift Boat charge against Kerry. The *Washington Post* investigated the events of March 13, 1969, the day Kerry rescued a member of his crew who'd fallen overboard in the Bay Hap River, to earn a

Bronze Star and his third Purple Heart. Kerry's tale of bravery, the paper found, largely checked out. Many outlets, including *Salon* and the *Los Angeles Times*, looked at the veterans' attack on Kerry's first Purple Heart; this one, too, was thin.

Among the most persistent reporters on the story was Michael Kranish of the *Boston Globe*, who has long covered Kerry. Just after the Swift Boat Veterans launched their ads, Kranish published a blockbuster piece that quoted George Elliot, one of the Swift Boat Veterans, saying that he'd made "a terrible mistake" in suggesting that Kerry had shot a wounded Viet Cong soldier in the back to earn a Silver Star. Elliot told Kranish that he believed that Kerry actually deserved the medal.

But the right-wing response to Kranish's piece proves the power of selective exposure and the strength of the tribe of supporters that Merrie Spaeth had cultivated over the preceding three months. Matt Drudge, the proprietor of the popular right-wing Web site the Drudge Report, posted Kranish's story but also added a sensational note suggesting that Kranish was not to be trusted because he'd been "commissioned to write the foreword of the Kerry-Edwards campaign book." *This* story then traveled around the right-wing blogs. Instapundit opined that Kranish's reporting "sounds fishy." Little Green Footballs said the Kranish story "is a lie." The Swift Boat Veterans immediately attacked Kranish; Elliot said he'd been tricked. In reality, Kranish had never been commissioned to write anything for the Kerry-Edwards campaign; Drudge's story was at best a mistake, at worst a fabrication. But attacking Kranish's credibility easily dimmed the import of his story. The partisans remained impervious to reality.

3

Trusting Your Senses: Selective Perception and 9/11

Boom!" Phillip Jayhan, a businessman and messenger who lives near Chicago, recently told an interviewer. "You could actually see a missile. Missile, rocket, incendiary device, whatever you want to call it—there is something that shoots out. You can actually see this projectile for a few frames. And you can definitely notice the cockpit going into the building, and the missile going in six or eight feet to the right. It's just plain as day." Jayhan is a clean-cut, chain-smoking fellow in his middle forties, with dusty blond hair and a quick, meandering, argumentative style. He was describing the apotheosis of his search for what "really" happened on September 11, 2001. It's a video he found online a few months after the attacks, and he says it proves something so definitive and unaccounted for that it will completely overturn all you think you know about that day.

I met Jayhan late on a warm summer evening in Santa Clara, California. He was in town for Conspiracy Con, an annual convention of adherents to fringe ideas. The speakers included some of the nation's most prominent proponents of MIHOP—the idea that the government Made It Happen on Purpose; Jayhan planned to interview many of them for a documentary film he'd been making on what he calls the "9/11 Truth Movement." In his hotel room, Jayhan asked me what I thought happened on 9/11. When I told him I believed the official theory, he raised an eyebrow in a way that suggested more sorrow than anger. Then he pulled out his laptop and logged on to his Web site, LetsRoll911.org, to show me the images that turned him around.

Jayhan's alternative theory of 9/11 began with a gleam in a photograph. Shortly after the attack, he was sifting through pictures of United Airlines Flight 175, the second aircraft to hit the World Trade Center towers, when he spotted what looked like a tubular bulge on the belly of the plane. Later, he discovered images that seemed to show an explosive flash in the same spot. Then, in a video clip that had been archived by a Web site called Camera Planet, Jayhan found the clincher.

If you play it at full speed, the footage, captured by one of the many television cameras that turned toward World Trade Center after the first plane hit, shows only the monstrously familiar. The towers loom in the picture. The one on the right, the North Tower, is partly occluded by smoke; the one on the left is serene, untouched. Then, in a snap, something breaks the expanse of blue sky bordering the South Tower. You begin to recognize it as the silhouette of an aircraft, but by then it's half gone. "The plane is absorbed into the World Trade Center as though it were made of butter," Jayhan wrote on his site. This is the disaster the world saw live, the nearly surreal moment when it dawned on you that what you were watching was something that someone had planned.

Jayhan spotted another possibility in the clip—the footprint of a more sinister history—only after he looked at a version that had been slowed down and that zoomed in tightly on Flight 175. The footage he showed me now, quite distorted from the manipulation, begins with the hulking silver mass of the South Tower filling the field. The scene moves so slowly that you can make out each individual frame of video. The aircraft seems to jerk, rather than slide, into the picture. As the first third of the plane enters the shot, you see that what you're looking at is its underside. Flight 175 is banking away from the camera, into the tower. Then, near the front of the fuselage, just where the body begins to taper into the cockpit, an indistinctly shaped bright light appears on the undercarriage of the plane. This illuminated slice, Jayhan believes, is the exhaust plume of a missile.

He pointed it out with no hint of hesitation. To Jayhan, the missile is as recognizable in the shot as the plane and the building. But I couldn't see it. For me, the video is too dim and blurry to discern any significant detail. You'd have a hard time making out even the United Airlines logo on the tail. The picture is drained of color; like so much about 9/11 and its aftermath, the scene is lost in shades of gray. Yet not only does Jayhan see a missile here, he sees it *move*, too. As the aircraft speeds to its doom, the bright spark shifts slightly lower on the plane's body, and then, at the same moment that the cockpit slips through the skin of the tower, there is a small explosion of orange.

The entire sequence takes place over the course of just a few frames of video—in less than a split second at the film's full speed. But Jayhan believes that in this quick moment, we're witnessing something dastardly: Flight 175 is carrying a projectile, and just before the aircraft hits the building, the missile jettisons from the plane, falls a few feet away, and then flies straight at the tower. The orange flash is the projectile—not the plane—making contact with the building. "What's better than a smoking gun?" Jayhan asked on his Web site. "How about a picture of the bullet! It's almost as if God's angels were aiming the cameras so as to make sure the day's events were duly recorded and archived for later criminal prosecution."

Four decades ago, a fifty-eight-year-old Russian immigrant living in Dallas learned that his political hero, the nation's popular young president, would be coming to town. The man, a manufacturer of women's clothing, had his offices in the city's textile hub, the Dal-Tex Building, on the downtown corner of Houston and Elm Streets, just across the road from the Texas School Book Depository and Dealey Plaza. The president's motorcade would be passing by this very spot. So on the afternoon of the visit, a bright, warm Friday, the man collected his secretary and his camera and walked to the top of a small promontory bordering Elm Street. The camera was the top-of-the-line home recorder of the day, a Bell & Howell Model 414 PD, which you wound by hand to capture thirty seconds of images on 8 mm film. The secretary was Marilyn Sitzman, whom the man needed to help him steady himself as he took in the scene (he suffered from vertigo). The promontory where they stood would come to be known as the "grassy knoll." It was 12:30 p.m. on November 22, 1963.

The sequence that Abraham Zapruder recorded that day runs for twenty-six seconds and offers the most definitive photographic account of the moment that John F. Kennedy was assassinated. About a dozen people were in the crowd that afternoon filming the presidential visit on movie and still cameras. Just four of them caught the fatal shot. But only Zapruder did so with any real clarity. His film became not only the most iconic document of what happened that day; in a real sense, it is the *only* document. If you close your eyes and picture the Kennedy assassination, it's the Zapruder film that plays back in your mind: The presidential limousine coming slowly down the street, bystanders in set-piece sixties fashions, oblivious of the calamity about to unfold. The stunning violence of that shot to the head. The first lady, in trademark pink and pillbox hat, in a panic, crawling up and back out of the limousine. The Secret Service man Clinton Hill leaping into the car before it speeds away.

Yet to watch Zapruder's film today is to realize not only its iconography, but also the technical limits of 1960s recording technology. The camera jiggles about, it loses focus, the colors bleed into one another and obscure much faraway detail. The film contains no sound. It's nearly impossible to tell, from just the viewing, how many shots rang out that morning, and when, and from which direction. Is the film even authentic? Has it been edited in any way?

To skeptics of the lone gunman theory, the film's history proves a cover-up: Zapruder sold the sequence to *Life* magazine, which published still images from the recording but would not allow broadcast of the full-motion sequence. It was only in 1975, more than a decade after the assassination, that the public got a look at the film (Geraldo Rivera played it on his late-night news show). After that, assassination theories began to take off. Lip readers, film effects specialists, physicists, logicians, and neurosurgeons have all been called in to decipher every instant that Zapruder captured. Their various findings support every argument. Depending on which way you see the president's head snap after he's shot, you can say that the Zapruder film shows that there is a gunman on the grassy knoll. Or, conversely, you can argue that it shows that Lee Harvey Oswald acted alone from a perch in the depository window. Some say the sequence in the film proves that Oswald wouldn't have had enough time to get off three shots; others say it illustrates exactly the opposite.

The Zapruder film may be the most perfect rendering we have of the chaotic half-minute surrounding Kennedy's murder. But the disputes it has fostered also illustrate the shortcomings of photography and of film. Zapruder's film tells us that in order to create a shared truth, a single image isn't enough; pictures and movies, like words, invite wide argument, and sometimes they're almost uselessly, infinitely interpretable.

We have tried to solve this problem, in the generation since the Kennedy assassination, by recording from vastly more vantage points: more cameras, more audio tape, surveillance of everything about us. Recording technology is now ubiquitous: Billions of tiny cameras. Flickr. YouTube. When a tsunami devastates the planet, when war ravages a far-off land, when the police brutalize a suspect, or when a dictator is hanged, we'll see it. Usually from many angles, and often it'll be amateurs, not professionals, wielding the cameras. The world is constantly watched; each of us, now, is Zapruder himself.

When United Airlines Flight 175 slammed into the South Tower of the World Trade Center on September 11, 2001, at least thirty television photographers caught the impact.* Countless still cameras, some in the hands of professionals and many held by ordinary people, observed it careering into Manhattan. And as the buildings in New York toppled from their full height into oblivion, photographers captured every angle of that scene,

---

* The crash of Flight 175 was one of few historical instances in which an act of homicide was shown on live television; the first and most famous such broadcast occurred two days after the Kennedy assassination, when the Dallas nightclub owner Jack Ruby killed Lee Harvey Oswald as he was being transferred from police headquarters to the Dallas County Jail.

too. There are recordings of 911 calls, of officials responding to the attack, and of eyewitnesses screaming their horror in the street.

When you experience events of extreme stress or surprise—when something comes at you out of the dark and upends everything you thought you knew about the world—you're apt to remember the moment in vivid detail, recalling for years and even decades later what you saw, what you heard, what it felt like to be there, then. Psychologists call these "flashbulb memories," and our society's classic flashbulb recollections involve the Kennedy assassination. If you were alive in 1963, you remember exactly where you were and what you were doing when you heard the president had been shot. That's exactly how people put it, too: people *heard* there had been a shooting in Dallas. Nobody had seen it. But if you were alive on 9/11, what you remember is what happened at the scene. You saw it unfold. Your flashbulb memory is of the thing itself.

What's strange is that despite the dazzling clarity of our documents, disputes over what actually happened on 9/11—arguments that seemed to begin the moments the planes broke the serenity of the New York skyline—rage on. Indeed, people who put their faith in MIHOP find proof of their theories in the thousands of photographs and sounds recorded that day. When Phillip Jayhan looks at videos of Flight 175, he sees a missile there. And he is not alone. A poll by Zogby International conducted in the spring of 2006 found that 42 percent of Americans believe that "the U.S. government and its 9/11 Commission concealed or refused to investigate critical evidence that contradicts their official explanation of the September 11th attacks." A survey by Ohio University revealed that a third of Americans think federal agents either carried out the attack or deliberately neglected to stop it "because they wanted the United States to go to war in the Middle East." Sixteen percent suspect that explosives were secretly planted in the World Trade Center towers before the attacks. More than a fifth say that a missile, rather than a plane, struck the Pentagon that morning.

Here is the paradox of living in a world that's constantly watched. It turns out that when you add more cameras, more tape recorders, and better systems to broadcast these documents—when you make it easier for people to capture and to disseminate documentary evidence from any event's ground zero—you don't necessarily bolster agreement about what's actually happening around us. In other words, you don't always strengthen the truth. Sometimes, in fact, more recordings lead to *greater* uncertainty.

We've got better images of September 11, 2001, than of November 22, 1963. But in the case of 9/11, just as in the case of Kennedy's murder, the truth has split. Opposing realities have taken hold. Getting to the bottom of this split—of why audio and visual proof is disintegrating in our networked world—requires a deeper understanding of how we process documentary evidence. Our eyes and ears now feast upon audio and video *proof*. Our minds, though, will have none of it.

In the fall of 1951, Princeton met Dartmouth in the final game of the Ivy League football season. Twenty-seven thousand fans, some who'd traveled all the way from Dartmouth, crowded into Princeton's Palmer Stadium for a match-up that many expected would resemble a coronation. Princeton's Tigers had been having a very good year. Not only were they undefeated, but they had a star halfback, Dick Kazmaier, who was the most gifted player in college football. He'd been featured on the cover of *Time* magazine and would go on to win the Heisman Trophy. Even the Dartmouth fans had come mainly to see Kazmaier play. And indeed, as expected, the Tigers, with Dashing Dick at their back, trounced the Indians 13–0 to win the championship.

But in the days that followed, the Princeton-Dartmouth meeting would be remembered not for any display of athleticism but instead for the feeling, which blossomed on both campuses, that the other school had played dirty. It was a very rough game. "Casualties on both sides," the *New York Times* reported, "were heavy." In the second quarter Kazmaier was tackled so hard that he suffered a broken nose and a mild concussion and was forced to sit out the rest of the game. Another Princeton man may have been kicked in the ribs (accounts, as we'll see, differ). In the third period a few Dartmouth players were dealt serious injuries, including Jim Miller, the second-string quarterback, who suffered a broken left leg.

At Princeton, the idea began to circulate that Dartmouth had deliberately set out to hurt Princeton's star, Kazmaier. That was the only way Dartmouth knew how to play, students said. Dartmouth fans, on the other hand, came to believe that Princeton was just whining—the game they remembered wasn't much worse than what one usually saw when two teams went hard to win. Kazmaier's injuries were unfortunate, but that was to be expected in a contact sport, folks at Dartmouth argued. The idea that anyone on their side had *tried* to go after Kazmaier was nonsense.

Albert Hastorf, a psychologist at Dartmouth, and Hadley Cantril, a sociologist at Princeton, first noticed the divergent views of the game in their respective campuses' student newspapers. The differences struck them as curious. How could people who'd watched the same game have come away with such contrary ideas of what had taken place on the field? The researchers came up with an intriguing way of digging into the problem. They decided to show groups at each school—two fraternities at Dartmouth, and two eating clubs at Princeton—a film clip of the game. They asked the students to act as unbiased referees, marking down all of the infractions they could spot. The results were remarkable. Although all students were shown the same film, each side "saw" a completely different game.

Dartmouth students found a roughly equal number of transgressions committed by each team—about four errors per side, as they counted it, although Dartmouth did notice the Princeton players making many more "flagrant," as opposed to "mild," infractions. Princeton students saw the game very differently; they watched the movie in wild-eyed anger at the Dartmouth team's clear disregard for the rules. Students at Princeton claimed to witness an average of almost ten infractions committed by Dartmouth during the game, the majority of them flagrant. Princeton fans saw *Princeton* players make only half as many errors, and most were minor.

The disparate reading of the film, Hastorf and Cantril found, was not a product of mere bias. The fans were not *choosing* to see actions in the game—or deliberately overlooking things—in a way that corresponded with their feelings. Rather, it was a matter of visual perception: their eyes were taking in the same game, but their brains seemed to be processing the events in two distinct ways.

In their report on the study, the researchers tell the story of a Dartmouth alumnus who ordered a copy of the film to show to a gathering of friends. When the alum received the reel, it didn't make sense to him. He'd heard that his side had played a dirty game, but where were those parts on the movie? He sent an urgent telegram to officials at Dartmouth: "Preview of Princeton movie indicates considerable cutting of important part please wire explanation and possibly air mail missing part before showing scheduled for January 25 we have splicing equipment." Of course, nothing was missing from his copy of the film. What was missing, instead, was in his head.

A football game, if you regard it with a certain expansiveness, bears some resemblance to a lot of things in life—indeed, you might say, to the whole business of living. Football is a social occurrence: what happens in a game hinges on a confluence of people, including not only the players but also, among many others, the coaches, the referees, the owners, the league officials, the committees who make the rules, the architects who design the stadiums, and the farmers who raise the animals whose hide goes into the manufacture of that eponymous spheroid orb.

Football is not a discrete event, either. A "game" is more properly thought of as a collection of plays that happen in sequence, each linked together, determining the fate of the next. The plays, in turn, are made up of many smaller actions—tossing, catching, running, blocking—and these, too, can be dug into deeper still, until you're analyzing the merest of details that make up what we think of as football. A specific quick-footed succession of passing steps. The beautiful snap of a quarterback's arm. The ungainly manner in which a star player is slammed into the ground, on his nose.

Football, in other words, is a lot of people doing a lot of things together over a series of overlapping time spans, and the thrill of it is that on some of these time spans there is so much going on that it's hard to know what's important and what's not. "There's an instant before it collapses into some generally agreed-upon fact when a football play, like a traffic accident, is all conjecture and fragments and partial views," Michael Lewis points out in *The Blind Side: Evolution of a Game*, his excellent exploration of modern football. But not only car accidents and football plays are like this; everything is. Think about a schoolyard at recess or a bank robbery or a baseball game or a business meeting or a political debate. Think about a terrorist attack or a presidential assassination. Or just think about all that happened yesterday: every "thing" that occurs is really a million smaller things involving a million people. But which of the million things and which of the million people do we notice? And which do we overlook?

Hastorf and Cantril argued that it is the stratified structure of football, and of life, that explains the difference between what the Dartmouth fans "saw" and what the Princeton fans "saw" when they watched an identical movie of the season-ending game. There are countless "occurrences" during a football game, but "an *occurrence* becomes an *event*"—it becomes something we notice—"only when that happening has significance," they wrote. The rub is that not everyone finds the same things significant. What each of us notices is a function of a personalized calculus—an idiosyncratic, unconscious filter, built up over a lifetime, that we apply to all that we take in. When the Dartmouth alumnus watched the film of the game, he interpreted the images through the prism of his own life. His was a mind reared at Dartmouth. To him, the idea of a Dartmouth footballer playing dirty did not—could not—register. So he could not see Dartmouth's rough play in the film.

You might wonder which side was right. Was it the Dartmouth fans or the Princeton fans who possessed the "correct" view about what occurred on the field? It is true that many news accounts of the day faulted Dartmouth. But there's also a sense in which we cannot really know what happened, and this is precisely the message of the Dartmouth-Princeton study. As in some spooky experiment out of quantum mechanics, the very reality of the game appears to waver according to the act of observing it. It's a strange notion. Hastorf and Cantril's work seems to confirm a fundamentally postmodern and faintly creepy thing about life: that what happens around us is as much in our minds as it is in the world. "It is inaccurate and misleading to say that different people have different 'attitudes' concerning the same 'thing,'" Hastorf and Cantril wrote. "For the 'thing' simply is *not* the same for different people whether the 'thing' is a football game, a presidential candidate, Communism, or spinach."

In the last chapter I told you about the phenomenon of selective exposure, which involved choosing your sources of information according to your preexisting biases. Hastorf and Cantril's study illustrates a different cognitive trap. *Selective perception* says that even when two people of opposing ideologies overcome their tendency toward selective exposure and choose to watch the *same* thing, they may still end up being pushed apart from each other. That's because they really won't be experiencing the "same" thing—whether it's a football game, a presidential assassination, or a terrorist attack, each of them will have seen, heard, felt, and understood the "thing" vastly differently from the others who have experienced it.

As I'll explain, the effects of selective perception have become more powerful now, in this fragmented age, but it is not a novel phenomenon. Hastorf and Cantril did their work in the middle of the last century, and the implications of their study have been explored by dozens of researchers in the decades since. You can see the mark of selective perception, for instance, in assassination researchers' various opposing interpretations of what's going on in the Zapruder film.

Perhaps the most famous well-researched instance of many people coming away with different ideas about the same thing occurred in the United States in the early 1970s. The thing was the sitcom *All in the Family*, featuring Carroll O'Connor as the right-wing bigot Archie Bunker. The show, which debuted in 1971, quickly became the number-one television program in the country, seen weekly by nearly a hundred million people. It was also beloved by critics, cultural commentators, and civil rights activists, who believed that it offered an honest portrayal of racists—especially the stupidity of racists—in America. Although Archie regularly spouted a torrent of racial and ethnic slurs—"jungle bunnies," "black beauties," "Heeb," "spade," "spic," "yenta," "gook," "chink"—he also said a good deal to reveal his ill-education: that he was "mortifried" or that something was "not German to the conversation" or that the death penalty was "a detergent to crime." The show's admirers—not to mention its creators—thought that everyone could see that Archie was a boob.

But could they? In the fall of 1971, the novelist Laura Hobson published a scathing critique of the show in the *New York Times*. She pointed out that Archie never used some of the most hateful racial slurs—he did not, for instance, say "nigger" or "kike." *All in the Family* was cleaning up racism. Archie was a "loveable bigot," and of the millions who regularly tuned in to the show, there were likely many who didn't realize that it was actually meant to be a parody—and not a celebration—of Archie's way of thinking. In other words, Hobson believed that the series was provoking selective perception on a national scale. Well-educated cultural commentators enjoyed the show because they thought it affirmed their beliefs. But to perhaps a vast number of Americans, Archie was someone to look up to—a hero of the working class—and these people loved *All in the Family* because it affirmed *their* beliefs.

A few weeks after Hobson's article appeared, Norman Lear, the creator of the show, shot back at her complaint. Hobson, he said, was raising "the age-old specter of the intellectuals' mistrust of the lower middle classes." To think that some people would fail to recognize the folly of Archie's ways, Lear declared, was itself a form of bigotry.

What were people seeing when they watched *All in the Family*? Was it a show about a simpleton whose views on the world were plainly antiquated or, rather, one about a plain-speaking man with the courage to describe the world honestly? Neil Vidmar and Milton Rokeach, two psychologists who were inspired by Hastorf and Cantril's study of the Dartmouth-Princeton game, decided to take up the question. They gathered a group of Americans—237 high school students from the Midwest, most of whom were male and all of whom were white—and asked them to fill out an anonymous questionnaire. Vidmar and Rokeach solicited the students' deepest feelings about life and television—or, at least, about what they thought of people who were different from them. To find out who was of "high" prejudice and who was of "low" prejudice, the researchers asked the students six probing questions, things like "Do you think white students and negro students should go to the same schools or to separate schools?" and "Do you feel there should be a strong law against homosexuals, or do you feel that if two adults want to be homosexual, that is their own business?" Finally, the researchers asked the students what they thought was going on in *All in the Family*.

It turned out that Norman Lear was wrong, and Laura Hobson was right. The majority of those surveyed found *All in the Family* hilarious. But bigots and nonbigots harbored vastly different ideas about what was happening on the show. When asked who seemed to win most of the arguments—was it Archie or his hippie son-in-law, Mike?—the bigots thought it was Archie. Those who weren't bigoted thought it was Mike. The two sides also disagreed about what the show was trying to tell us about Archie. Those whom Vidmar and Rokeach classified as "low prejudice" thought Archie was "a bigot, domineering, rigid, loud, and that he mistreats his wife." People of "high prejudice" had the opposite take: Archie was "down-to-earth, honest, hardworking, predictable, and kind enough to allow his son-in-law and daughter to live with him." It was a classic case of selective perception.

Norman Lear had set out to make a show that skewered hatred with satire. Nearly everyone who shared Lear's worldview thought that he'd done just that. Rooting out bigotry "has defied man's best efforts for generations, and the weapon of laughter just might succeed," Jack Gould, the *New York Times* critic, wrote when he first saw the show. But not everyone in America got the joke. Thanks to selective perception, some people were getting a *different* joke. Even when the whole country is watching the same thing, in fact, we aren't. Not really.

The 9/11 attacks profoundly unsettled Phillip Jayhan, as they had everyone else. But for him, the enormity of the disaster registered not as fear but as doubt. Jayhan is a preternatural skeptic. He has long harbored a deep distrust of the government and of the institutions that exert power on the world, a fact that became evident during the course of our interview in Santa Clara. As I pushed him to divulge more about his belief that 9/11 was carried out by government agents, he revealed what he said were the secret ways of the world. He showed me how when you fold up 5-, 10-, 20-, and 100-dollar bills a certain way, you can create pictures resembling the World Trade Center and the Pentagon on fire. "This is a parlor game that the elites are playing with us," he said. "They're mocking us."

Jayhan also described an extensive theory of satanic cultism that he said actually fuels many of the shifts of power we see in society. His idea, inspired by *The Franklin Cover-Up: Child Abuse, Satanism, and Murder in Nebraska*, a book by former Nebraska state senator John DeCamp, is that Satanists routinely kidnap children and provide them to politicians for sexual trysts; the cult then keeps the politicians in line through blackmail.

Finally, Jayhan implored me to investigate a theory that George W. Bush was involved in the ritualistic murder of seventeen people in Brownsville, Texas, in 1984.*

Given his worldview, it was obvious that Jayhan really believed that he saw a missile shooting out from Flight 175. Or, to put it more accurately, he *really did see it*. If you think about what Hastorf and Cantril's football fans saw in the game replay, Jayhan's interpretation seems understandable. A billion things happened to a million people on 9/11, and if you watch all the videos and listen to all of the audio, there's a lot that you'll find significant and there's a lot you'll overlook. Some of it you've really got to puzzle out. Jayhan puzzles it out according to his own thoughts about how things work in society. As a consequence of his ideas about the world generally, he is naturally prone to seeing something in those pictures that I—as a consequence of my own vastly different beliefs about the world—do not. There's a bright spot on the belly of the plane, it shifts slightly, and then there's an orange flash. To me—and to many others who've examined Jayhan's ideas—the sequence represents nothing more than the sun's reflection off the plane. To Jayhan, it's unmistakably a missile. That's selective perception.

But unlike the controversy over what *All in the Family* really means, the question of whether a missile was mounted under Flight 175 obviously has only one correct answer. The evidence (beyond Jayhan's pictures) supports one side completely: all major investigations into the attacks—the 9/11 Commission's report, the two major federal engineering studies that looked into what happened to the towers, and even the many assessments by other MIHOPers—lend no support to Jayhan's idea. The

---

* I did, and came upon a widely circulated story from the 2000 presidential race headlined: "Bush 'Refuses to Dignify' Mass-Murder Allegations: 'That's Not What This Election Is About,' He Says." It was published in the March 8, 2000, issue of the satirical weekly *The Onion*.

theory also fails the test of logic: Why would the plane shoot a
projectile at the building? Why would government plotters have
risked using a missile—wouldn't they be worried that someone
would catch it on tape?

Jayhan conceded that he can't answer these questions but
said that the presence of the missile proves, at least, that the
government isn't divulging the full story. He added that "just
because you can't figure out why there's a missile there doesn't
mean there isn't one."

The most powerful proof of Jayhan's error, though, can be
found in other photographs of Flight 175. In a sequence released by the National Institute of Standards and Technology,
which extensively analyzed the cause of the towers' collapse, you
can see the aircraft approach the South Tower from a vantage
point directly underneath the plane. The shot is clearer than
the video Jayhan showed me. And when I look at it, it's obvious that there's no missile there. Another video clip released by
CNN shows the flight approaching head-on, as if it were coming toward you. This a small, grainy segment of video, but you
can see here, too, that nothing hangs from the bottom of the
aircraft. Furthermore, when you study photographs of what an
ordinary Boeing 767 looks like during flight, you see illuminated
cylindrical segments on the underside—places where the sun
is reflecting off the body. The pictures look so much like the
bright spots that Jayhan sees in the 9/11 videos of Flight 175
that they would seem to have closed the case: what we're seeing
in Jayhan's videos must be the sun.

But it's here that we arrive at the special problem that selective perception poses to a fragmented world. Jayhan does not
include the exculpatory photos on his Web site. He did not point
them out to me during our interview, either, and I found them
only after digging into his theory on my own. You can think of

Jayhan's propaganda, then, as a product of both selective exposure *and* selective perception. It wouldn't matter much if Jayhan alone saw something odd in a few videos taken on 9/11. But the videos, accompanied by Jayhan's analysis, traveled online in much the way that the Swift Boat Vets' ideas did—in underground selective-exposure networks, and without much mention that there were other photographs less susceptible to a selective interpretation of the facts.

Several 9/11-doubting Web sites and discussion boards, a few amateur radio shows, and even early versions of the 9/11-truth documentary films *Loose Change* and *In Plane Site* took up Jayhan's cause. Soon, then, others were claiming that a missile hit the South Tower. Selective perception was spreading. "I see what I think is a missile," one fellow noted in a discussion group after Jayhan posted his finding. He added, "Of all I have seen, this is by far the most convincing." Another advised Jayhan, "Be very careful of your personal security. You are a true patriot and that is a dangerous thing to be these days." These were people who shared Jayhan's worldview; just like him, they could really *see* it.

This is how pictures and sounds deceive us today. The problem with the old world, Abraham Zapruder's world, was that it contained too few recordings. The only clear film we had of the Kennedy assassination could be made to prove everything, and thus it ended up *proving* nothing. But Phillip Jayhan's error shows us that the opposite situation is equally unhelpful—that too *many* images can also be made to prove everything. The promise of our world, the world of YouTube and Flickr, was that hundreds of photographs and videos would be analyzed together to converge upon a single truth. What we're finding is that the convergence isn't clean. If it's not impossible, it's at least impractical to analyze every video, every photograph, every bit of audio recorded on 9/11. In the thousands or millions of pictures taken of any event, a fraction will inevitably be so vague as to allow for vastly discordant interpretations of reality.

Selective exposure suggests that we'll most likely end up looking at the documents that can be most readily viewed in a certain convenient light. And selective perception says that when we do come upon these, we'll think of them as proving what we'd always suspected. Remember the euphoria with which Jayhan described the epiphany of coming upon the video in which he sees a missile: "It was as if God's angels were aiming the cameras so as to make sure the day's events were duly recorded and archived for later criminal prosecution."

Reality splits, and then the split reality spreads. We think that what we see in pictures or what we hear on tape gives us a firm hold on fact. But, increasingly, the pictures and the sounds we find ourselves believing may only be telling us one version of true.

Early in April 2004, Ibrahim Hooper, the communications director for a Washington-based civil rights group called the Council on American-Islamic Relations, received a mysterious photograph in his e-mail in-box. The picture shows a white man dressed in a military uniform standing with two dark-skinned boys in what appears to be a desert setting. Behind them is a ramshackle structure, perhaps a cabin or a makeshift bunker. The man and the boys are under this structure's lean-to roof, posing, happily, for the camera. The man grins, the boys smile shyly, and all flash a thumbs-up sign. There is, however, something amiss with the scene. One of the boys is holding up a piece of cardboard on which, in black marker, is scrawled, "Lcpl Boudreaux killed my dad. then he knocked up my sister!"

The picture came with no information about who's in the picture or where they are or when it was taken. But to Hooper, what was going on was obvious. The photo, as he saw it, showed an American soldier making fun of two Iraqi children by having them hold up a sign they didn't understand. Hooper's group, which goes by the acronym CAIR, had long opposed the war in Iraq, and to Hooper, the photo was proof of how ugly the battle had become. He rushed off a press release, pointing reporters to the picture. "If the United States Army is seeking to win the hearts and minds of the Iraqi people, this is the wrong way to accomplish that goal," chided Nihad Awad, CAIR's executive director.

You can understand CAIR's chagrin. Wars today are won and lost with the click of a shutter, the capture of light on a digital camera's photo-sensitive charged-coupled device. Just a few weeks after Boudreaux's picture hit the Web, the world would see photographs of Americans abusing Iraqis at Abu Ghraib prison. There might have been a chance, before those pictures, for the United States to scratch out some kind of victory in Iraq. The photos ended it. That's the singular power of visual "proof." The press had long covered allegations of abuse at Abu Ghraib, but there was no story until there were pictures. Images transform statistics and anecdotes into fact. Between 1986 and 1990, almost two thousand residents of Los Angeles filed complaints of excessive force against the city's police officers. But the brutality became a problem on March 3, 1991, only when it was caught on tape.

In response to CAIR's press release, the military launched an inquiry into the photograph. It found that the man pictured was a Marine reservist, Lance Corporal Ted J. Boudreaux of Houma, Louisiana, a small town about fifty miles southwest of New Orleans. News of the investigation sparked a small outcry against

Boudreaux; his local newspaper said that by taking such a photo, he had "embarrassed himself, the Marine Corps and, unfortunately, his home state." But when confronted with the image, Boudreaux did something unexpected: he called the photo a fake. And, indeed, just as the Naval Criminal Investigative Services began to look into the case, several other versions of the picture popped up online. Some were obviously phony—one version had the boys holding a sign that reads, "We wanna see Jessica Simpson!" But at least one picture appeared just as real as the image CAIR received, and this one showed a decidedly friendlier message: "Lcpl Boudreaux saved my dad. then he rescued my sister!"

Which picture was the real picture? The manner in which Phillip Jayhan arrived at his missile-theory of 9/11 shows how documentary evidence is dissolving today through the processes of selective exposure and selective perception. The two mysterious pictures of Lance Corporal Boudreaux tell a related story. They are intriguing because they put forth a lie—one or both of the scenes pictured never really happened—but their real power has to do with the truth. The pictures show how fakery—or, really, the mere possibility of fakery, the ever-present suspicion of digitally abetted fraud—will weaken all images and sounds supporting stories that many would prefer not to know: stories like that of what really occurred between a marine and a couple of kids in the Iraqi desert, or at a prison called Abu Ghraib, or to a man named Rodney King.

In 1987, Thomas Knoll, a computer scientist studying robotic vision, wrote a small program to manipulate digital images. He showed it to his brother John, who worked as a special-effects designer at George Lucas's film-effects company Industrial Light and Magic. John was blown away by the program's capabilities. He could do things with his brother's software that he couldn't do with anything he had at ILM, and he convinced Tom to turn the application into a commercial product.

A few years later, the brothers licensed their code to the Silicon Valley company Adobe Systems, which put the program on store shelves early in 1990. It was called Photoshop, and it would forever alter how we think of photographs. Suddenly, every picture was malleable. With just a little bit of training and some creativity, Photoshop allowed designers to edit images in profound, sometimes imperceptible ways. You could make Oprah skinnier, turn O. J. Simpson more menacing, and pin George W. Bush's face on Osama bin Laden's body. But Photoshop today is more than a ubiquitous piece of software; it's a metaphor for the age.

Virtually every document we interact with—every photograph we shoot, every song we play, every movie we watch—is, at heart, a digital file, strings of binary code that can be understood by machines. Digitization has been good to us; it's given us the Web, DVDs, and the iPod, among other wonderful things. But computerized documents have also deepened the disconnect between what we perceive through our senses—what we see and what we hear—and what's actually going on in the world.

Lance Corporal Boudreaux has said that he was horsing around in Iraq in the summer of 2003 when he snapped a photo with two local boys. He used a digital camera, and he sent the file across the planet over e-mail to his mother and a few other relatives. The picture, he said, was innocent. The sign he put in the Iraqi boy's hand read "Welcome Marines." But Boudreaux can't prove it; his mother's computer blew out in a lightning storm, and she lost everything on it, including the picture. Somewhere in the transfer, somehow, his photo must have leaked out on the

Web, he said. Photoshop intervened, and a nice scene in the desert turned into a disaster.

Boudreaux's story is certainly plausible. Online, you're constantly treated to pictures that aren't real. Here is the president reading a book upside down, and here he is fishing in a flooded New Orleans—someone made those scenes up. During the 2004 presidential campaign, a skilled Photoshopper swiped a 1971 shot of John Kerry at an antiwar rally in Mineola, New York, from the Web site of Corbis, a photo agency, and stitched it seamlessly with a 1972 image of Jane Fonda at a rally in Miami Beach, Florida. The composite photo shows a thoughtful, appreciative Kerry next to an agitated Fonda. It was given a border, a headline, a caption, and an Associated Press credit and was made to look like an authentic newspaper clipping that proved Kerry's close association with a reviled Hanoi Jane.

The image quickly flew around the Web, even catching the attention of some in the media; the *New York Times* reported its existence, describing the picture in detail but noting that its origins were "unclear." Finally, it reached Ken Light, a veteran photojournalist and a lecturer at the University of California at Berkeley Graduate School of Journalism. He knew it was a fake; he'd taken the original Kerry picture used in the scene, and he had the film negative to prove it.

Light has thought a lot about how his photo came to be involved in deceptive propaganda, and he is less concerned about the incident than you'd expect. He notes that the false image didn't do much lasting damage. The truth got out, and, as he wrote in the *Washington Post*, "If you use a search engine to look for my Kerry picture now, you'll find the hoax explanations before you see the photo itself." To Light, the real danger of living in the age of Photoshop isn't the proliferation of fake photos. Rather, it's that *true* photos will be ignored as phonies.

When every picture is suspect, all pictures are dismissible, and photography's unique power to criticize will decline.

"My work is about witnessing my time and events," Light told me one afternoon. "My career as a photographer has been based on seeing America through a lens that is critical of institutions and of the culture." Among other things, Light has photographed the Texas death row, the poverty-stricken Mississippi Delta, and migrant workers crossing the Mexican-American border. His pictures are important precisely because they're credible—because they document what we think of as reality. If you're a supporter of the death penalty, you can read ten thousand words on the horror and loneliness of death row and still come away unmoved, dismissing the whole thing as one subjective writer's bluster. But Light's haunting photograph of a twenty-one-year-old waiting for execution could surely rattle you from your settled view. This is what attracts Light to photography. It's difficult to shake criticism that comes through a camera, he says, because "people sense a deeper truth in photographs" than they do in other media.

There are already signs, though, that our trust in pictures is slipping away. Ed Lake is a retired weather observer who lives in Racine, Wisconsin, and is known to the world as the Fake Detective. Lake gets his name from his curious pastime. He spends many hours analyzing the numerous naked photographs of celebrities that pop up on the Web. He is the Internet's leading authority on the silhouette of Gillian Anderson's breasts or the precise curvature of Sandra Bullock's behind. Lake, who has been detecting fakes since 1996, says that in the early days of the Web, people used to get fooled all the time by images of nude celebrities they saw online. But over the years skepticism has set in. Now, Lake says, "Most of the e-mail I get is about real pictures. Now they automatically think it's fake."

I asked several digital-imaging experts—including Lake—to examine the two photographs of Boudreaux and the boys in the desert. None of them could say which, if either, was real; many said both could be fake. The marines conducted two investigations and could not get to the bottom of the issue. The case against Boudreaux went nowhere, and he's now back at home.

Online, though, the commentary was illustrative. People pointed to all kinds of reasons favoring one version or another, but often the "evidence" they cited seemed to satisfy their own beliefs. On Free Republic, a discussion site dominated by partisans on the extreme right wing, some pointed out that the soldier appeared to be wearing army fatigues, which didn't fit with the U.S. Marine Corps' ranking of lance corporal. (Boudreaux doesn't dispute that it's him in the picture, though, and he's wearing the correct uniform.) Others pointed to flaws they saw in the handwriting or in some of the shadows in the "knocked up" sign. But beyond anything in the image, for many Freepers— which is what denizens of Free Republic call themselves—the biggest clue that the picture was doctored was that CAIR said it was real. They didn't trust CAIR. Why, they asked, should they trust a picture that the group says it received by e-mail?

In the digital world, a picture, a video, or a bit of audio isn't assessed on its own terms. You are no longer responsible for believing your own eyes or ears; only if you trust the person who produced the photograph should you conclude that it shows what it purports to show. Otherwise, you can guiltlessly conclude that it's a fake.

"A photograph passes for incontrovertible proof that a given thing has happened," Susan Sontag once wrote. "The picture may distort; but there is always a presumption that something exists, or did exist, which is like what's in the picture." What she was getting at is the same quality of photography that Ken Light reveres, which is really what we all revere: the photo's evidentiary value, its intimacy with the truth.

But technology is changing that relationship. The number of pictures we are now capable of making, the slanted ways in which we transmit them and understand them, and the ease with which we can manipulate them have pushed open the distance between what really happens and what we think has happened when we look at the picture of the event. This holds true not only for still photography, which was Sontag's muse, but also for motion pictures and for recorded audio. If you go on the Web and search for the freighted keywords that surround 9/11—Pentagon, World Trade Center towers, and so on—you'll immediately find, among many unconventional ideas about the attacks, the work of a young man named Dylan Avery. And it's here that you'll begin to understand the full scope of the problem I'm describing.

Avery is a clever, daring fellow in his early twenties from the central New York town of Oneonta. For as long as he can remember, he has wanted to make films. It used to be that this was a dreamer's idea of something to do with your life; the movie industry was a place where ambition and talent could take you only so far but never nearly far enough. As with everything else, though, technology has greased the grip of the tight-knit social networks that rule the business of which movies get made and which get seen. Today, if you've got a very specific kind of creative spark, you can quickly make yourself a star, at least on the Internet.

So goes the rough description of Dylan Avery's career. It began a couple of years after 9/11, when he came up with an audacious idea for a movie. Its premise was fictional: a group of young people, ordinary kids not unlike Avery and his friends, somehow stumble upon proof that the official story of 9/11 is a cover-up. But then Avery logged on to the Web and began to research the attacks, and what he found undid him. "You learn things, then you learn more things, and it was only a matter of time before I'd come to realize it," he says. 9/11 was an "inside job."

In the spring of 2005, Avery released *Loose Change*, a feature-length documentary that challenges the official story of the attacks. Half a year later he put out an expanded, polished version of the film, *Loose Change: Second Edition*, and he's currently working on a final cut. At least a half-dozen 9/11 "truth" documentaries now circulate on the Internet and on the conspiracy convention circuit. They are all of a type—which is to say, less than fully entertaining. *Loose Change* is something else entirely, the ne plus ultra of 9/11 skeptic films.

Set against a breezy pop-synth soundtrack and narrated in a hipster patois by Avery himself, the film resembles nothing so much as an MTV production. The style accounts for its popularity. *Loose Change* does not have a distributor and has never been released in theaters. But Avery's company, Louder Than Words, has sold more than a hundred thousand DVDs of the film, and *Loose Change* has hovered for many months near the top of the charts on Google Video and other online movie libraries. Some of Avery's fans describe *Loose Change* as "the red pill," referring to the drug that takes Keanu Reeves down *The Matrix*'s rabbit hole. For many who watch it, the film represents a comprehensive, startling introduction to a set of ideas commonly banished from mainstream discourse. *Loose Change* is the 9/11 skeptic's gateway drug.

The trajectory of *Loose Change* shows how easy it has become to fashion yourself a propagandist. Avery produced the first edition of his film using off-the-shelf video software on his laptop computer. It set him back less than $2,000. The second edition cost three times that much, so he took jobs at Red Lobster and Starbucks to finance it. Distribution, too, was easy and cheap; the price to press hundreds of DVDs is almost nothing, and distributing a video online actually does cost nothing. (Avery sells DVDs of *Loose Change* for as much as $18 each, but he encourages people to make their own copies and pass them out to everyone they know.)

Avery's process of researching *Loose Change*, meanwhile, was of such sparkling efficiency that it would make a Japanese automobile plant operations manager smile. Little in the film is actually new; most of Avery's ideas are instead appropriated wholesale from the Web. *Loose Change* brims with documents and videos collected from other sites, investigations conducted by an army of amateur sleuths dedicated to the cause, and tips sent in from fans. Wikipedia, the fantastically successful online encyclopedia whose articles can be edited by anyone, serves as a model. Avery is in charge of the production, but his film represents the ideas of many in a larger online movement.

This novel approach has not resulted in an entirely consistent argument. In the first version of the movie, Avery put forward Phillip Jayhan's idea that the second plane to hit the World Trade Center carried some kind of projectile or bomb on its belly. The film also argued that United Airlines Flight 93 was shot down by the U.S. military—it was not, Avery says, brought down as a result of a revolt by passengers over Shanksville, Pennsylvania, as the official story has it.

In the second version of *Loose Change*, however, released just months after the first, Avery dropped his original "9/11 truths" and proposed an altogether new parallel reality: now there's no mention of the Jayhan's missile, and instead Avery argues that the planes that hit the World Trade Center were remote-piloted drones carrying no passengers. The planes were decoys; they were there to trick the public into blaming terrorists, but actually, according to Avery, the towers were brought down by the sort of controlled demolition that is used to destroy old buildings. And he contends that something even stranger happened to Flight 93: it was not brought to the ground by its brave passengers, nor was it shot down, but instead it landed safely in Cleveland, where the plane unloaded two hundred passengers* and was never seen or heard from again. Avery's other main argument is a mainstay of the 9/11-skeptic movement. He says that the Pentagon was most likely damaged by a missile, not by a passenger jet.

Both versions of *Loose Change* contain a number of errors and logical fallacies and skip over necessary details of the case (e.g., what would be the government's motive for committing the crime?). The film's popularity has prompted many damning counterarguments online, the best of which are actually maintained by other MIHOPers themselves, who tend to see *Loose Change* as a liability to the movement. (You could say they worry that it offers a weak consonant argument.) If *Loose Change* were an indictment, a judge would toss it out of court. But the point here is not that *Loose Change* is faulty. What's interesting, in fact, is what its flaws mask: a certain devious calculation in the way Avery handles documentary evidence.

---

* Avery speculates that the two hundred people who landed in Cleveland were the passengers from the four planes that the official story says crashed that day. He doesn't know where the passengers are now, or why the government would go to the trouble of flying them safely to Cleveland if it was willing to kill so many thousands of people in the buildings. But others in the movement, including Jayhan, suggest an idea right out of John le Carré: the passengers whom we think of as being victims that day might actually have been the operatives who carried out the whole thing. Having the world conclude that they died in the attack was their way of clearing their identities.

Avery uses a slate of photographs, videos, and audio recordings to make his case. (The entire film is something of a pastiche
of found footage; Avery has not secured the rights to much of
what he uses, so its legality is thus dubious.) At one point, as
the film takes on the case of what happened at the Pentagon,
Avery asks, "Why is there no discernible trace of Flight 77?"
And the images pile up, one on top of another, all showing little discernible aircraft debris around the crash site. Then he
shows pictures of the structural damage the building suffered.
There is only "a single hole" in the wall of the Pentagon, he says.
And he's right—you can see it right there on your screen, and
it doesn't make sense. "A Boeing 757 is 155 feet long, 44 feet
high, has a 124 foot wingspan, and weighs almost 100 tons," he
notes. "Are we supposed to believe that it disappeared into this
hole, without leaving any wreckage on the outside?"

Well, are we? Watching Avery make his case about the
Pentagon, you feel yourself starting to slip into the mood of his
alternative reality: *he certainly seems to have the facts on his
side.* He moves on to the scene in New York. In a series of
videos showing the North Tower as it collapses, Avery points to
visible puffs of air and debris that shoot out from the building;
the puffs move down the building as it falls, about twenty stories below what he calls the "demolition wave." What are these?
Avery says they're the fingerprints of a controlled demolition—
explosives placed in the building are going off, causing debris
to shoot out from the tower.

Avery plays a series of clips from live TV news coverage that
morning in which anchors, reporters, and eyewitnesses all say
that they can feel and hear explosions—in other words, signs
of a controlled demolition—in the towers. "There were two or
three similar huge explosions and the building literally shook, it
literally shook at the base of this building," says one unidentified

man with a British accent. A man interviewed on the street says, "A big explosion happened, all of a sudden the elevator blew up, smoke, I dragged the guy out, his skin was hanging off, and I dragged him out and I helped him to the ambulance." Another eyewitness: "We started coming down the stairs from the eighth floor. Big explosion. Blew us back into the eighth floor."

Then there's a reporter saying, "We just witnessed some kind of secondary follow-up explosion on the World Trade Center number 2," after which a news anchor says, "We understand now there has been a secondary explosion on Tower 2." You see a Fox News reporter say that he's just heard a very loud sound and then he corners a police officer and asks, "Do you know if it was an explosion, or if it was a building collapse?" "To me it sounded like—to me it sounded like an explosion," the rattled officer says. Avery shows a helicopter shot depicting all of Lower Manhattan engulfed in smoke. The Fox News title on the bottom of the screen reads: "10:38a: 4th explosion rocks remains of world trade ctr."

Near the end of the film, Avery examines the phone calls that passengers and crew in the hijacked planes are said to have made to their families and authorities on the ground in the final minutes of their lives. The calls, of course, play a pivotal part in the official story of 9/11. It is through conversations with people on the ground that passengers on Flight 93 learned of the fate of the other three aircraft, and it's from the phone calls, too, that we've assembled some of our most enchanting narratives about what happened that morning.

Todd Beamer, an account manager at the software firm Oracle and a passenger on Flight 93, tried to call his wife from an onboard phone, but instead he got through to Lisa Jefferson, a GTE operator at a call center near Chicago. Beamer and Jefferson spoke for thirteen minutes. He told her about his wife—she was named Lisa, too, he said—and his kids. He told her that passengers had decided to take over the plane. He asked her to recite the Lord's Prayer with him, and the two of them did. "Jesus help me," he said. Then another passenger asked, "Are you ready?" "Roll it," Beamer said, referring to a food cart the passengers used as battering-ram, and their attack began.*

Avery argues that the phone calls never happened. In the film, he plays a recording of a call made by Betty Ong, a flight attendant on American Airlines Flight 11, talking to a reservations agent on the ground. "The cockpit is not answering their phone," she says in a calm voice. "And there's somebody stabbed in business class. And there's—we can't breathe in business class. Somebody's got mace or something. Okay. Our Number One got stabbed. Our purser is stabbed. Nobody knows who stabbed who, and we can't even get up to business class right now 'cause nobody can breathe." It's a fake, Avery says. Nobody who was on that plane could have remained so tranquil. "Does Ms. Ong sound like a woman on a hijacked plane who just saw three people murdered?" he asks. "Why is nobody in the background screaming?"

Avery notes that many other phone calls were "peculiar." Mark Bingham, a public relations manager on Flight 93, called his mother and began, "Mom, this is Mark Bingham." Avery asks, "When was the last time you called your mother and used your full name?" What actually happened that morning, Avery then argues, was probably the product of a military

---

* Early news accounts reported that Beamer's final words were "Let's roll!" The phrase became a national rallying cry in the months after the attack, and it remains one of our hallmark myths about 9/11. In his 2002 State of the Union speech, President Bush invoked the phrase to describe how the attacks had altered the national character: "For too long our culture has said, 'If it feels good, do it.' Now America is embracing a new ethic and a new creed: 'Let's roll.'" A couple of weeks after 9/11, Lisa Beamer applied for and was granted a trademark for the term.

"voice-morphing" technology, which allowed the government to fool the passengers' family members into believing they had received calls from the air.

A lot of this, of course, sounds foolish. There is no evidence that the government has any technology to mimic people's voices in a way that Avery suggests; this is just a wild supposition, one of many in the film. Yet you get through *Loose Change* feeling overwhelmed. How can you not? Avery shows you just so much, he absolutely drowns you in pictures and sounds that seem to corroborate his story. And it does raise real questions: Why *don't* we see any aircraft debris at the Pentagon scene? What *are* those explosive puffs ejecting from the towers? What about the people who claimed to hear explosives at the scene of the World Trade Center?

The whole thing is a trick of selective exposure and interpretation and of dismissing as fake the evidence that doesn't jibe with your views. Avery had a vast trove of audio and video to choose from for his film—hundreds of hours of video recorded during just that morning. The choices he made shaped his narrative. But had he chosen differently, he could have told a different story. There are, if you look for them, at least a dozen high-quality images showing what look like remains from a passenger aircraft at the scene of the Pentagon. There's a picture of an engine assembly, of various large mechanical parts found inside the building, of large pieces of the aircraft in the yard, and of human remains, too. There are also many photographs of the damage done to the building, and these absolutely contradict Avery's idea that there was only a "single hole" in the wall of the Pentagon. If you look at these photographs—that is, if you step outside the reality constructed by *Loose Change*—it seems nearly impossible to doubt that what happened there is what the official story says.

What about the puffs of smoke and the "explosions" that people reported hearing that morning? When Avery watches this evidence, he concludes that there must have been a controlled demolition. But that's his selective interpretation of what's in the scene; what he sees there happened as much in his head as it did in the world.

Structural engineers and demolitions experts I spoke to watch the same scenes and see no such thing: explosive puffs from a controlled demolition would have occurred much faster than those we see in the videos; there would have been a great deal more of them, and they would have gone off in an orderly, predictable pattern. The small explosive puffs we see flying away from the towers are just puffs of air rushing out from the building, they say—what you'd expect when a building collapses, with large sections of the walls and the floors tumbling down and "pistoning" the air inside the towers out through the windows. The "explosions" that everyone heard that morning are also what you'd expect when buildings as big as the towers are damaged as thoroughly as these were; as the structure weakens, as many critical systems in it are subject to the harsh heat, things snap, large structures fall, fireballs erupt, and things just explode. This is nothing like what would happen in a controlled demolition, where the explosions would be orderly and would all occur at roughly the same time, not in an unpredictable sequence.

Then notice how Avery deals with the tape of flight attendant Betty Ong's phone call from the air, one of the bits of evidence that is most damaging to his theory. He concludes that it's a fake. In the same way that right-wingers looked at the photograph of Lance Corporal Boudreaux and spotted flaws in the clothing, Avery decides that Ong just doesn't sound as if she's for real.

He does a similar thing with the famous videotape in which Osama bin Laden appears to confess to having planned the attacks. Bin Laden, who is left-handed, doesn't seem to be eating and writing with the correct hand in the video. "The man in the video looks and acts nothing like bin Laden," Avery says, as if he knows the real Osama. The Ong and bin Laden tapes were both released by the government, and doctoring either scene wouldn't have been especially hard. To Avery, they are thus easy to ignore; why should anyone take the government's evidence as proof?

Members of the 9/11 Commission, the bipartisan panel that handed down the official theory of how the attacks occurred, began their effort by looking at previous such investigations, particularly the official inquiry into the Kennedy assassination. They wanted to avoid its mistakes. In 1964, after ten months of investigation, the Warren Commission concluded that Oswald was solely responsible for Kennedy's death. Their story was simple, unbelievably so: Oswald fired three shots at the motorcade from a sixth-floor window on the southeast corner of the book depository. Two of those shots hit Kennedy, including one—the so-called magic bullet—that passed through the president's throat and then struck Texas governor John Connally, seated in the front seat of the open limousine, in the back, the right wrist, and finally his left thigh.

Many Americans initially accepted the finding. But within a year a hail of criticism began to fall, and the lone-gunman theory spiraled out of public favor. Today, the vast majority of Americans believe that Oswald acted as part of a conspiracy.

The Warren Commission's main failing was secrecy, many 9/11 commissioners concluded. Its report lacked documentary proof. To exculpate foreign governments and various U.S. agencies from responsibility for the assassination, the commission had relied on a trove of covert intelligence data. But because it couldn't present or even describe the evidence to the public, it could not support many of its conclusions.

Members of the 9/11 Commission decided that their work would be different. It would be open. They had the same thought that Merrie Spaeth did when she was arguing with some of the Swift Boat Veterans about what kind of anti-Kerry campaign to launch: evidence matters. The pages of its final report, which the commission released in the summer of 2004, bulge with descriptions of the extremely sensitive information it received from the government. In general, the report accounts for all that it asserts (its section of endnotes alone makes for a weightier tome than the volume you hold in your hand). "We were trying to be as comprehensive and transparent as possible," Jamie Gorelick, a member of the commission who served as a deputy attorney general in the Clinton administration, told me, "so people would know what we had looked into even if there were unanswered questions."

But it didn't work. In a world that can give us something like *Loose Change*, openness and more evidence don't necessarily translate into shared national truths. Not long ago, Gorelick was speaking at a conference of business leaders in Boston. After her presentation, a prominent executive in the audience approached her and posed a sensitive question: "Is there any proof to the story that a missile hit the Pentagon on 9/11?" Gorelick pressed the executive on where she'd heard such a thing, and the woman said that her daughter had told her about it. Gorelick has a distinctively grave speaking style that brings to mind a brook-no-nonsense schoolteacher. As she described the incident, her voice took on a strained pitch, as if she were reprimanding a student who'd neglected to turn in his homework. "The daughter was attending a very reputable college," Gorelick recalled. "Apparently, she and all of her friends believed this to be the case."

4

Questionable Expertise: The Stolen Election and the Men Who Push It

Ⅰ n June 2006, Robert F. Kennedy Jr., the attorney, activist, and third child and namesake of one of the most beloved men of recent American history, published an article in *Rolling Stone* magazine with a teasing, blockbuster headline: "Was the Election Stolen?" The piece ran for several pages and ruminated on the myriad controversies surrounding the 2004 presidential vote, but Kennedy answered his provocative question within the first few paragraphs. "After carefully examining the evidence," he wrote, "I've become convinced that the president's party mounted a massive, coordinated campaign to subvert the will of the people in 2004."

George W. Bush's second term was by this time well under way. He'd been reelected with more than 62 million votes nationally, 3 million better than John Kerry. In the pivotal electoral state of Ohio, Bush won by a margin of 118,601—about

2 percentage points. But Kennedy counseled readers to dismiss the official count. The results in Ohio, he argued, were missing more than 350,000 votes meant for Kerry—enough for the Democrat to have won the state, and with it the White House. The whole thing, Kennedy insisted, was rigged.

To many on the left, Kennedy's article represented the ultimate endorsement of long-bubbling concerns over the integrity of the American electoral process. The 2000 election had climaxed in a chaos of hanging chads and butterfly ballots, installing into office the candidate with fewer votes, as elementary a subversion of democracy as it is possible to imagine. That debacle prompted many in Washington to vow to fix the system, but their reforms amounted to little. In the months before the 2004 vote, observers were predicting that Election Day would be a mess. It was.

The punch-card machines that bungled the Bush-Gore contest in South Florida were still in wide use, including in Ohio. Even more troubling were the systems that many jurisdictions had chosen as a replacement—electronic voting machines that kept election results locked away on computer memory cards, uncountable manually by any human being. The voting process in many states, furthermore, continued to be managed by officials with a political interest in the result. This was of particular concern in Ohio, where the secretary of state, a conservative Republican named Kenneth Blackwell, issued a series of capricious preelection rulings that seemed to be designed to limit broad participation in the vote. For instance, a few weeks before Ohio's voter-registration deadline, Blackwell ordered local elections offices to process only registration forms that had been printed on heavy cardstock paper, a ruling that immediately invalidated thousands of registrations marked up on lighter-weight paper. He rescinded that decree just days before the deadline—late enough that hundreds of voters' registration forms might have been skipped by local officials. On November 3, 2004, John Kerry conceded the race in a short speech at Faneuil Hall. As the senator stepped gently back into history, activists on the left began to point to the many flaws in the race. They went to work proving that Kerry had been robbed.

At first, the activists met little success. They were instantly dismissed—or, worse, ignored—by the press and by politicians. Authorities acknowledged that there had been many voting problems in Ohio; most worrisomely, tens of thousands of voters, mainly in African American areas, were forced to wait in voting lines for many hours, a situation that likely kept many people at home. Still, there was no evidence, the authorities said, of a conspiracy to rig the race. Moreover, Bush's winning margin was wide enough that even if everyone who'd stayed at home due to long lines—or whose registration had been hampered by Blackwell's cardstock ruling—had intended to vote for Kerry, the final result would not have changed. Bush would still have won the state. But the activists, suspicious of elections officials, didn't buy these explanations. Online, they found their métier. As the Swift Boat Veterans had managed months earlier, election protestors built an electronic protest organ of surprising and beautiful efficacy. Working in small bands, they drew up mission statements, collected donations, and produced elaborate reports. They dug for evidence and found it everywhere.

There were numerous small allegations of fraud, instances that weren't especially consequential to the final count but that suggested a terrible record—a claim, for instance, that in Miami County, Ohio, thousands of votes were added to the result *after* the polls closed.* But the muckrakers lavished their energies on one main charge. They claimed that Republicans in Ohio—with help, likely, from Republicans elsewhere—had deliberately rigged voting results in counties all over the state, either by manually stuffing the ballot or by tampering with voting machines. As evidence, they cited what they considered the shining gem of their analysis: the Election Day exit polls, which news organizations compile to project election results, showed Kerry ahead. The dissidents argued that the exits were a peek at the honest outcome—what the voters meant to choose, a Kerry victory—before it had been purloined by Bush's forces.

The people offering these arguments possessed little training in the fields you'd expect. They weren't experts in polling methodology and didn't have backgrounds in political science or in the monitoring and running of the voting process. The activists were, in the purest sense of the word, *amateurs*, led by, among others, a former high school math teacher, an economist, a professor of media studies, and a scholar in something called organizational dynamics. They brought an unconventional eye to the study of the race, searching for evidence of fraud in circuitous ways, using techniques that surprised and baffled insiders. Often, they saw cause for alarm in aspects of elections that experienced observers recognized as nothing out of the ordinary.

---

* Along with several other journalists, I investigated these claims and found many lacking. For instance, as the investigative reporter Mark Hertsgaard first pointed out in *Mother Jones*, votes were not added to the Miami County results after the polls closed. The explanation for why it appeared that way to activists is technical: It was Miami County's convention to consider a voting precinct as being "reported" even if only one vote from there had been counted. This means that for a brief while, the software that posted the results to the Web showed 100 percent of the precincts reporting, even though votes were still being counted.

Nevertheless, by the spring of 2006 their theories had spread far and wide online, and they'd managed to seduce many adherents, not least Robert Kennedy Jr. Kennedy's article contained no new findings or any novel analysis of what happened in Ohio in 2004. Instead, he pointed to the claims of the amateurs online, whom he praised for their diligence. For the activists, it was a huge break. Kennedy had won fame as an environmental activist, and he'd long championed out-of-the-way causes, styling himself as a protector of the public good. In *Rolling Stone*, he had previously argued that drug companies were hiding the truth about how an additive in children's vaccines might cause autism. (The claim has been refuted in multiple studies.) Now he was alerting Americans to another injustice. It was a position that worked well in the media. Cable news networks, *The Colbert Report*, Charlie Rose, and talk radio shows across the nation invited Kennedy to argue his point on the air.

But Kennedy's article made no mention of experts who'd questioned the amateurs' work. In the year and a half since the vote, many academics had looked into Ohio's 2004 race. Although several had found that the vote had been far from perfect, not a single study conducted by any professional—by anyone who made a living working with polls or in the academic fields related to voting—had determined that Kerry had won Ohio. Kennedy ignored these findings, and highlighted the amateurs' interpretation instead.

Mark Blumenthal, a professional pollster in Washington, runs a blog called Pollster.com, where he has analyzed in extravagant technical detail the argument that exit polls proved a Kerry victory. Blumenthal, like many other survey experts, doesn't see much to the idea; in every American presidential election since 1988, the exit polls have predicted the Democratic candidate doing better than he eventually did in the final result. Kennedy didn't mention this track record. His article's section on exit polling was informed entirely by people who hadn't previously conducted political surveys. Yet it sounded definitive. "I had this conversation two dozen times with friends and friends of friends who read the article," Blumenthal recalls. "They would say, 'My God, I put the thing down and I was just blown away.' People found it very convincing."

In the late 1980s, the political scientists Benjamin Page and Robert Shapiro set out to measure how the many voices that we encounter in the media shape public opinion. To understand their inquiry, imagine that you are producing a segment for the evening news, and it's your job to feature the most influential speakers on either side of a topic of great national concern—a war, say. Whom would you choose to invite on your show? One obvious person would be the president. But who else? Members of the opposition party? How about a retired military general? Foreign leaders? Protesters? What if, in a radical departure from policy, the anchor of your news network offered to make a passionate on-air statement outlining his or her own view—would that leave a powerful impression on people watching at home?

The choice isn't obvious. Each of these sources is plainly unique. A general would offer thoughts on the war based on his military experience, while a president's opinions might be colored by the next election. Naturally, then, each speaker should affect viewers in a different way. Page and Shapiro have long been interested in the flow of public opinion—how and why mass attitudes change in response to what we see, read, or listen to. Now, by examining just the sort of TV news broadcast I'm describing, they devised a clever study to find out how speakers of different backgrounds push mass opinion in different ways. It was painstaking work. They looked at hundreds of news segments aired during several periods of boiling controversy, noting every authority who spoke out in the debate. Then they compared the news coverage to national opinion surveys taken just after the news had aired. Would they see any pattern, they wondered, in the public's response to what had been broadcast on TV?

The pattern, indeed, was unmistakable. Presidents, for one, don't matter much, they found. For every broadcast featuring a president advocating a certain message, public opinion will move only by about a third of a percentage point in the direction the president favors, Page and Shapiro found.* Other politicians—whether of the president's party or the opposition —also don't push the public a great deal. Neither do foreigners, friend or foe. When Osama bin Laden shows up on TV, as is his habit, Americans are less likely to pay attention to him than they are to the way American leaders *react* to him, the research suggests. Interest groups and activists, meanwhile, can push the public *away* from positions they're advocating, most likely because Americans see them as self-concerned. There are few better illustrations of this than the mass protests against the Vietnam War in the late 1960s and early 1970s, which actually increased support for the war. Page and Shapiro cite a CBS News survey from 1970 that asked respondents whether "college student protests and demonstrations in general have gone too far, and should be stopped." Eighty-one percent agreed.

If presidents, politicians, foreigners, and activist groups can't move the public, who can? News anchors and experts. Page and

---

* Of course, a president does get to go on TV a lot, so over time he could move the public a great deal. But Page and Shapiro also found that there are diminishing returns—"talkative presidents" could not pump up their ratings indefinitely by going on TV often. The president's popularity also matters. Presidents with approval ratings under 50 percent have almost no effect on public opinion.

Shapiro discovered, to their surprise, that a single commentary by a news anchor can prompt as much as a 4 percentage-point change in public opinion—a startling power, although one that I'll save for discussion in the next chapter. "Experts" are also extremely powerful. These are the academics, think-tank insiders, former government officials, former members of the military, scientists, and all the other bespectacled, lab-coated, many-lettered men and women who pop up on the news to explain a subject that's foreign to most of us. Experts, Page and Shapiro found, can push public opinion more than 3 percentage points toward the position they're calling for.

Why experts should hold such power over us isn't a mystery. Experts contextualize, they interpret, they deconstruct. They spin wisps of hypothesis and theory into the substantial stuff we think of as fact. Capitalism pushes us toward lives of narrowness and specialization—the butcher, the baker, the candlestick maker—and, increasingly, hyperspecialization: the organic butcher, the gluten-free baker, the reclaimed-wood candlestick maker, each of us familiar with just a vanishingly small section of society. At the same time, civic life demands that we harbor ideas on matters that are far beyond our direct experience. You are not a macroeconomist, a scholar of global development, or an international relations theorist. But in the course of following social or political debates, you're asked to consider questions that are the domain of such experts—such as whether an increase in the minimum wage might affect unemployment, or whether international aid hurts African nations more than it helps, or how the rise of China might affect the strategic goals of the United States.

Expert opinion is the soul of modern media. Reporters are preternatural generalists, but, like eager Italian waiters armed with pepper mills, they sprinkle the wisdom of experts upon everything they send out to us. They corral real estate experts to tell us when to buy and when to sell, fashion experts to tell us what to wear, and nutritionists to tell us what to eat. Consequently, if you examine many of your most cherished ideas about the world, you're likely to find some expert or another lurking down beneath. What's the basis, for instance, of your thoughts on the threat of global warming, or embryonic stem cell science, or the business prospects of Google? As the controversies that dominate our lives become ever more complex, as arcane information from outside our own experience overwhelms the public discourse, the world is increasingly rendered comprehensible only through the eyes of the expert.

Consider, for instance, one example from not-too-distant American history: the political debate over SALT II, the nuclear arms limitation agreement that President Jimmy Carter signed with Leonid Brezhnev, the Soviet premier, in the early summer of 1979. Cold War–era weapons theory was a generally impenetrable subject, the sort of thing that the public, if people paid attention to it at all, understood mainly according to the sardonic sensibility of a Stanley Kubrick film.

But even by these standards, SALT II was difficult. The treaty aimed to limit the U.S. and Soviet arsenals of "strategic nuclear delivery vehicles" to 2,250 each by the end of 1981. But nuclear treaties never really focus on such broad goals; like all formal contracts, they attempt to constrain the wide range of human possibility into a narrow channel of acceptable action, and they're preciously technical and legalistic. It took negotiators more than seven years—spanning three American presidential administrations—to assemble SALT II. In its issue reporting on the signing of the treaty, the *New York Times* had to publish a glossary of terms used in the agreement that included such wondrous acronyms as FROD, ASBM, SLCM, and GLCM. (These stood for functionally related observable differences, air-to-surface ballistic missiles, sea-launched cruise missiles, and ground-launched cruise missiles.) Carter argued that SALT II "reduced the danger of nuclear war." But any citizen unschooled in nuclear theory would have found the document about as comprehensible as a homeowner's insurance policy.

In surveys, Americans had long expressed strong approval of a plan like SALT II. But many were also ignorant of its provisions; according to one poll, less than a third even knew which countries were involved in the accord. Treaties are signed by presidents, but they do not take on the force of law until they are ratified by the Senate. Now, during several weeks of congressional hearings, a parade of diplomats and retired generals— that is, people whom the public considered experts in nuclear strategy and weapons technology—argued that SALT II was flawed.

William Westmoreland, the general who commanded U.S. forces in Vietnam during the 1960s, said that ratification would weaken America's non-nuclear forces. General Alexander Haig, who had just retired as NATO's supreme allied commander in Europe, criticized the treaty's limits on cruise missiles. Henry Kissinger, the dean of the nation's foreign policy establishment, called on the Senate to add several provisions to SALT II to strengthen the U.S. hand. Public support plummeted. By the fall, after weeks of hearings, even senators friendly toward the treaty began urging Carter to remove it from consideration. Early in 1980, when the Soviet Union invaded Afghanistan, he did. The critics had profoundly shifted public opinion, just as Page and Shapiro's work suggests will happen when experts take on a cause. The experts had killed SALT II.

But the most interesting thing about the debate on SALT II isn't that experts pushed Americans to oppose it—it's that the experts who did so weren't the ones who represented the consensus view. Experts didn't kill SALT II; *some* experts, the ones who'd made it on TV and in the papers, killed SALT II. Many of the weapons theorists who testified in the Senate actually spoke out in favor of the accord. They worried that rejecting SALT II would spark a dangerous arms race. These were also retired military men of high rank and arms negotiators who'd long pondered the great strategic dilemmas prompted by nuclear weapons. They were experts. But their names weren't as well-known as those experts in opposition, and the news media and, in turn, the public, ignored them.

We arrive once again at the doorstep of multiple realities. SALT II was a hard question. And in any debate over difficult subjects, one naturally finds people of scholarship and achievement arguing passionately for opposing ends. As I discussed in previous chapters, "reality" splits when people selectively expose themselves to different facts, or when they interpret the same evidence in divergent ways.

Expertise presents another mechanism for reality to shatter: we choose our personal versions of truth by subscribing to the clutch of specialists we find agreeable and trustworthy. The American public had no way of determining which side was actually right on SALT II. People didn't choose a position on the issue based on a private assessment of the facts; after all, many didn't even know which countries were signatories to the treaty. Rather, they put in their lot with the experts they liked. They chose their reality based on personalities they found trustworthy.

Something similar has happened in the debate over who truly won the 2004 election. Surveys suggest that about a third of Americans believe that Bush was not fairly reelected in 2004. Every political scientist and pollster who's studied the case feels differently. But as in so many other current controversies, a subset of the population, including luminaries such as Kennedy, has chosen to trust another set of experts, those who propose a different truth.

It's a pressing problem of the fragmented age. Today, experts come at us from all directions, in every medium, through every niche. But their quality—their education, their experience, their reputation, their ideological and financial allegiances— is growing ever more difficult to ascertain. We consult experts specifically to learn something about which we are ignorant. The transaction is inherently treacherous because ignorance puts us at a disadvantage, too. How can we know whether the "experts" who dominate the public discourse really are expert?

The day after the 2004 election, Kathy Dopp, a mathematician who lives in Park City, Utah, was poring through voting results from across the country when she stumbled upon a statistical peculiarity that suggested something nefarious in Florida. Dopp is a pleasant middle-aged woman with shaggy silver hair and big glasses. Early in 2004, she began hearing about computer scientists' objections to touch-screen electronic voting machines. The machines, as Dopp and many other election observers around the country worried, were a disaster, bedeviled by a fundamental design flaw: when a voter casts a ballot on such a system, the voter sees no proof that it has accurately recorded her choice. This makes recounting the vote impossible; the machines simply spit out the number they've stored in the database, giving no assurance that it represents what voters wanted. Worse, many of the touch-screen machines now in wide use have been shown to be vulnerable to surreptitious hacking, and the authorities responsible for testing them have proved to be less than adequately rigorous.

A few months before the election, Dopp founded a group, Utah Count Votes, to oppose the introduction of electronic voting machines in her state; across the country, many such citizen groups had come together to oppose touch-screen voting, and many had succeeded in raising widespread concern about the reliability of the systems. After the race, Dopp was hoping to find some mathematical smoking gun pointing to touch screen–enabled electoral fraud somewhere in the nation. To her surprise, though, she saw something very different—an apparent problem in several Florida counties that employed another kind of voting procedure known as optical scan. These systems use a computerized reader to count ballots that voters mark by hand (not unlike the process of a standardized school exam). Optical-scan voting is considered tougher to rig on a wide scale because its paper ballots can, as a last resort, be tallied in a manual recount. Yet in results from many optical-scan counties in Florida, Dopp noticed something very strange: the votes for George W. Bush greatly exceeded the local population of registered Republicans.

The 2004 election was a terrifically partisan contest. Nationally, 89 percent of Democrats voted for Kerry, and 93 percent of Republicans voted for Bush. So the vote in a place like Baker County, a rural area in north Florida, was unusual, Dopp noticed. Of the 13,000 registered voters there, slightly more than 3,000 identified themselves as Republicans. But Bush won 7,738 votes in Baker, vastly more than Kerry's 2,180. Dopp also saw a similar pattern in Holmes County, in the Panhandle, where 73 percent of the voters were registered as Democrats, but 77 percent of votes went to Bush. She spotted as many as a dozen such counties—places with high registration for Democrats but lots of votes for Bush. And they had all used optical-scan voting systems. The suspicion seemed warranted: why had so many counties that employed similar voting technology all seen so many Democrats vote for Bush?

Dopp posted her full analysis on the Web, including some eye-popping charts that seemed to converge upon a provocative question: "Is it possible to rig op-scan voting systems?" she asked in one post in a lefty-leaning message board. Was it possible that Bush didn't win it after all? To crestfallen liberals, the data looked miraculous. I was investigating election problems for *Salon* at the time, and I remember the e-mail coming in as if from a loosed spigot, all of it pleading for me and other reporters to publicize Dopp's work. Thom Hartmann, a liberal columnist, was the first journalist to report on Dopp's discovery. Hartmann's article in Common Dreams, a popular left-wing Web site, carried the headline: "Evidence Mounts That the Vote May Have Been Hacked."

But on closer inspection, Dopp's theory broke down. After reading Hartmann's article, Walter Mebane, a political scientist at the University of Michigan, noticed an obvious flaw in Dopp's work. The pattern that she considered suspect—high Democratic registration but lots of votes for Republicans in optical-scan counties—had actually occurred in the same areas in many previous elections, even before the counties had adopted optical-scan voting. This wasn't an anomaly. It was a local idiosyncrasy. Democrats in these parts often vote for Republicans. To understand why, you have to ask an expert like Mebane, someone who's studied voting patterns in Florida.

What Dopp and her supporters had missed can be summed up in a single word: "Dixiecrats." Many of Florida's largest counties, such as Miami-Dade and Palm Beach, moved to upgrade their voting systems only after the punch-card blowup of 2000. They purchased paperless touch-screen machines because these were the newest thing then on the market. But Florida's small and midsized counties, especially those in the northern, rural parts of the state, upgraded their voting machines in the 1990s, when the best technology available was optical scan.

The demographics in these parts are unusual. Political sentiment runs much closer to that of neighboring states—Alabama and Georgia—than to the rest of Florida. People are extremely conservative, but out of Civil War–era contempt for Republicans, they've long been registered as Democrats. For much of the twentieth century, they've voted for conservative Democrats, too. But the civil rights movement and Nixon's Southern Strategy to attract white voters transformed the politics of the rural South, and in the 1970s, these Democrats began to vote the other way. In the last thirty-five years, the only Democratic presidential candidates to win electoral votes in Alabama and Georgia were Bill Clinton and Jimmy Carter, both of whom were Southern governors (and Carter was *from* Georgia). John Kerry's losing margin in Alabama and Georgia was in the double digits. It wasn't a surprise, then, that he'd lost in the Florida counties right across the border—and it had nothing to do with the voting machines.

Notice that Dopp's error was not one of fact. To dig into the race, she had to get her hands on several bits of data: county-by-county vote counts from across Florida; the number of registered voters, broken down by party, in each county; and the kind of voting machines each jurisdiction used during the race. A decade ago, Dopp would have had to phone the elections office in every county in the state to get such stats. Just finding the data would have taken her weeks of work. In 2004, she got the figures on election night from the Web. But this was the easy part. The hard part was determining what the numbers meant. And that's where she erred. Kathy Dopp is a mathematician. She has

worked as a math teacher and an actuary, she once founded an
Internet service company, and she has designed a house powered by solar energy. But the politics of the rural American
South were simply lost on Dopp and her acolytes. "This was a
case of just not knowing about Florida or American elections in
the South—which is to say, American elections," Mebane says.

It is a common mistake in the digital age. New technology
gives us access to vast new stores of data and tools with which
to understand them. On the Web you can find seemingly any
number you want: an instantaneous county breakdown of live
election results; a census of illegal immigrants in the United
States (between seven and twenty million); how much sea levels will rise as a result of global warming (between 110 and 770
millimeters in this century); the price at which any stock is trad-
ing at this very second. Through my local library's Web site, I can
get thirty-year-old American public opinion surveys regarding
SALT II without ever having to leave the house. Academic journal articles once buried in dusty tomes in the narrow, vertiginous
stacks of far-flung, ivy-covered campuses are now available to
all online.

All of this data is empowering, certainly. It gives us a peek into
fields where only experts once dared to tread. It breaks down
barriers. It allows us to check on the elite. Yet at the same time,
in the absence of expert comment, we find ourselves drowning
in a sea of facts divorced of meaning, trying to keep afloat in
all the numbers. And it is amateurs—people like Dopp, folks
with no particular experience on the issues at hand—who are
popping up as our purported lifesavers.

Many reporters (myself included) cited Walter Mebane's research to show that Dopp was wrong. But the experts' opinions
did not seem to greatly hurt Dopp's standing among those who
questioned the election results. Two days after Kerry's conces-
sion, three Democratic congressmen—John Conyers, Jerrold

Nadler, and Robert Wexler—asked the Government Accountability Office to investigate the race. They pointed to Dopp's finding as one of the "troubling" signs of a breakdown. Dopp, meanwhile, began to cultivate the accoutrements of authentic expertise. She founded a group, USCountVotes (later renamed the more official-sounding National Election Data Archive), whose mission was "to investigate the accuracy of elections" by analyzing "data for the entire United States."

Dopp attracted several mathematicians and statisticians to her cause. Together, over the next couple of years, they would release several dense reports on the 2004 race, arguing in different ways that the election was not legitimate. Dopp had never studied the American political scene. Her first major attempt at investigating an election resulted in failure. But now she was calling herself an expert. And in some quarters of the Web, people were listening to what she said.

In the early 1970s, John Ware, then a young researcher at the University of Southern California School of Medicine, decided to play an impish trick on a few of his colleagues—although as he tells it, the gag was mainly intended to further science. Ware had recently seen a comedian on television whose shtick involved saying a whole lot in a style that suggested something of great import but that was actually complete nonsense. Gobbledygook. Because Ware had once read a book called *The Presentation of Self in Everyday Life*—in which the sociologist Erving Goffman explored the importance of theatrical presentation in human interaction—he was quite interested in gobbledygook. Could people really be fooled by nonsense? Could someone who knew nothing about a subject skate by on personal style and good humor alone, convincing others that he was some kind of expert in the field? Ware's colleagues, a group of distinguished psychiatrists, psychologists, and social workers, would soon be holding a training conference in Lake Tahoe. "And so I had this idea," Ware recalled recently. "Why don't we hire that guy from TV to do a lecture for the faculty?"

The gobbledygook guy from TV, though, was unavailable, so Ware got another television actor of very small repute, Michael Fox (not to be confused with Michael J. Fox), whose biggest role was as the TV detective Columbo's veterinarian. Ware turned Michael Fox into Dr. Myron Fox and presented him to a group of about a dozen faculty members as a highly regarded expert on a comically abstruse topic, "the application of mathematics to human behavior." Dr. Fox's lecture for the afternoon was titled "Mathematical Game Theory as Applied to Physician Education," and Ware instructed him to deliver it with a surfeit of humor, physical expression, double-talk, neologisms, non sequiturs, contradictions, and references to unrelated topics.

Dr. Fox spoke for an hour, and then he opened up the forum for a half-hour of questions and answers. Throughout the session, he said nothing of substance, mainly rattling off jargon that was superficially related to mathematics and game theory. "There was a moment in the discussion where he said, 'Now let me summarize my main points,'" Ware recalled. "Of course, there weren't any main points—he wasn't making any points at all. So he told a joke about the opera *Tosca*. One person raised a hand and said, 'You really didn't present a basis for your conclusions. What's the scientific evidence?' And I remember he walked to the side of the room and he looked out the window. 'Here we are in Lake Tahoe,' he said. 'It's beautiful. We could get into a lot of technical details about my work—I could try to impress you with all my publications. But let me ask you, how many articles have you published in this field? What work have you done?' He totally intimidated this professor, who really backed down."

Afterward, Ware handed out a questionnaire to see whether the group had seen through Dr. Fox. Remarkably, they hadn't. Indeed, they swooned. "Did he stimulate your thinking?" the questionnaire asked. Everyone said Dr. Fox had. "Did he use enough examples to clarify his material?" Ninety percent thought so. Almost everyone said that Dr. Fox had "presented his material in a well-organized form." Among the comments people wrote down were, "Excellent presentation, enjoyed listening," and "Has warm manner. Good flow, seems enthusiastic."

"The results were so incredible—to fool an audience that was all professors and faculty members with a talk that communicated absolutely nothing of substance," Ware recalled. But he wondered whether the whole thing was a fluke. And so he tried it again. A few weeks later, Ware played a videotape of Dr. Fox's lecture to another group of mental health educators. They, too, loved it. When asked whether Fox had "dwelled upon the obvious," every one of these people said no—what he was saying truly fascinated and intrigued them. One person was so convinced of Dr. Fox's expertise that he reported having previously read articles by the scholar. Ware showed the tape to another group—students enrolled in a graduate-level course on educational philosophy—and saw the same reaction. "His relaxed manner of presentation was a large factor in holding my interest," one of them reported. Another said, "Good analysis of subject that has been personally studied before."

John Ware became deeply captivated by these sessions, and over the following years he staged multiple experiments to pin down what came to be called the "Dr. Fox effect." "It shook the foundations," he said. The suggestion that a person's speaking style could so strongly seduce an audience—that the way you said something might be more important than what you'd said—"really makes you look twice at how the public evaluates so-called experts," Ware says.

The most comprehensive Dr. Fox study that Ware conducted was a controlled experiment involving undergraduates at Southern Illinois University. About two hundred students were broken up into several groups, each of which was shown a videotape of an actor delivering a lecture. The lectures covered identical topics but varied widely according to two variables—the level of "content" each conveyed, and the "expressiveness" of the lecturer. Lectures of "high" content covered dozens of teaching points, while low-content lectures covered only 15 percent as many. Lectures that were highly expressive featured the teacher acting in the same jokey, warm way as Dr. Myron Fox in Lake Tahoe; "low-expression" lectures were delivered "in a dry, stand-behind-the-lectern way, no affect, the way a lot of professors do it," Ware told me.

Here the Dr. Fox effect was stark. Of all the groups, the students who were shown lectures that were high in both content and expressiveness reported the most satisfaction with their professor. That is, teachers who are both knowledgeable *and* exciting elicited the greatest response from their audiences. Crucially, though, Ware found that expressiveness carried a lot more weight than did content. Thus the lectures that were extremely expressive but very low in content also rated highly with students. In fact, students preferred the low-content, highly expressive lectures to those that were high in content and low in expressiveness. In other words, professors were better off teaching very little very enthusiastically than teaching very much very badly.

That American society prizes style over substance is so widespread a criticism that even to note it might seem clichéd. After all, nobody thinks Rush Limbaugh is the most popular guy on the radio because he's the smartest guy in the country; he's good on the radio *despite* his ignorance, because he can talk about what little he knows in a way that's exceedingly interesting (to people of a certain persuasion). But the Dr. Fox experiments suggest that style is even more powerful than the cliché indicates. We tend to think of expertise as a measure of scholarship and experience and other factors that are easily quantified. You'd never guess that a fast-talking ignoramus could fool *you*. But that's exactly what Dr. Fox says can happen.

Ware has tracked the phenomenon far beyond the classroom. He once hired Michael Fox to play a medical doctor and to hold mock encounters with patients. Ware wanted to see whether people would trust a warm, personable doctor who gave out bad advice over a cold, impersonal doctor who was extremely knowledgeable. And that's what happened: the patients preferred friendly quacks. If you think about it, this isn't really a surprise. Make a list of some people you consider influential in your life. Do you trust them because of how much they know? Do you even *know* how much they know—do you, for instance, have any independent verification of your own doctor's medical knowledge? Or do you trust her for other reasons—perhaps personal warmth, rhetorical style, how smartly she's dressed, how wealthy she seems to be, which medical school she attended? The people we listen to aren't necessarily those whom we've determined know the most. We listen to those who seduce us in other ways. And we're easily seduced.

Ideally, of course, people would navigate the world rationally, analytically, rigorously, even skeptically; you'd be constantly on the lookout for the slick and the sly, and you'd evaluate every claim—every Dr. Fox who comes to your classroom—with careful, deep rumination. But the world clearly doesn't always work this way. To understand why, it helps to look at the psychological mechanisms by which humans make decisions.

In the 1980s, the psychologists Richard Petty and John Cacioppo proposed that people form their attitudes on certain subjects by employing one of two distinct cognitive methods. In some cases, we look at a problem through the "central route," which describes a diligent attempt to investigate the facts of a case. If you decide to search for a new car by spending weeks researching the performance and safety statistics of every sedan on the market, you're using the central route of cognition. On the other hand, instead of taking the time to look through a mountain of data, you might simply choose to buy a Volvo because *Consumer Reports* rates it highly. In that case you'd be employing the other cognitive pathway, what Petty and Cacioppo call the "peripheral route." Here, we use "cues"—like emotional reactions or what an expert or a celebrity or some other trustworthy figure thinks—to guide us toward a decision. You might choose a Ford because your parents always bought Fords, or a Hummer because Arnold Schwarzenegger has several, or a Toyota because you like the bombastic pitchman whom the local dealership features in its TV spots.

What determines when people use central processing or peripheral processing to find the answer to a specific question has been a matter of extensive research in psychology. Generally, you use the peripheral route when you're trying to save time or if you're confronted with questions that are beyond your capacity to answer. *Consumer Reports* has the resources to test every car on the market, and you do not. So if the magazine says that Volvo's the way to go, you listen. This isn't always a bad strategy. After all, how often is *Consumer Reports* wrong about some product endorsement? Rarely, or else it wouldn't be as vaunted as it is.

The psychologists Daniel Goldstein and Gerd Gigerenzer have shown that heuristics—simple rules of thumb that we use to quickly decide what to make of the world—can often yield very good results. Goldstein and Gigerenzer once asked a dozen German students, "Which city has a larger population: San Diego or San Antonio?" All of them picked the right answer: San Diego. But when a dozen American students were asked the same question, only two-thirds chose San Diego. How could Germans do better than Americans on a test of American cities? Because the Germans, Goldstein and Gigerenzer found, were using a simple peripheral processing trick to guess the right answer: San Diego was the only city in the pair that they'd heard of, so they figured it must be bigger.

The trick is called the "recognition heuristic," and it's basically a little rule that tells us to assume that something we've heard of is more valuable (in this case, more populous) than something that's new to us. The Americans who were asked the question couldn't employ the recognition heuristic because they'd heard of both cities. Instead, they had to puzzle out the answer in a more systematic way, through the central route. And some of them, inevitably, got the wrong answer. The irony, of course, is that the American students possessed more knowledge about the topic—U.S. cities —than the Germans did. The Americans knew *too much* to use the shortcut that led to the right answer.

The German students used a trick because they didn't know the subject, and this is an important point about peripheral processing. It's something we reach for when we possess "frugal" information. In other words, we tend to make decisions peripherally when we simply don't understand the details of the case at hand, especially if we're overwhelmed by details. To see what I mean, imagine that I asked you to read and try to decipher the following seemingly incomprehensible paragraph in only twenty seconds (no cheating):

> The eraser is made of good quality rubber and it is matched to be about the same size and shape as the usable portion of an ordinary lead pencil eraser. The flat end is cemented to a small disk-shaped mount of relatively stiff, strong materials such as metal or plastic. The mount has a rigidly connected device protruding from the side opposite the eraser. It is of small diameter and is helically shaped like a corkscrew and terminates in a pointed outer end. It can be threaded into a stub or base part of a worn-down eraser in a ferrule on the end of an ordinary lead pencil. Short tabs are provided on the periphery of the mounting disk. They prevent the pencil from rolling on a flat surface even if it has a slight slope. Also, the tabs tend to prevent the pencil from falling or being thrown out of the pocket. They are useful for the fingers to engage when the user is screwing the device into an eraser stub.

The text comes from a patent-application description that the researchers S. Ratneshwar and Shelly Chaiken once used in an experiment to see whether people's ability to comprehend a subject affects how they make decisions about it. Let me ask you this: Do you think that what you just read describes a successful product? What if I told you that the inventor was a highly re-garded professor of industrial design at Stanford who'd invented many things in the past? Would that guide your views about its possible success? That's just what happened in Ratneshwar and Chaiken's experiment. When subjects who were given only twenty seconds to read the patent description were told that the inventor was a Stanford professor, they tended to give the new invention high marks. But subjects who were told that the in-ventor was a realtor—rather than an inventor—didn't think too highly of it. Objectively, these factors shouldn't have mattered at all. Everyone had been given an identical description of the product. But they didn't understand the description. So they made up their minds by looking at other, peripheral cues.

You could argue that the peripheral route makes sense in this case. Perhaps an inventor's background is a good way to measure his product's chance of success—a Stanford professor of industrial design might very well create a best-selling product. That may be. On the other hand—how do we know? What if the professor's previous inventions had nothing to do with pencil erasers? What if his design experience had been mainly theoretical, rather than practical? How do we know that he's not a complete fraud? Consider, after all, Dr. Fox. John Ware's colleagues must have felt the same press of incomprehensibility when confronted with the fake expert who visited them in Lake Tahoe. His talk made no sense to them, just as the patent description made no sense to the participants in Ratneshwar and Chaiken's study. But the peripheral factors—Dr. Fox's credentials, his résumé, his warm personal manner, and the very fact that he'd been invited to speak to the group—suggested someone of great importance. So they rated him highly. And they were completely duped.

This is the basic problem with the peripheral route. The particular cues we choose to pay attention to may not be the ones that best guide us toward the truth. Indeed, they might obscure the truth. In the fall of 2004, Kathy Dopp appeared to know what she was talking about. She was a mathematician, a peripheral cue suggesting that you could trust her numerical analysis of registration versus vote counts in Florida's optical-scan counties. She was also the head of Utah Count Votes, which sounded official and well-intentioned enough to indicate that she knew about politics in the United States. There were other cues as well. The stinging recent history of unfair elections was a cue to be on the lookout for errors in the casting and counting of votes. The voting machines were a cue, too: nobody trusted them. And then there was Bush himself. Peripheral processing all but invites us to introduce biases into how we make decisions—and for many on the left, it just didn't seem likely, and maybe not even plausible, that Bush, after all he'd bungled, could fairly win the vote.

None of these factors mattered to the substance of Dopp's argument. But they bolstered her case anyway, in the same way that credentials and humor gave people a reason to believe in Dr. Fox. The peripheral cues were a quick way of seeing that Dopp's idea could be real. To find flaws in her analysis, you had to go through the central route—that is, you had to dig into the substance of her theory, learn about the Dixiecrats, and test her numbers against previous elections. Only if you did all of this did her argument fall flat. But who does all of that?

One of the skeptics who joined Kathy Dopp's effort was Steven Freeman, a scholar of organization studies who has dedicated much of his life since the election to proving that the exit polls showed that Kerry really won. In 2006, Freeman fashioned his research into a book, *Was the 2004 Presidential Election Stolen?* (it was coauthored by the journalist Joel Bleifuss). The book, in turn, formed the spine of Robert F. Kennedy Jr.'s argument in *Rolling Stone*. Freeman's rise, even more so than Dopp's, illustrates the power of peripheral cues and the new amateurization of expertise. How he managed to displace bona fide scholars of polling and politics—to convince Kennedy and tens of thousands of others of his own unconventional analysis of the election's outcome—is a case study in the ways that complex topics can be distorted by people who put on the garb of experts.

Freeman is a tall, imposing fellow with a long mane of black hair that he pulls tightly back into a ponytail. It's a faintly dowdy look that suggests the life of an academic, a suspicion that's confirmed with a peek at the man's résumé. Freeman is impressively lettered. He's earned a bachelor's degree in philosophy and a master's degree in social systems sciences from the University of Pennsylvania, as well as a doctorate in organizational dynamics from MIT's business school.

Freeman's primary research interest involves the way companies make decisions and respond to change. He earned his PhD, for instance, by examining the U.S. motor vehicle industry's sluggish response to advances by the Japanese. As part of his dissertation, Freeman argued that organizations deal with "loss"—a business downturn, say—according to the five stages that the psychiatrist Elisabeth Kübler-Ross proposed for how people respond to grief: denial, anger, bargaining, depression, acceptance. Freeman is also interested in the role of morality and ethics in companies. After the terrorist attacks on September 11, 2001, he studied how the investment firm Sandler O'Neill & Partners, which was based on the 104th floor of the South Tower of the World Trade Center, responded to the catastrophic loss of more than a third of its employees. The company thrived. Within months, its revenues and profits had recovered to previous levels. Freeman and his coauthors argued that Sandler O'Neill succeeded because people at the firm became galvanized by the attacks. They were determined not to see the business fail, and the secret to their resilience, Freeman believes, was a force often overlooked by scholars of business: what he calls "moral purpose."

Freeman says that he has taught classes in survey design, but the main thrust of his work was far removed from the science of exit polling in U.S. elections. Indeed, before November 2, 2004,

Freeman hadn't given much thought at all to the machinery of democracy. But on election night he was shocked into action. At the same moment that television anchors were predicting a Kerry loss based on official counts coming in from across the country, Freeman was looking at CNN's Web site, where he caught a slate of exit poll data that he says showed a decisive Kerry win.

Exit polls are compiled through interviews with voters just as they leave voting precincts. In 2004, a consortium of national news organizations hired two polling firms—Edison Media Research and Mitofsky International, led by the veteran exit pollster Warren Mitofsky—to conduct the poll. Pollsters staked out about fifteen hundred precincts throughout the country and attempted to ask a random sample of voters how they had cast their ballots. By the end of the day the pollsters had conducted more than 114,000 interviews. The results looked good for the Democrats. As Freeman saw on CNN's site, the exit polls were predicting that Kerry would take Ohio by more than 4 percentage points and Pennsylvania by almost 9 points. Florida, another battleground state, was extremely close, with the exits showing Bush leading by 49.8 percent to Kerry's 49.7.

The official results, though, defied these numbers: Bush won Florida by 5 points and Ohio by 2.5 points. He lost in Pennsylvania, but only by 2 percentage points, not by anywhere near the margin that the exit polls predicted. Freeman was astonished by these differences. How had the polls been so off? When "neither reporters, nor pollsters, nor the Democrats, nor political scientists raised the obvious questions," he wrote in his book, "I thought that, well, perhaps this is my job as much as anyone else's." He began to investigate.

There can be only three possible explanations for the large difference between the exit poll prediction and the final count: Option One is that there was some problem in how the *poll* was conducted (for instance, if pollsters showed a bias in how they selected voters to interview, choosing slightly more Kerry voters than Bush voters to be included in the survey). Option Two is that there was a problem in how *the election* was conducted (that is, the vote was rigged). And Option Three is that there was a *random sampling error* in the poll results. This is a technical but important point: every survey, even a well-designed, perfectly run poll, runs the risk of being completely wrong because, by coincidence or sheer chance, the people picked in the survey aren't representative of the total group.

While it's difficult to calculate the odds of Option One or Option Two from above, determining the likelihood of a survey being off due to random error involves a relatively straightforward bit of math. Freeman's first effort, then, was to rule out this last possibility. It took him just a couple of weeks to do so, and the end result was an eye-popping number that was destined to make waves. In a paper he published on the Web, Freeman showed that the odds against the exit poll failing due to random error simultaneously in three key states—Florida, Ohio, and Pennsylvania—"are 662,000 to one." He wrote, "As much as we can say in social science that something is impossible, it is impossible that the discrepancies between predicted and actual vote counts in the three critical battleground states of the 2004 election could have been due to chance or random error."

A 662,000-to-1 probability sounds big, it sounds definitive, and it sounds scary. Actually, though, the number's true meaning was exceedingly subtle, and, if you understood it, exceedingly tame. Freeman was only saying that it was highly unlikely that the discrepancy between the exit poll and the final count was a coincidence. In other words, the number simply meant that *something* had gone wrong—either Option One, the possibility that the poll had over-sampled Kerry voters, or Option Two, that the vote count was rigged. Everyone in the debate, though, including the pollsters, agreed that *something* had gone wrong; the important question for the pollsters was what it was.

For many activists, however, Freeman's long-odds number quickly came to stand for proof that the election had been stolen. Many cited it as a measure of the unlikeliness of the official results. Freeman, Dopp, and their colleagues released several other such stats of dubious meaning. One involved the exit poll's prediction that Kerry would win the national popular vote by 3 percentage points. The researchers calculated that the odds against this projection being off as a result of random error were also astronomical: 1 in 455,000. Once again, the number meant only that *something* had gone wrong—it did *not* measure the odds that the election had been stolen. But here's how Robert F. Kennedy cited it. With the exit polls showing Kerry "winning by a million and a half votes nationally," he wrote, "the statistical likelihood of Bush winning was less than one in 450,000."

Big-number statistics offer a classic path to the peripheral route; to nonexperts, numbers can easily be made to look freighted with meaning, when in truth they may signal nothing out of the ordinary. The pollsters who'd conducted the 2004 exit poll considered the amateurs' long-odds numbers irrelevant because right from the start, they, too, had ruled out a random sampling error.

Warren Mitofsky, the man who ran the 2004 exit polls, was highly regarded in American public opinion circles, and he had managed several national exit polls since 1990. Mitofsky died in the fall of 2006, and though he was by all accounts generous to others in the field, he was also, at times, brusque and defensive about his work. In the immediate aftermath of the race, he seemed reluctant to fully account for what had gone wrong with the exits. He once shot off an e-mail to a blogger who'd criticized how his poll had performed: "We have never claimed that all the exit polls were accurate. Then again, neither is your reporting." Still, the day after the election, Mitofsky did offer a very early idea about why the polls had differed from the final count. He told the PBS program *The Newshour* that there had been a substantive flaw in his exit poll: Option One, Kerry voters had been overrepresented in the survey. "Kerry was ahead in a number of the states in margins that looked unreasonable to us, and we suspect that the main reason was that the Kerry voters were more anxious to participate in our exit polls than the Bush voters," Mitofsky said.

In January 2005, Mitofsky published a thorough report outlining this theory. It ran for seventy-seven pages and was as dense as mud—anyone who wasn't a pollster would have had to read it several times just to understand the polling team's technical descriptions of what had gone wrong. But in the thicket of details, the report strongly argued against election fraud. It pointed out, for one, that there was no significant difference in exit poll errors across voting technologies. If Bush had won as a result of rigged paperless electronic voting machines, you'd expect to see a bigger difference between the exit poll and the final results in places that used such devices. But voting locations with touch-screen machines saw essentially the same discrepancy as optical-scan and punch-card machines—in other words, the exit poll was not "more wrong" in these locations, a strong suggestion that the machines had not been tampered with.

In his report, Mitofsky suggested a complex mechanism for his theory about why the poll had predicted a Kerry win—his idea that Kerry voters were slightly overrepresented among respondents. Exit polls are conducted by an army of interviewers—usually people looking for a good short-term job, including many college students—who are stationed at preselected voting precincts across the nation. Because the accuracy of any poll depends on its respondents being chosen randomly, each of the interviewers that Mitofsky hired was assigned a number, from 1 to 10, that represented the "rate" at which they were supposed to approach a voter leaving the polls. An interviewer given a rate of 1 had to try to interview every single voter who left a polling place; an interviewer with a rate of 10, reserved for large precincts with many voters, was expected to approach only every tenth voter for an interview.

The ideal exit-poll interviewer should operate something like an automaton, Mitofsky told me after the election. Interviewers should have been constantly counting people as they left the booth and approaching whomever the count dictated. They were not allowed to choose people who seemed friendly or people who were closer to their own age or people who looked like they weren't in a hurry. If an interviewer asked the female half of a couple to participate in the poll and she refused but offered up her spouse, the interviewer was not supposed to talk to him instead. "What they're told is not to deviate from this number, not to make any exceptions," Mitofsky said. But the data, he believed, suggested that in places where conducting interviews was difficult, the interviewers had made some exceptions.

Mitofsky pointed out that precincts where the exit poll had deviated most from the actual election results tended to be the same places where pollsters had been assigned large interviewing rates. In precincts where pollsters were asked to interview every voter, the difference between the exit poll prediction and the official count was slight. But as interviewers were given more leeway—if they were asked to interview every fifth voter, say, in a larger area—the error grew. In the areas where interviewers were forced—according to rules that varied by jurisdiction—to stand more than twenty-five feet away from the polling place (as they were in Ohio), the exit poll was more off. Where the weather was inclement (as in many very rainy Ohio neighbor-hoods on Election Day 2004), the poll was more off. Where interviewers were younger or had less training, the poll was more off. "What that means to me was the interviewers were selecting people not in accordance with our instructions but ac-cording to their own judgment," Mitofsky said. Consequently, the survey lost some of its randomness and, by a slight margin, included more Kerry voters than Bush voters.

Mitofsky's theory made intuitive sense to many political poll-sters. Studies have long shown that Republicans are more wary than Democrats of talking to people from the news media.* In an experiment conducted during elections in New Jersey and New York in 1997, the pollsters Daniel Merkle, Murray Edel-man, Kathy Dykeman, and Chris Brogan looked into whether voters would be more willing to participate in an exit poll if in-terviewers carried folders stamped with logos of national news organizations, thus clearly identifying themselves as nonparti-san representatives of the media. The researchers found that participation rates did increase in these areas—but not in an unbiased way. The logos attracted Democratic voters but put off Republican ones. Exit-poll interviewers did not carry fold-ers bearing news-media names in the 2004 race, but they did wear badges showing that they were from the media, and the questionnaires they held were marked with logos representing ABC, CBS, NBC, CNN, Fox News, and the Associated Press. Interviewers were also instructed to tell each voter that the poll was being carried out by the media. These factors, polling ex-perts reasoned, could plausibly have introduced a slight bias into the poll.

---

* The reluctance likely has roots in the bedrock right-wing belief that the main-stream media are unreasonably liberal, a topic that I'll explore in the next chapter.

Such a bias would not have been unusual. For many political pollsters, the most compelling reason to trust the official count over the exit polls was that exit polls in the United States do not have a perfect record. They've been off before. In 2003, Mitofsky and his polling partner Joe Lenski published an article in an academic journal pointing out that the Democratic vote was overstated in 38 percent of the exit polls conducted for Senate and gubernatorial races in the 1990, 1994, and 1998 elections. Presidential exit polls have overstated Democrats' margins in every election since 1998. The 2004 race had the biggest error of recent years, but the error in 1992 was almost as large: the exit polls predicted that Bill Clinton would win that race by 2.5 percentage points more than he actually did. The only reason there wasn't an outcry then was that the race wasn't close enough for the overstatement to have mattered. That is, Clinton still won. The 2004 race was much tighter. And in close races, a slight bias in the survey can cause a lot of heartache.

Mitofsky's report put to rest many of the questions that people in the political polling world had raised about the skew in the exits. His theory was seconded in 2005 by the Election Science Institute, an election-reform group that organized a team led by Fritz Scheuren, then the president of the American Statistical Association, to analyze exit poll data from Ohio. The group concluded "that the non-response rate theory"—that is, Mitofsky's theory about Kerry voters—"is much more likely than the fraud accusation theory to account for most, if not all, of the observed discrepancy between the exit polls and the actual results." Mark Blumenthal, of Pollster.com, says, "Among campaign pollsters and among media pollsters, I don't know of anyone who believes that the exit poll discrepancy of 2004 was evidence of fraud."

But Freeman, Dopp, and their colleagues pounced on Mitofsky's report. They threw at it an operatic barrage of math and charges of cover-up and argued in several papers that it "did not come close to justifying" the idea that Kerry voters had participated in the poll more readily than Bush voters. Their allegations were unyieldingly recondite and were quickly refuted by other analysts. In many cases, their mistakes echoed the trap Dopp had fallen into before; the amateurs were simply ignorant of how elections and exit polls actually work. Freeman, for example, frequently argued that exit polls enjoy a vaunted history of accuracy. He pointed to the exit polls that the television network ZDF conducts in Germany; according to his calculations, the ZDF poll has differed from the official count by less than three-tenths of a percentage point in recent German elections.*

Freeman is also fond of the story of the Ukrainian presidential election of 2004, where exit polls predicted that the opposition candidate Viktor Yushchenko would defeat Viktor Yanukovych. When the official count didn't bear this out, the discrepancy was an immediate indication to everyone in the world that the election results were fraudulent. When Ukraine held another election, Yushchenko prevailed. So if an exit poll discrepancy proves that the vote was stolen in Ukraine, why doesn't it prove the same thing in the United States?

But again, Freeman's theories gloss over some important points, ideas that were obvious to experts—pollsters and political scientists—looking at his work. The exit polls in Germany, as Blumenthal notes, don't tell us anything useful about the accuracy of U.S. exit polls because the two surveys are conducted in completely different ways. The German polls are simply much more thorough. In Germany, more than 80 percent of voters who are asked agree to participate in the polls. In the United

---

* They were not nearly as accurate in Germany's 2005 parliamentary elections; the leading television network, ZDF, was off in its prediction by 3.8 percentage points, according to a calculation by Mark Blumenthal.

States, it's around 50 percent. In Germany, two experienced pollsters are stationed at each chosen polling place throughout the election. In the United States in 2004, there was one pollster at each precinct, and most of them had never worked an exit poll before. In Germany, the interviewers stand right outside the door of the polling location, and they never leave. In the United States, they stand as far as a hundred feet away, and they leave three times during the day to call the national office with their results. These are all substantive differences, the sort that, combined, have a direct bearing on the quality of the poll. They go far in explaining why the German polls are so often accurate and why the polls in the United States failed. But Freeman ignored these distinctions.

Comparing the Ukraine vote to that in the United States, as the MIT political scientist Charles Stewart has pointed out, is similarly spurious because the two elections and the two nations are so different. In Ukraine, one exit poll showed opposition candidate Yushchenko winning 54 percent to 43 percent nationally. The final national poll in the United States put Kerry at 51 percent and Bush at 48 percent, a much tighter margin. The poll was also much closer to the actual result, which had Bush at 51 percent and Kerry at 48 percent. Moreover, Stewart noted, *preelection* polls in Ukraine agreed with the exits, bolstering the case that Yushchenko was the true winner. In the United States, though, polls taken before the election tended to show either a very close race or a Bush win. The final tally was well within these predictions. But Freeman skipped over these nuances.

If some of this sounds abstruse, the truth is, I haven't even yet covered the most esoteric bits of opposition that Freeman and his compatriots leveled at Mitofsky's theory that the exit poll was simply faulty. For more than two years after the election, Freeman continued to claim more and newer signs that, in fact, the exit poll's numbers had been correct, and that widespread vote-stealing on the part of Republicans had led to Bush's win in the election results. "When you look at the numbers, there is a tremendous amount of data that supports the supposition of election fraud," Freeman told Kennedy. He went on to list a king's bounty of examples. "The discrepancies"—between the exit poll and the voting results—"are higher in battleground states, higher where there were Republican governors, higher in states with greater proportions of African American communities and higher in states where there were the most Election Day complaints."

Every one of these allegations breaks down on further scrutiny. But investigating them is heavy work. There is difficult math, there is the intricate parsing of Freeman's selective statistics, there is the need to dig into what he misses and what he misinterprets. The political scientist Mark Lindeman, of Bard College, has produced a thorough refutation of the work of Freeman, Dopp, and their colleagues. It's forty-one pages long. Mark Blumenthal's paragraph-by-paragraph response to Kennedy's section on exit polling—which draws heavily from Freeman's theories—runs more than twelve thousand words. Longer, that is, than this chapter so far. On exit polling alone.

The honest debate on the exit polls is difficult—nearly incomprehensible, actually, to most Americans. There are portions of it that would test the mettle of statisticians. As you plow deeper into the matter, then, the line between comprehension and ignorance begins to blur, and the central route can't hold. You begin to care not about what's being said but about who's saying it, and how. You start to look at all the peripheral cues.

Not long ago, I went to see Steven Freeman give a talk to a group of scientists in San Francisco. Freeman lectures in the manner of an academic, softly, slowly, abetted by PowerPoint.

He is, nevertheless, compelling. There's a rumor of East Coast authority to his accent, and he ends each of his rhetorical points with an upward lilt that suggests deep self-confidence.

After his talk, a member of the audience asked him how many people would have had to have been in on the fraud he says happened in Ohio. "Literally a handful of people can alter millions of votes," Freeman said, definitively. "There are three companies that sell 80 percent of the voting machines in this country and they're very tightly intertwined. It's a trivial matter, it really is trivially easy to program fraud into these machines. You need two lines of code buried within a million. 'Beginning at six o'clock on November 2, 2004, switch one out of 10 votes from Column A to Column B.' 'At 9:00 p.m. on November 2, 2004, delete this line and the line above it.' Anyone who's taken a first-year programming course in college could do that. Really, a handful of people could switch votes system-wide."

What Freeman did not talk about is the great decentralization of the voting process in Ohio—the wide variety of voting technology, and the large number of election administrators managing the vote in each precinct. The majority of the machines in the state were punch-card and optical-scan systems (not, as is often alleged online, electronic touch-screen systems), so you have to imagine that anyone stealing the vote would have been okay with doing so even with a paper trail. And, anyway, hacking these—the punch-card and optical-scan counters—would have required many more than a handful of people. You'd have needed accomplices in the counties; you'd have needed accomplices in the precincts. Quickly, it becomes a conspiracy.*

---

* Freeman is understandably touchy about the label "conspiracy theorist." In a telephone interview, I asked him to explain why he's so certain that the 2004 exit polls were correct when we know that previous exit polls showed a Democratic bias, notably the exits of 1992 and 1988. His answer is that previous discrepancies can be explained by a long history of undercounting Democratic votes. In other

Freeman, furthermore, does not talk about the most definitive study of the vote in Ohio, by the University of Michigan's
Mebane, which matched voting patterns in 2004 to those of
previous elections and found no reason to suspect systematic
vote-switching.

These factors go through the central route. They are things
you have to look at rigorously and critically—but we're past
that here. The thing is so complicated that you're only looking
at it peripherally. You're paying attention to the cues. Freeman's credentials: UPenn, MIT, the letters PhD. Then there
are the various labels people apply to him. On the Web, you can
find him referred to as a statistician and an expert in surveys.
Kennedy wrote that Freeman "specializes in research methodology." And Freeman told Kennedy, "I am a survey expert."
Never mind that his eight-page résumé does not mention these
accomplishments. Freeman told me that his work with surveys

---

words, Freeman thinks that previous polls have been right, but election counts
are usually a little bit wrong. In his book he goes on to note that elections where
exits have been most off share a consistent, very suspicious feature: "[T]he candidate whose official number far exceeded exit-poll results was named George
Bush." He added that "in each case, the George Bush in question was running
for election with the benefit of incumbency. In 1988, Bush Sr. was the incumbent
vice president. In 1992, he was, of course, president, as was Bush Jr. in 2004."
The implication, unstated, is that the Bushes win through election theft; the exits
always show them doing worse than they do. Freeman did not explain how such
a fraud might have occurred, or why they couldn't have been more successful at
it in 1992 (when George H. W. Bush lost the race). In the interview, he told me
that the issue was "one that honestly it would be easy for you to make me look bad
on," and he declined to discuss it in any detail. "I'm a little bit concerned about
telling you this because based on what you've said before, I can see a hatchet
job being done," he said. "I don't know. What are you going to do with this?. . . I
mean, are you going to actually do that, would you refer to me as a 'conspiracy
theorist'? Is that the way you might write this?" I answered that I've never called
him a conspiracy theorist, and he said, "I know you haven't said it, I'm just asking
is that something you would do? Where do you think you're going with this?"
Then he said that he needed to take another phone call and that we could talk
again in ten minutes' time. He didn't answer my subsequent phone calls.

was limited to workshops that he's taught, although these aren't mentioned in his résumé either. But no matter. This is how Freeman comes to us. He's a PhD, he's affiliated with the Ivy League, he's a statistician and an expert in surveys, and he says that the exit polls prove the election was stolen.

On the other side you have the late Warren Mitofsky. The peripheral cues here are impressive as well. Mitofsky was a world expert in polling, and he knew more about the 2004 exits than anyone else alive. Still, as Freeman points out, there's the problem of conflict of interest. "If this guy was remotely seen as partisan, could he ever get another contract like this?" What Freeman means is that Mitofsky couldn't come out and say that his exit poll proved fraud. "I'm not directly attributing malfeasance on his part," Freeman says, "but I am saying that you can't accept it as something without using your own intelligence." This is another peripheral cue: Mitofsky had some motive for a cover-up.

Here, then, is your decision. Two experts are saying two opposite things, and it's your job to choose. It's a choice that comes right out of the literature on selective exposure—like the smokers I told you about in chapter 2, you're going to listen to the people who are saying what you want to hear. Reality splits along the lines of our preexisting beliefs. For people on the left, those who'd long been worried about voting in America, and who were devastated by Bush's win, the choice was clear. They had an expert who was telling them they were right, that their guy really won.

There is one more wrinkle in the difficulty we're facing with expertise, and it has to do with the labyrinthine world of academia. When you're outside a closed group, you tend to think of it as being monolithic: that all biologists know all biology. But in academia every discipline is studded with subdisciplines, and the subdisciplines contain several more narrow specialties, each of which may be animated by particular intrigues or bits of received wisdom or philosophical tendencies that folks on the outside will simply never understand. "Science is an extremely specialized activity, much more specialized than a lot of other stuff that people in life do," Naomi Oreskes explains. Oreskes is a science historian at the University of California San Diego, but before she came to academia she worked in the private sector. In the business world, she points out, it isn't uncommon for people to be called on to do what needs to be done, even if the work is beyond their expertise. You may work in accounts receivable, but if the payroll man is out on vacation, you might find yourself picking up his job for the week. You'd be a fool to tell your boss that this isn't in your contract.

"Academia is almost completely the opposite of that," Oreskes says. "You build your whole career by being a specialist on a very small piece of territory." One doesn't get ahead in climate research by trying to learn *everything* about global warming. One gets ahead by trying to become the world's expert on *something* about global warming, and there may be only a handful of other people in the world studying the same *something* as you. "More often than not, these people are actually not experts on other areas that to you or me or the public might seem closely related," Oreskes says. "We might expect that scientific experts are able to speak on all aspects of global warming, but the reality is that the person who studies the ice-albedo effect might know relatively little about, say, paleoclimate research."

This stratification is true of any field worth looking into, but it's particularly apparent in areas that are very complex—like the study of the climate—or in fields that are just emerging, such as academic investigation into the accuracy of elections. In political science, the study of whether a given election has yielded the right outcome is a topic that didn't exist ten years ago, and it only barely exists today. If you look into who's publishing and doing actual research on the question, you'll find only a handful of names. There is Michael Herron, of Dartmouth. There's Jasjeet Sekhon, of U.C. Berkeley. There's Jonathan Wand, at Stanford, and MIT's Stephen Ansolabehere. And there's Walter Mebane of the University of Michigan, who has looked more closely at the 2004 race than any of the amateur researchers have—and has found no reason to believe that Kerry actually won it.

Mebane is a stocky black man in his late forties with a round, friendly face and close-cropped hair, and he talks about his research with the plain exuberance of a kid in a playground. It's a field that he's taken to calling "election forensics," although in reality the topic is so new and so small that even the name is not yet fixed.

Broadly, Mebane is looking for mathematical techniques to determine whether a particular election was fair. The work speaks to his long focus on the qualitative, empirical study of U.S. politics—Mebane's interests run toward the geeky, scientific side of political science, with his publications carrying titles like "Coordination among American Voters with Heterogeneous Expectations" and "Poisson-Normal Dynamic Generalized Linear Mixed Models of U.S. House Campaign Contributions."

After the 2000 race, Mebane, along with several colleagues, spent months developing a mathematical model to compare Reform Party candidate Pat Buchanan's vote count in Florida's Palm Beach County with his results in three thousand other U.S. counties. The researchers found that Buchanan's performance in Palm Beach was so anomalous, it could only have been caused by a particular quirk of the election there—the infamous butterfly ballot, which had fooled many Al Gore voters into accidentally punching the hole for Buchanan. In a paper published in a peer-reviewed journal, the *American Political Science Review*, a year after the election, Mebane and his colleagues reported the bottom line: Gore lost at least two thousand votes—and thus the race—as a result of the butterfly ballot.

In his work on elections, Mebane is fastidious, abundantly concerned with data, and excessively cautious about speculation. He works for months or years gathering numbers before issuing his conclusions. There is, of course, nothing special about that process: it's how academics work. Kathy Dopp spotted something odd in Florida and put out her findings the day after the race. Steven Freeman's first paper calling into question the election results went live within a month of the race. Walter Mebane isn't nearly so quick to yield to his initial impressions.

When he does arrive at an answer, Mebane is no shrinking violet. In April 2004, after rigorously studying ballots that had gone uncounted in the 2000 presidential race, Mebane published an academic article with the unwavering title "The Wrong Man Is President! Overvotes in the 2000 Election in Florida." Since then, Mebane has found a number of new statistical techniques to look at elections, and he's been doing so around the world. Mebane was a natural choice to investigate what had really happened in Ohio in 2004. Early in 2005, the Democratic National Committee asked him whether he was interested in doing so. Mebane says he was wary of working with the party. "I was very much afraid of the DNC wanting to do a political report—of them saying, 'We have our conclusions and so go find the evidence for us,'" he says. On the other hand, investigating Ohio was a difficult thing, and the Democrats could provide the enormous resources that such an endeavor would require. Mebane made it clear that he'd do the work only if he could go where the evidence took him.

The study, which he conducted with Dartmouth's Herron, revealed a great many terrible facts about elections in Ohio. Through a statistical analysis of voting results and voting technology they gathered from each precinct in Ohio, they found that elections officials in the state badly misallocated voting machines, leaving tens of thousands of voters to vote at precincts without enough machines. This led to some extremely long voting lines, especially in African American areas—places, that is, that would very likely have chosen Kerry. Mebane's study determined that throughout Ohio, between 2 and 3 percent stayed home in 2004 most likely due to delays caused by voting lines. But crucially, there weren't enough disenfranchised Kerry voters in this lot to have given the senator the election; Mebane used survey data plus a close analysis of voting records to determine that half of the black voters who were turned away by the lines went back to the polls later on in the day—meaning that long lines did not disproportionately affect Kerry's count.

Mebane's most interesting finding concerned whether votes for Kerry and votes for Bush had been systematically switched— one of the amateur election activists' key attacks on the 2004 race. To look into this possibility, Mebane and Herron and their researchers tracked down voting results from each precinct in the state, which proved arduous. "I wanted to look at every scrap of data that I could think of and could get my hands on," Mebane told me. "That sounds easy, but it wasn't. The precinct data that we got from the state turned out to have errors in it." They cleaned up the errors through a detailed comparison with voting results they'd obtained from other sources, which took about a month of work. Because they wanted to see how votes had changed between Ohio's 2002 election and the one in 2004, Mebane and Herron also had to find out which precincts had changed their boundaries since the previous election, a process that took more back-and-forth with elections officials in the state.

Months passed. Data trickled in. They ran hundreds of calculations. And in the summer of 2005, they found an answer. John Kerry didn't win Ohio. In precincts across the state, there were strong similarities between votes for Kerry in 2004 and votes in 2002 for Tim Hagan, the Democratic candidate for governor. Where Hagan's vote had been high in 2002, so had Kerry's in 2002; where Hagan had done poorly, so too had Kerry—a pattern that would not have held had Kerry's and Bush's vote been switched, as a result of rigged machines. Moreover, Kerry's votes in the state were also correlated with votes for Eric Fingerhut, the 2004 Democratic candidate for the U.S. Senate, and were negatively correlated with support in precincts for Issue 1, a state constitutional amendment banning gay marriage. Mebane still has a lot of concerns about the race in Ohio. In June 2005, he became furious that the Justice Department closed its investigation into how voting machines had been dispersed in Franklin County, where Mebane found that—either through malice or incompetence—African American voters had been given far fewer machines than their registration should have dictated. But he's sure that John Kerry didn't win the state. "I'm absolutely certain of it," he told me. Every bit of data he's looked at supports the case. And he noted that others can look at all of his vote-precinct numbers, too—he put up all of his data on the Web, as well as all of the calculations he used to come to his conclusion.

Mebane's study is the most thorough analysis of Ohio's 2004 race that we have, and probably the most thorough that it is possible to perform. Neither Freeman, Dopp, nor any other activist has managed to find any flaws in it. Indeed, they rarely even mention it. While Kennedy was researching his piece for *Rolling*

Stone, a researcher at the magazine interviewed Mebane about his thoughts on the race. Mebane e-mailed the researcher with data showing why Kennedy's assertion that the Kerry and Bush votes were switched didn't hold up. Kennedy ignored Mebane's analysis. Instead, he chose Freeman.

A few weeks after Kennedy's article was published, Bill Clinton gave a talk to the Association of Alternative Newsweeklies' annual conference, in Little Rock, Arkansas. A member of the audience asked Clinton what he'd thought of Kennedy's argument. "I must say, I read Robert Kennedy's article in *Rolling Stone* and I think all of you should if you haven't," Clinton said. "And before I read it, I was convinced that President Bush had won Ohio." Clinton hedged a bit, explaining how he was sure Al Gore really won Florida in 2000 but didn't know what to make of Ohio in 2004. But then Clinton added, referring to Kennedy, "He sure as heck raised a—he made a compelling case. Those numbers that he said, in some of those precincts the probability of the vote total being that much at variance with the exit polls was one in six hundred thousand."

For Clinton, then, just as for Kennedy, and for a great many other Americans who now believe that Bush did not truly win the 2004 presidential race, a sticker-shock number put out by a scholar of business organization just weeks after the election had come to seem a great deal more important than what trained pollsters and political scientists had determined over several months of thorough inquiry. The peripheral route takes over.

5

The Twilight of Objectivity, or What's the Matter with Lou Dobbs?

The CNN anchor Lou Dobbs has a fleshy round face, broad shoulders, a thinning cap of golden hair, and a big, booming voice that's instantly recognizable amid the comfortable background drone of twenty-four-hour news. More than just about anyone else on television, Dobbs, who is six-two and round as a pro wrestler, fits the cartoon image of a fat cat; you can easily picture him lounging in a chaise somewhere on the Mediterranean coast as women in coconut bikini tops fan him lovingly with palm fronds, and bunches of grapes dangle at his lips.

For a long while, too, Dobbs cultivated just such an epicurean image. In the 1980s and 1990s, as the host of *Moneyline*, Dobbs assumed the role of the businessman's best friend. He covered U.S. enterprise in the way that CEOs wanted it, with a heavy focus on the cold rationality of markets. But in recent years

Dobbs has shifted his gaze. He has traded rationality and even objectivity for what he calls news with a point of view. It's a point of view that is supremely suspicious of the very CEOs he once feted. Now, he regularly accuses businesses of "selling out" American workers, and he excoriates politicians who he says have left the nation vulnerable to migrant hordes. Lou Dobbs, suddenly and without apparent explanation, is a man on a mission.

Seven nights a week, Dobbs headlines *Lou Dobbs Tonight*, an hour-long catalogue of the outrages carried out upon Americans, who are, in the Dobbs lexicon, always "hardworking," always honest, and in a continual epic struggle against forces far beyond their control. The passions on cable news run generally hot—it's rare to turn on CNN or Fox without seeing something "breaking"—but Dobbs's show runs hotter than most. Alarm is always in the air.

A typical segment goes like one broadcast in the fall of 2006, in which the anchor warned of a new proposal by "some corporate business leaders and their political allies that could erode the United States' sovereignty." The report concerned a federal plan enacted under the North American Free Trade Agreement, or NAFTA, to allow Mexican truck drivers to carry their freight across the border and into the United States. Lisa Sylvester, one of Dobbs's regular correspondents, told Dobbs that the trucking plan was the first step in a push by corporations to blur the U.S. borders with Canada and Mexico. Proponents of the plan want to create a "NAFTA superhighway that would stretch from Texas all the way to Canada," Sylvester reported. Their ultimate goal, she suggested, was a "North American Union" modeled after the European Union. Her report featured a member of the John Birch Society who warned that "a super-elite are taking control" of U.S. affairs.

And thus the anchor's outrage was stoked:

DOBBS: These three countries, moving ahead . . . without authorization from the American people, without congressional approval. This is as straightforward an attack on national sovereignty as there could be, outside of war.

SYLVESTER: And they are doing this behind closed doors, as you mentioned. Congress has been left out of the loop. People don't even know what they are coming up with. But what's clear at this point is that they are moving ahead with this North American Union and putting these plans in place. Very frightening.

There's another side to the trucking story, one not mentioned on Dobbs's show. The government has outlined rigorous safety guidelines and instituted inspections of all trucks coming into the country; vehicles would be required to be insured by U.S. firms, and their drivers would be tested at the border to make sure they read and write English. This doesn't mean that letting Mexican trucks into the United States is a good idea; the plan, though, is far less alarming than Dobbs lets on.

The "NAFTA superhighway," meanwhile, is a longtime figment of antiglobalist anxiousness, and it's not very real beyond that. Although some businesses have formed lobbying groups aimed at improving transportation lines connecting the United States, Mexico, and Canada, no government agency has proposed building new roads, let alone a "superhighway" spanning the continent. As for the "North American Union," it, too, is inspired more by suspicion than by substance; there are no plans for creating a common currency with our neighbors or for overturning U.S. regulations in favor of North American laws or for merging the nations in any other way. If you watch Dobbs's report, though, such moves hardly seem far-fetched. In Dobbs's TV universe, they're a near certainty.

When Ted Turner founded CNN in 1980, he famously skimped on the salaries he paid to on-air talent. At CNN, he said, the "news is the star." For a time, Turner's phrase became the network's internal motto. But Turner left CNN long ago, and so, too, has the notion that what CNN produces is something so banal as "news."

Now, many of CNN's reports come with what some in the company have called "an edge." Since taking on his populist mantle, Dobbs has become one of the network's highest-rated anchors—his show garners more than eight hundred thousand viewers a night, fewer than those for any prime-time program on the rival Fox News, but phenomenal for CNN. (Larry King's interview program, which draws more than a million people on a typical night, is the only CNN show that does better.)

Anderson Cooper, the salt-and-pepper-haired Adonis of news, is also a big CNN star, thanks to his edge. Cooper made his name during Hurricane Katrina, when, during a live broadcast, he castigated officials for their slow response to the disaster. On Cooper's show the edge isn't ideology but instead Cooper's own personality: empathic, intimate, slyly combative, always in the foreground.

CNN's sister network, Headline News, was once a staid disseminator of no-nonsense bulletins, playing a straightforward stream of the day's big stories. Now it, too, comes with sass. Nancy Grace, a former prosecutor who runs a nightly legal-news show on the network, snarls at every argument made by any defense attorney, whatever the merits of the case at hand. On her show, anyone who's ever charged with a crime is deemed guilty forever, even after the defendant's been acquitted. Headline News also features a right-wing blowhard named Glenn Beck, something of a poor man's Bill O'Reilly. Beck, Cooper, Grace, and Dobbs represent the new CNN, where entertainment and opinion reign, and objectivity has left the building.

Attitude, of course, is not unusual on cable. Up and down the dial, you find people spewing opinions rather than giving you the news, and the granddaddy of this tradition, the Fox News Channel, continues to dominate the ratings. There's little surprise in this trend; indeed, the polarization we see on the news is actually a natural response to information fragmentation. So far in this book I've examined what happens to audiences—that is, we ordinary people—in a world of unprecedented media choice: we begin to select our reality according to our biases, and we interpret evidence (such as photos and videos) and solicit expertise in a way that pleases us. But there's another side to this dynamic: how *news outlets* must change to satisfy audiences in a culture of niches. You can see it play out in what's happening to CNN and, in particular, what's happened to Lou Dobbs.

Whenever we're confronted with ideologues in the media, it's tempting to ask about their motivations. Does Bill O'Reilly really mean the things he says, or is he just doing it because it makes good TV? Can *anyone* sincerely believe, as Anne Coulter says she does, that Joseph McCarthy is an American hero, and that the widows of men who died on September 11, 2001, are basking in their celebrity—or does she say such things only because doing so sells a lot of books? Lou Dobbs studied economics at Harvard; does he *really* put stock in the anti-immigrant, protectionist drivel he glorifies on TV? Or is he, instead, simply venal?

But when you investigate the roots of bias in the media, Lou Dobbs's personal motivations begin to appear less important than the system in which he operates. It's this system—the multichannel, watch-what-you-want-to-believe world—that produces characters like Dobbs, and it's this system that is now naturally working against the sort of "objective" news CNN used to produce. Daniel Henninger, who writes for the CEO-friendly *Wall Street Journal* editorial page, once wondered whether there was something supernatural about Dobbs's transformation from a hard-nosed business journalist to a barker of antiglobalist fervor. "It's as if whatever made Linda Blair's head spin around in *The Exorcist* had invaded the body of Lou Dobbs and left him with the brain of Dennis Kucinich," Henninger wrote.

But Lou Dobbs is not a raving idiot. He just plays one on TV. Given the circumstances, he'd be a fool not to.

Every couple of years, the Pew Research Center for the People and the Press calls up more than a thousand Americans to find out how they get their news and what they think about the people who provide it. This is one of those cultural assessments you dive into expecting the worst: given the state of the world—the data points about your countrymen's ignorance regarding geography and geopolitics, those dispiriting stories about high-schoolers' failures at math, your general certainty that people these days are more apt to be wrong about simple things than at any time in the recent past (in a way, the very premise of this book)—a survey of how (or whether) Americans stay informed seems sure to provoke a strong urge to emigrate.

But Pew's statistics on the broad national appetite for news actually prompt little alarm. In 2006, when the group asked people whether they'd read, watched, or listened to the news in any medium yesterday, more than 80 percent said they had. The number is slightly lower than in some previous surveys—in 1994, it was 90 percent—but the last decade's data shows no discernable trend in the desire to be informed. Americans aren't turning off the news.

What is changing, to no one's surprise, is where people are getting their information. In the early 1990s, the vast majority of Americans said they regularly watched the nightly network news, and more than three-quarters turned on local TV news. When Pew asked people whether they'd recently read a newspaper, more than half said yes. Audiences for all of these things have steadily fallen since. Today, instead, about a third of Americans say that they get their news from cable TV and the Internet. Since the 1990s, people have also grown far more skeptical about what they watch, read, or listen to. The numbers for CNN are illustrative of what's happened throughout the industry. In 1998, 42 percent of the people whom Pew surveyed said that they believed "all or most" of what they watched on the network. In 2006, only 28 percent said the same thing.

The Pew data also supports the notion of partisan news "realities." There are Republican news organizations and Democratic news organizations, and each side feels deep antipathy toward the other side's sources. A third of Republicans regularly watch Fox News, and they believe the network is highly credible. But Fox attracts comparatively few Democrats, most of whom find the network not at all believable. CNN and National Public Radio, by contrast, are popular with the left but are among Republicans' least favorite sources. In 2006, 30 percent of Democrats said that they believed pretty much everything they heard on NPR. Only half as many Republicans said so.

In order to understand the forces pushing apart Red News and Blue News—and, in a larger sense, to understand what's pushing Lou Dobbs off the cliff—it's useful to take an extended detour through the work of Lee Ross and Mark Lepper, two psychologists at Stanford University who have done groundbreaking work on how people understand the sort of purposedly objective information we encounter in the news. In the 1970s,

Ross and Lepper became fascinated by a phenomenon in social psychology called "biased assimilation," which is highly relevant to many of the ideas I've discussed in the book so far. Biased assimilation says that people tend to interpret and understand new information in a way that accords with their own views. Imagine that you are staunchly opposed to capital punishment, and I present you with a stack of empirical studies concerning the death penalty's deterrence effect on murder. Some of the data I give you suggests that capital punishment does reduce crime, while other numbers say that it does not. Taken together, in other words, the studies present an inconclusive case. Which side of the argument would you buy?

By now, you might be able to guess the answer: you'll believe the data that support your view. Working with the psychologist Charles Lord, Ross and Lepper looked into this question in an experiment using undergraduates who were either advocates or opponents of capital punishment. When the students were shown a pair of reports that presented a mixed picture of the death penalty—one study supported the deterrence effect, the other questioned it—people accepted at face value the data that aligned with their position. But they picked apart the data that challenged it. "It seems the researchers studied a carefully selected group of states and that they were careful in interpreting their results," one pro–death penalty student in the experiment said of a pro-deterrence study. But the same person was dubious of a paper suggesting that states with capital punishment actually saw higher rates of homicide: "The research didn't cover a long enough period of time to prove that capital punishment is not a deterrent to murder." People on the anti–death penalty side, meanwhile, responded exactly opposite—they thought the studies showing a deterrence effect were hopelessly compromised, but that the ones on their side seemed to make a lot of good sense.

This led to a funny result. People in the study became polarized. Taken together, the two reports they'd been given suggested that it was hard to know whether or not capital punishment deterred crime; after looking at the research, then, a truly dispassionate person should have moderated her extreme position. But people moved the other way instead. Because they believed they'd found mistakes in the research they disagreed with, and because they accepted the research that conformed to their views, the undergraduates *reinforced* their long-held positions. Those who had always favored the death penalty favored it more passionately after looking at both sides. The people who had opposed it from the start opposed it even more fervently at the end.

As I've stressed often in this book, sometimes getting more information about a controversy doesn't produce a better foothold on the facts—sometimes, strangely, more information actually pushes us deeper into the cocoon of our long-held views. The death penalty study underlines this thesis perhaps more elegantly than any other experiment in psychology.

Lee Ross is a tall, aging man with white hair and piercing pale blue eyes.* He speaks with a slight, pleasing Canadian accent, and he is animated when he discusses his long-ago work on biased assimilation because the idea forms the basis of his more far-ranging inquiry into a theory called "naive realism." The label refers to the way Ross believes that we understand the world,

---

* Aside from his work on bias, Lee Ross is famous in psychology for having coined the term "fundamental attribution error." This describes the common human tendency to explain people's behaviors as being a consequence of their essential disposition, rather than as something arising out of the specific situation they're in. If a sports car screams past you on the highway at a sinful speed, your first thought might be to curse the driver for being a dangerous delinquent. You're far less likely to consider, instead, the reason the fellow might be speeding. Maybe he's taking his pregnant wife to the hospital? That's the fundamental attribution error: we assume that people do what they do because that's how they *are*.

and it suggests an intriguing idea about why we see "bias" in ostensibly objective news reports.

It's important to remember that the death penalty advocates and opponents in Ross and Lepper's study didn't know that they were interpreting information in a skewed way. Indeed, Ross says, each of us thinks that on any given subject our views are essentially objective, the product of a dispassionate, *realistic* accounting of the world. This is *naive* realism, though, because we are incapable of recognizing the biases that operate upon us. Think of the Dartmouth and Princeton football fans I told you about earlier. When they looked at identical film clips of a game, each side "saw" a different reality. They did not know—and really, could not know—that their perception of the event didn't match the reality of it because, for them, the perception was indistinguishable from its reality. How they "saw" the game was how it really was.

What's dangerous about this naiveté is that it spins out into our appraisals of other people. We're jarred and offended when other people don't agree with what, to us, is so brilliantly clear. "If we think we see the world the way it is," Ross explains, "then we think that reasonable people ought to agree with us. And to the extent that people *disagree* with us, we conclude that they are not reasonable—they're biased." Ross and his colleagues have tracked people's tendency to assume bias in others in several experiments. "You can do a simple study and ask people something specific like, 'What should the United States' response be in Iran?'" he says. "If we let you look at other people's responses, we find that exactly to the extent that the other person disagrees with you, you think they're biased. You think their opinion reflects biases rather than rational consideration." Nowhere was this more evident than in a famous experiment that Ross and Lepper conducted early in the 1980s. It's a study that returns us to the topic at hand: how and why we perceive bias in the news.

On the evening of September 16, 1982, a militia associated with the Lebanese Maronite Christian political party the Phalangists entered the sprawling Palestinian refugee camps of Sabra and Shatila, in West Beirut, and set about killing hundreds of civilians. The massacre unfolded over four days and is remembered as one of the most brutal events of the Byzantine fifteen-year Lebanese civil war. It set off a round of international recriminations. Israel had invaded Lebanon that summer, and Israeli forces had been surrounding the camps while the militias carried out their attacks.

In the immediate aftermath of the massacre, details of what had taken place were murky. In fact, they remain murky. The exact number of people killed and the roles that various parties played in the massacre will likely never be known. But in wartime—especially in the bruising wars of the Middle East, where enmity stretches back to the biblical age—a lack of details rarely precludes people from taking a stand. Proponents of the Palestinian cause quickly blamed Israel for what had happened; Israeli forces should have stopped the killings, they argued. Staunch supporters of Israel, meanwhile, absolved the country of any responsibility for what a third party—the Phalangists—had done.*

---

* There were many in Israel, however, who blamed the government. A couple of weeks after the attack, hundreds of thousands of Israelis rallied in Tel Aviv to demand an independent probe into the country's role in the massacre. They also called on Menachem Begin, the prime minister, and Ariel Sharon, then the defense minister, to resign. The government ultimately launched an inquiry; the report, published the following year, found that Israeli forces and senior officials were "indirectly" responsible for what had happened, and that Sharon bore "personal responsibility." Sharon was forced to step down as defense minister.

For Lee Ross and Mark Lepper, the controversy over who deserved blame for Sabra and Shatila presented an ideal vehicle
to examine something they'd long been interested in—people's
tendency to see bias in news reports of deeply felt issues. A few
weeks after the massacre, Ross and Lepper, along with their
colleague Robert Vallone, recruited 144 Stanford students from
three different places on campus—from the pro-Arab and pro-
Israeli student associations, as well as people from introductory
psychology courses, who were presumably neutral on the issue.
The researchers showed the students six news segments covering the massacre; the news, which came from all three TV
networks, was intended, in the way that network news is, to be
a broad, mainstream, nonpartisan recounting of the events in
question. Then the participants were asked to rate the programs
in several ways, all covering the same basic point: how fairly had
the networks presented the case of Sabra and Shatila?

People who were neutral on the issue of the Israeli-
Palestinian crisis came down somewhere in the middle. They
didn't think the media were particularly skewed toward either
side's point of view. But partisans in each camp thought the news
was biased. Supporters of Israel said that the news set a double standard against Israel—the programs were "blaming Israel
when they would have excused some other country," people
said. The news accounts focused "too much" on Israel's role in
the massacre, instead of looking at how other parties had acted.
Pro-Israel students suspected that the segments would likely
push neutral viewers to turn against Israel. Supporters of Israel
also thought that they could divine the basis for the bias they
saw: the reporters and the editors who'd produced the news,
they said, were probably very pro-Arab.

Students on the other side of the debate saw the opposite bias.
They thought that the networks were "excusing Israel when they

would have blamed some other country"; that the news accounts didn't focus enough on Israel's role in the massacre; that the segments would prompt neutral observers to take Israel's side; and that the journalists who'd put together the stories were probably advocates of Israel. To people in both camps, the segments were thoroughly unfair.

You might notice an apparent contradiction between these results and those of Ross and Lepper's death penalty study. In that experiment, people who looked at both sides of the issue dismissed the other side; it was too weak to merit consideration. Here, after watching news segments presenting both sides, people said that the other side—the camp they opposed—was being presented as the stronger position. The difference has to do with the third party now on the scene. In the death penalty study, people were evaluating the research for themselves. But in the experiment involving news segments on Sabra and Shatila, a reporter had already evaluated the evidence and was now sitting in judgment of it. "If I see the world as all black and you see the world as all white, and some person comes along and says it's partially black and partially white, we both are going to be unhappy," Ross says.

Remember naive realism. We all think our views are essentially objective, and when people disagree with us, we're apt to decide that they're not being reasonable. They're being unfair. So if you feel strongly about an issue, you're bound to think that the reporter, the editor, the news network, or the pundit "has given inappropriate weight to facts favoring the other side," Ross says. "You think there are more facts and better facts on your side than on the other side. The very act of giving them equal weight seems like bias. Like inappropriate evenhandedness."

A war of attrition has long been waged in the United States— and probably in every civilized society ever to live under the cloud of a mass media—concerning news bias. Whatever the issue, everyone claims that the media are stacked against them. For decades, conservatives have complained about a liberal bent to mainstream news; that the press leans left is an ancient Republican rallying cry, as cherished as the call for smaller government and old-fashioned family values.

In a recent book on the subject, the journalist Eric Alterman chronicles a long train of right-wing attacks on the media, beginning with Dwight Eisenhower and continuing all the way to George W. Bush. In 1969, Spiro Agnew, Richard Nixon's vice president, delivered the definitive attack. In a speech called "On the National Media," he took issue with "commentators and producers" who "live and work in the geographical and intellectual confines of Washington, D.C., or New York City" and who "wield a free hand in selecting, presenting, and interpreting the great issues of our nation." The vice president added this endlessly quotable quip about the press: "In the United States today, we have more than our share of nattering nabobs of negativism. They have formed their own 4-H club—the hopeless, hysterical hypochondriacs of history."*

When Eric Alterman, who leans to the left, looks at the news, he finds little evidence of the anticonservative slant that made Agnew anxious. Alterman called his book *What Liberal Media? The Truth about Bias and the News*, and its main purpose is to document what he says is much clearer proof pointing the other way—that the news is actually biased *against* liberals. "Conservatives are extremely well represented in every facet of the media," Alterman wrote. There's Fox News, there's right-wing talk radio, and there are all those righty pundits—Robert Novak,

---

* The alliterative assessment was authored for Agnew by aide William Safire, who would advance, assiduously, to the Op-Ed page of the *New York Times*.

William Bennett, Kate O'Beirne, Jonah Goldberg, David Brooks, Tucker Carlson. Together, these constitute a "massive conservative media structure that, more than ever, determines the shape and scope of our political agenda."

Alterman is not alone in this view. In recent years liberals have taken up arms against the media no less pugnaciously than have conservatives, forming battalions of attack-dog outfits to document pro-conservative bias in the news. On the left now, just as on the right, people believe that the press is out to get them.

The Pew Research Center's surveys of Americans' attitudes toward the news bear this out. Republicans and Democrats each claim to see some media sources as routinely favoring the other side. Claims of media bias, though, are like allegations of unfair umpiring. You support them only when they're on your side. When the other guy suggests a systematic bias in the news, the argument inevitably seems disingenuous. "Both sides think the other side is just being strategic," Lee Ross says. "It's as if the other side *knows* that they control the media, but they're engaging in special pleading." That's just what Alterman, for instance, argues. "Smart" conservatives understand that the press isn't really against them, he writes; their protestations otherwise are merely a tactic, an effort to force better coverage of their issues. "The right is working the refs," Alterman writes. "Much of the public believes a useful, but unsupportable, myth about the SCLM"—the "so-called liberal media"—"and the media [themselves] have been cowed by conservatives into repeating their nonsensical nostrums virtually nonstop.*"

What's beautiful about the study on Sabra and Shatila is how completely it undercuts this argument. Ross and Lepper called their finding the "hostile media phenomenon," and it tells us

---

* Apparently a little alliteration always assists allegations of media bias.

something just as important—and just as bizarre—about human perception as does the experiment on football fans in the Ivy League. The people in the experiment weren't lying. They weren't being strategic. There was something deeper going on. "When we asked about what they'd seen on the news, they actually remembered more arguments and facts favoring the other side than their own side," Ross says. Just as the Dartmouth and Princeton fans had "seen" different games, each side of a punishing war had observed something hostile to their side in the news. The bias we see in the news isn't strategic. It's real. It's real to us, at least, and that's as real as it gets.

During several elections in the late 1970s and 1980s, Ross and Lepper examined how the hostile media phenomenon affects the way people watch televised presidential debates. Ever since the first TV debate—Nixon versus Kennedy in 1960—surveys have shown that partisans who've just watched a match-up often think that their own side prevailed. This is biased assimilation: when given new evidence—your candidate's performance in the debate as compared to the other guy's performance—you're likely to interpret it in a way that strengthens your position.

Ross and Lepper asked people another question—not who they believed had won the debate, but who they thought had won the *media coverage* of the debate. "And what we demonstrated," Lepper says, is that people "would routinely believe that the coverage had been prejudiced in favor of the other candidate. They believed neutral viewers who had seen only *the debate* would agree with them that their candidate won. But neutral viewers who had seen only the *news coverage* of the debate would be persuaded—persuaded unjustly, from their point of view—that the other candidate had done better."

Over the years, many other experiments—a few more on how people watch news about the Middle East and others involving abortion, genetically modified food, and the wisdom of medical research on animals—have confirmed Ross and Lepper's findings. Two people on opposite sides of a controversy can watch the same news story, and both will come away feeling honestly, genuinely misrepresented by it.

Journalists know this well; audiences complain bitterly about bias in stories while seeming to miss facts that are sympathetic to their side. There is one news subject where this pops up regularly enough that it merits chronicling. It concerns a war that readers will be surprised to learn still sees much hot fire, but one in which, it turns out, combatants are surprisingly quick to mobilize against any perceived media slight. It is the war over, of all things, computer operating systems.

Not long ago, David Pogue, who reviews technology for the *New York Times*, wrote about Windows Vista, the latest version of the ubiquitous operating system made by Microsoft. Pogue has a light prose style, and his assessment of Vista was typically good-humored. He admired the program's aesthetics, and he was thankful that, compared to previous versions of Windows, it was fortified against viruses. But Pogue also noted several times that Microsoft seemed to have borrowed much of its innovation from Apple, whose Macintosh operating system long ago sported many of Vista's purportedly new features. "You get the feeling that Microsoft's managers put Mac OS X on an easel and told the programmers, 'Copy that,'" he wrote.

Pogue characterizes his piece as a "balanced review." He had offered a lukewarm endorsement of Vista but pointed out that in the end it didn't matter what he thought because Windows' place in the computing ecosystems was secure. "Windows isn't going anywhere, the landscape won't be changing anytime soon, and the corporate world will still buy it 500 copies at a time," he wrote. Sooner or later, he added, Windows Vista is "what most people will have on their PCs."

There are many tribes in the tech world, agglomerations of like-minded folks who, for some reason or another, develop nearly cultish devotion to certain companies and their products. There's a tribe of TiVo lovers. There's a Blackberry cult and an oppositional one devoted to the Palm Treo. There are people who can't get enough of the Roomba, a robotic vacuum cleaner so given to anthropomorphization that owners often name them. But there is no bigger tribe, and none more zealous, than fans of Apple; ask any tech journalist about these people and you'll get an earful, and probably the word *rabid* will come up more than once. Windows, by contrast, attracts few devoted followers—instead what you have are those people who simply hate the preening superiority of the Apple fanatics. Pogue's review of Vista attracted the worst of both camps. The response was straight out of the literature on the hostile media phenomenon. The readers, that is to say, went nuts.

"The Mac people saw it as a rave review for Windows Vista," Pogues says, "and the Windows people saw it as a vicious slam on Windows." People on the Windows side apparently missed Pogue's complimentary language—his praise for the software's looks, his certainty that Vista would continue Microsoft's dominance. This didn't surprise Pogue, because he's got a reputation among some tech obsessives of being friendly to Apple products. (People call him an "Apple fanboy," which he can't stand.)

Pogue's rep, though, was no help in placating Mac fans, many of whom heroically misread his review as some kind of endorsement of Windows over the Mac. If you're agnostic on the question of computing platforms, it'd be difficult to find in Pogue's column anything approaching such a recommendation—but this is how it goes with fans of Apple products, who are infamous for their sensitivity to slams, real or imagined, against their beloved company. "It's funny—even if I write a generally positive piece about Apple, I still get more complaints from Apple partisans," says Walt Mossberg, the *Wall Street Journal*'s influential technology reviewer. Mossberg has even coined a term for the effect. "I call it the Doctrine of Insufficient Adulation."

As an example, Mossberg cites an article he wrote in the fall of 2004 about Apple's iMac desktop computer. He absolutely loved the thing; you can tell from his first paragraph, which would not have been out of place at a beatification: "I am writing these words on the most elegant desktop computer I've ever used, a computer that is not only uncommonly beautiful but fast and powerful, virus-free and surprisingly affordable."

He went on to note that the system "performed flawlessly and speedily," "was nearly silent," and that it "actually costs less than comparable Windows machines." He had only two tiny complaints. The iMac lacked a built-in card reader to access pictures stored in digital cameras, and "Apple scrimped on memory," adding far fewer megabytes of the stuff than was common on Windows computers. Mossberg's column ran for about 900 words; just 70 of them, or 8 percent, by my count, suggested anything even approaching negative criticism. Apple loved the review so much that it excerpted it in advertisements. Steve Jobs, the company's CEO, quoted it in speeches. But Mossberg's mailbox told a different story. *What did he have against Apple?* people wanted to know.

Except they said it in slightly different language. The anonymity afforded by the Internet liberates people from strict social norms, and Pogue's and Mossberg's correspondents are inevitably nasty. They lob accusations of corruption, laziness, cognitive handicaps, and unusual sexual proclivities. A few years ago, in a quite positive review of Apple's iPod Nano, Pogue mentioned that per gigabyte of music-storage space, the new product was more expensive than the iPod Mini it replaced, and that it wasn't (at the time) available in multiple colors. These small slights prompted several of Pogue's readers to wish him continued happiness in "licking Bill Gates's balls."*

Neither Mossberg nor Pogue claims to be objective. They're critics, and they trade in that slipperiest, gooiest of all media productions: personal opinion. At the same time, each is unfailingly ethical and intellectually honest. Their articles brim with justification. Neither will tell you that he simply hates the newest Sony digital camera—he'll tell you that its battery drains faster than Niagara Falls or that its manual reads like a translation from Japanese to French to English or that every picture comes out sepia. If you're nonpartisan, this is all you could want from a tech reviewer. The style likely accounts for Mossberg's and Pogue's enormous popularity. But fans of Apple often want more. They care little for honest opinion. They want to pick up the paper and see in it a reflection of their own nearly religious zeal for the thing they love. They don't want a review. They want a hagiography.

Americans as a whole aren't really very different. Many say they care about objectivity in the news. In Pews polls, an overwhelming number of respondents routinely claim not to be interested in getting "news from sources that share your point of view" and prefer instead "sources that don't have a particular point of view." In the business of reporting, too, "objectivity" is a value held in high regard. It's in the theology of journalism to provide a view of a subject that closely matches what's referred

---

* Pogue ignores the least substantive letters, but he says that he frequently corrects people who appear to have simply misperceived what he wrote. "They'll say, 'You couldn't find one damn nice thing to say about Microsoft's five years of effort?' And so I'll paste in three paragraphs from the review and say, 'Well, I consider these nice.'" Both Pogue and Mossberg say that when they respond to the e-mailers this way, people usually moderate their attitudes, apologizing for their previous boorish behavior.

to as the "reality" of it. The problem, as we've seen in so many studies, is that "reality" rarely goes without its quotes.

For people who feel strongly about an issue—for Apple fanatics, for abortion partisans, for folks who think they know the truth about global warming or what's going on in the Middle East—reality feels distinct and luminous, and journalistic "objectivity" inevitably produces a muddier picture. People say they want objectivity, but they don't mean it the same way reporters do; as naive realism suggests, they believe that their own point of view *is* objective, and thus any journalistically "objective" look should resemble the reality in their heads. When it does not—as it cannot—the audience assumes the worst. The reporter must be licking someone's balls.

This is the first part in the story of what makes a man like Lou Dobbs possible—and not only Dobbs, but the entire partisan media infrastructure we've seen rise up in the last decade. And not only possible but inevitable. For news organizations, there is a clear directive in how Americans respond to the news: if people are never going to be happy with "objectivity," why not provide something more suited to the palate? Why not create news that conforms to the partisan views? "There is a population who will see biased broadcasting as appropriate," Lee Ross says. "They see the world a particular way. And they're very grateful to have someone who finally tells it like it is."

Toward the end of World War II, Henry Morgenthau, Franklin Roosevelt's treasury secretary, outlined a plan for severely limiting Germany's capacity to ever again attack its neighbors. The proposal called for partitioning the nation, dismantling its military and heavy industries, and returning the population to an agrarian livelihood. The Morgenthau Plan alarmed many in the Roosevelt administration; Cordell Hull, the secretary of state, estimated that if it were implemented, 40 percent of Germans would die. Among the most inflammatory critics was a Stanford economist named Karl Brandt. Brandt traveled around the United States giving long, ranting speeches against the Morgenthau Plan. He was not a man to step lightly around a subject; Brandt's main rhetorical trick was to equate Morgenthau with the Nazis. Each of them, he said, shared the ultimate goal of starving all of Europe.

Brandt was eager to put out a book to this effect. Big New York publishing houses, though, would have nothing to do with him. But late in 1945, a wealthy young man in Chicago heard about Brandt's thesis. The young man was bright, ambitious, and full of ideas that were verboten in the popular press—including sympathy toward the defeated German people. He had long been thinking about getting into the publishing business, and he saw Karl Brandt as his chance. So the young man arranged to put out a speech by Brandt in pamphlet form. The pamphlet, called "Germany Is Our Problem," did well, filtering out to a wide audience through mail subscriptions and on some newsstands. Thus was born one of the leading right-wing media publishing outfits of our time.

The fledgling publisher was Henry Regnery, a small, intense man with a wide, keen smile. Regnery had studied math at MIT, but his passions ran toward politics and philosophy. He was squarely opposed to communism, he was suspicious of Roosevelt and the New Deal, and he had doubts about America's goals in the war.*

---

* Regnery's father, a textile magnate, was a founding member of the America First Committee, which led the call, in 1940 and 1941, for U.S. neutrality in the war. America First's chief spokesman was the aviator Charles Lindbergh, who identified the British, Roosevelt, and the Jews as the primary agitators for war.

Indeed, suspicion and doubt constituted Regnery's prevailing ethos. In his 1985 autobiography, *Memoirs of a Dissident Publisher*, Regnery described how, at the climax of the war, U.S. newspapers were filled with accounts of Allied bombing raids over "Berlin, Tokyo, Hamburg, or some other unfortunate city." Regnery wished that he could share the papers' enthusiasm. "It occurred to me that it must be easier for those who could accept all this at face value," he wrote. But he could not. What the papers were saying about the war, about the president, about politics—all of it struck Regnery as off. Roosevelt, Regnery felt, was acting "on the same level of irresponsibility" as Hitler, but nobody in the news dared to say it. What the country needed—and what Regnery would set out to create—was an opposition media, an ardent, vital, thriving press to challenge the "governmental and intellectual establishment" of the day.

Today Regnery Publishing, the company that Henry Regnery founded out of his dissatisfaction with World War II, is a major force in conservative circles. In 2004, it published *Unfit for Command*, the Swift Boat Vet John O'Neill's best-selling anti–John Kerry polemic, which helped to upturn a presidential election. Regnery has also published books by such conservative luminaries as Ann Coulter, Hugh Hewitt, David Horowitz, Michelle Malkin, Laura Ingraham, Barbara Olson, Oliver North, and Newt Gingrich. In 1996, Regnery put out "Inventing the AIDS Virus," an HIV-denial manifesto by Peter Duesberg, a molecular biologist who questions the link between HIV and AIDS.

But Regnery's current fortunes belie a more muted history, one of long stretches of little popular success. The hostile media phenomenon tells us *why* there's an appetite for slanted news in America. But Regnery's up-and-down history suggests a difficulty in feeding that appetite. It shows that slanted reporting works only in certain conditions. Today, the conditions are ripe, but for a long while, for Regnery, the partisan media game just didn't work.

Henry Regnery did not get into publishing for the money, and his early books prove the point. Many were devoted to criticizing U.S. policies in postwar Germany, a position that never gained mass appeal. A typical title was *The High Cost of Vengeance*, by the English author Freda Utley, who, like Karl Brandt, claimed that what the Allies were doing to Germany was far worse than what the Nazis had done to anyone*—a position that stands in stark relief against the flag-waving patriotism of Regnery's current slate of authors.

It was William F. Buckley who put Regnery on the map. In 1951, Buckley, who would go on to become one of the conservative movement's leading minds, had just come through Yale, where he felt he'd been pickled in liberal ideology. Buckley's *God and Man at Yale*, which Regnery jumped at the chance to publish, argued that the purpose of higher education in the United States was to instill in students a respect for God and individual rights, and that places like Yale were instead teaching godlessness and "collectivism." The book caused a stir and,

---

* Utley was particularly incensed by what she called the "brutal" postwar expulsion of German citizens from Poland and Czechoslovakia. Nazi crimes, she said, paled in comparison to what Germans had to endure on their long march back home. "Hitler's barbaric liquidation of the Jews has been outmatched by the liquidation of Germans by the 'democratic, peace-loving' powers of the United Nations," she wrote. Indeed, Utley added, the Jews killed by Hitler probably met a more peaceful end than these Germans, who "may have thought that a quick death in a gas chamber would have been comparatively merciful." Utley was not a Holocaust denier, but rather what the historian Deborah Lipstadt, in *Denying the Holocaust: The Growing Assault on Truth and Memory*, calls a "relativizer." Utley believed, as she wrote, that "it was high time we stopped talking about German guilt, since there was no crime the Nazis had committed which we or our allies had not also committed." Relativizers like Utley, Lipstadt argues, provided the early intellectual underpinnings for the more strident Holocaust denial movement that would follow.

along with Russell Kirk's *The Conservative Mind*, establis.....
Regnery as the foremost outlet for conservative intellectuals.
Perhaps the greatest sign of Regnery's importance to right-wing
thought came in 1985, when Ronald Reagan sent the publisher a
note from the White House thanking him for all the books he'd
put out and for the "heroic part" he played in the "climactic
struggle for the human spirit."

But Regnery's bank balance told a different story. For more
than thirty years, he scarcely made a dime on conservative
books. Despite his high standing with people like Reagan, Regnery's titles were serious and unflinchingly oppositional, designed to appeal only to a small fringe—and the fringe simply
couldn't keep a publishing house in the black. In the 1970s,
Regnery lost control of the firm to more commercially minded
insiders. It was rechristened Contemporary Books and focused
on subjects like auto repair and sports, rather than on right-wing
agitation. Regnery's house went through several other transfor-
mations in the 1980s and the 1990s; eventually, it was bought
out by Eagle Publishing, a conservative media conglomerate,
and Regnery's son Alfred took over daily control.

Henry Regnery died in 1996, at the age of eighty-four. The
same year, his publishing house saw its first mega-bestseller.
The book was *Unlimited Access*, by Gary Aldrich, an FBI agent
who'd worked security in the Clinton White House and had
come away with a terrible impression of the president, the first
lady, and their aides. Aldrich's book was a departure from previous Regnery publications, which had rarely covered political
scandals.

Aldrich's entire thesis was scandal: through many second-,
third-, or more-handed sources, he reported that compared to
the staff of George H. W. Bush, the Clinton people were slobs
("They throw garbage on the floor, or they throw cups of

coffee and miss the waste can and it splashes all over the wall," a cleaning lady told him), and they'd turned the White House into something like a porn pleasure palace (staffers were given to liaisons—homosexual, naturally—in offices and locker rooms, and they hung sex toys on the Christmas tree). Aldrich also reported that Hillary Clinton had had an affair with Vincent Foster, the former White House deputy counsel, whose 1993 suicide has long stirred extremist suspicion. And Bill Clinton, according to Aldrich, often secretly slipped out of the White House to meet a woman—unidentified, possibly a celebrity— at a nearby Marriot.*

Unlimited Access rocketed to the best-seller list, and it lingered there for a remarkable nineteen weeks, selling, according to some figures, half a million copies. Its success is understandable; 1996 was an election year, and the Clintons were terribly unloved by the right. But there was something else in the air, too, a new force that had just begun to sweep through the culture and that would permanently alter the character and the fortunes of ideological outlets like Regnery. It was the year of the great media crack-up. The news was just beginning to splinter.

"Fox News started in 1996," Marji Ross, Regnery's current president and publisher, points out. So, too, did MSNBC. Talk radio was a hot ticket, and on the Web, which was doubling in size every six months, political magazines like *Slate* and *Salon* were getting off the ground, and the biggest must-read for

---

* In 1997, Aldrich seemed to recant the story in an interview with *New Yorker* magazine's Jane Mayer. "The Marriot thing was not quite solid," he said. "It was hypothetical." The tale was tracked down to David Brock, the one-time right-wing attack-dog journalist who later disavowed his ways in *Blinded by the Right: The Conscience of an Ex-Conservative*, a searing confessional. Brock said that he once asked Aldrich about a rumor of Clinton's hotel-room dalliances—Aldrich apparently took Brock's question as a sign that the rumor was the truth, and he published it.

journalists was a tabloid scandal sheet called the Drudge Report. In a foreshadowing of the Swift Boat story, Aldrich's *Unlimited Access* would make the rounds in all these media. The White House tried to strike it down, beseeching TV networks not to cover it. In the past, the plea may have worked—networks and the big newspapers would have been reluctant to tout as unhinged an account as Aldrich's. But by 1996 they had little choice; if it was on Drudge, if it was on cable, if it was on the radio, the rest of the media couldn't keep *Unlimited Access* a secret.

The Aldrich book would become the first in an amazing series of Regnery best-sellers. In 1997, the firm published *Murder in Brentwood* by Mark Fuhrman, the Los Angeles detective who gained notoriety in the O. J. Simpson murder trial when audiotapes of his racist banter were discovered by the defense team. Fuhrman had been turned down by more than a dozen publishers, but Regnery made a killing on the book.

The late 1990s saw several anti-Clinton Regnery tracts hit big; Marji Ross says that some people in the publishing world thought the run would not last. "They'd say, 'Gosh, what are you going to do when you don't have Bill Clinton to kick around anymore?'" But Regnery's fortunes only ballooned in the new millennium's era of Republican dominance. In 2002, it published *Bias: A CBS Insider Exposes How the Media Distort the News*, by the former network reporter Bernard Goldberg. *Bias* fed into the very fears of a liberal press slant that had pushed Henry Regnery into the book business. It transformed such anxieties into publishing gold. Ross says that about a third of the titles Regnery now puts out become best-sellers, an astonishing statistic in the publishing world.

What fuels these hits is instructive. It's a marketing strategy built upon a sliced-up media world. "I don't really believe in mass media," Ross told me. "I think the more 'mass' an outlet is, the less engaged their audience is." Ross said that if she faced a choice of putting one of her authors on NBC's *Today* show—which attracts about six million viewers every weekday morning—or on the Fox News weeknight program *Hannity & Colmes*, which gets fewer than two million people, she'd choose *Hannity*. The Fox News audience, while smaller, would be far more engaged with what a Regnery author had to say. "We have also found that talk radio is a terrific vehicle for promoting our books," she said.

But there's one media source that Ross considers more powerful than all the rest: the Drudge Report. "Everyone looks to Drudge to see what news is breaking, and if you can get your news on Drudge, then you've captured the attention of a lot of people in the media." All of Regnery's biggest books—including John O'Neill's—have broken first on Drudge.

Henry Regnery once dreamed of using the printing press to forge a culture that reflected his conservative views. But during his lifetime, the plan didn't take. He managed to build a publishing house of tremendous influence among the elite. Some of his readers even went on to run the country. Yet his books hardly sold, and their ideas rarely filtered beyond the fringe. In a time of three networks and a few big newspapers, Regnery's views were stuck. Look at what happened in 1949, when he published Freda Utley's pro-German polemic. The *New York Times* dismissed it, in a review, as "such a compilation of half-truths, rumors, and demonstrable untruths that it is difficult to make an appraisal of Miss Utley's thesis." And that was that. The book, like many of Regnery's authors' ideas, died on the vine.

Fragmentation has changed the story. You can think of it as the second cause of—the other key ingredient in—the news media's drive away from objectivity. When the news began to split up and audiences gained control over where to get their information, competition became a factor. The new news outlets needed to offer products that would catch the eye. They needed to differentiate themselves. And it was only then that Regnery took off. For Fox News, for the Drudge Report, and for others on the right, Regnery's books became a deliciously valuable source. Regnery promised actual reporting (of a sort) that perfectly fit a right-wing perspective. It was news with a point of view. In the Regnery universe, the Clintons were sex fiends, John Kerry was a dishonorable liar, and CBS was out to liberalize your children. They were partisan, sensationalistic, and thinly sourced—not very different, really, from Freda Utley's assertions that the Allies were no better than the Nazis. But Utley didn't have the fragmented media at her back. Sensationalism and partisanship simply sell better today.*

On the northeast coast of North Carolina, on the wide banks of the Perquimans River, there is a quaint, picturesque little town called Hertford. This is historic country, one of the earliest settlements in the nation, a place of paddleboats, fishing, hunting—the signal symbols of Americana. Towns like Hertford are the stuff of Lou Dobbs's mythology; populated with few high-skilled workers and dependent on manufacturing companies for their economic livelihood, they're being inundated in the roiling sea of what Dobbs calls unfair global competition.

---

* There is a coda to this story. Seeing Regnery's success with right-wing books, in the last few years several mainstream publishers—the ones that people at Regnery call the liberal New York publishers—have opened their own conservative divisions. It used to be that Regnery would print the authors who'd been rejected by everybody else. Now Regnery's writers have become a hot commodity in the marketplace. Ann Coulter, one of the right's leading provocateurs, published her first book with Regnery. It was a best-seller. Then Crown Forum, Random House's right-wing imprint, snapped her up. Partisanship is now a hot commodity.

In the early 1990s, the Apricot Textile Company, one of Hertford's biggest businesses, employed hundreds of workers. Apricot made shirts, it made flags, and it made townspeople happy. Then came the North American Free Trade Agreement, which quickened the pace of imports coming in from Mexico and Canada. Dobbs, in his book *War on the Middle Class: How the Government, Big Business, and Special Interest Groups Are Waging War on the American Dream and How to Fight Back*, he writes that within thirty days of NAFTA's passage, Apricot's fortunes plummeted. Its revenue fell from a million dollars a month to less than a million a year.

Apricot was owned by a man named Carl Terranova, and over the next decade he would look for all kinds of new ways to keep his business alive. He tried making football jerseys. He tried making chefs' uniforms. But even such specialty products failed against foreign competition, Dobbs says. Eventually, Terranova, who suffered two heart attacks during the ordeal, was forced to close Apricot down.

The story of Apricot Textile, which Dobbs's correspondent Lisa Sylvester investigated during a special State-of-the-Union broadcast of *Lou Dobbs Tonight* in 2006, presents a difficulty for anyone wishing to accuse Dobbs of slanting the news. The difficulty is that the tale is true; indeed, Sylvester's report brims with supportive facts. In 1993, there were about 265,000 textile jobs in North Carolina, Sylvester noted, and the state has lost 65 percent of these since NAFTA was passed. This is accurate. So, too, is the fact that Apricot's closure will leave its employees in unhappy conditions—"people who are in their forties and fifties, and cutting and sewing is all they know," as Sylvester observed.

Bobby Darden, a local official in Hertford, told Sylvester, "In North Carolina the last ten-plus years, there's been a big decline in the number of manufacturing jobs, a lot of plant closings, and that's really hurt a lot of the county economies, especially rural county economies." This doesn't sound like the unglued opinion of a partisan—it's a level-headed summary of economic distress, and if you study North Carolina's economy over the last ten years, you'll find reams of data supporting it.

This is the funny thing about Lou Dobbs: his show is not *complete* fiction. Dobbs omits facts, he exaggerates (as in the story of the "NAFTA Superhighway"), he sees tenuous connections and conspiracies where cooler minds see nothing much, and he offers analysis that, to his many critics, appears unmolested by a single synapse of rational thought. At the same time, he frequently offers stories like that on Apricot Textile, stories that fit the template of actual news. They're full of honest information that CNN has obviously spent money and time digging up. Five correspondents work on such reports for Dobbs's show. They travel around the country to interview "victims" of free trade, they follow people who are trying to protect America's "broken borders," they shower viewers with stats on how globalization has ruined this or that economic sector, they seek out and chronicle every outrage of corporate greed. But in some respects their work is a puzzle; why do they go to all that trouble to track down the truth?

Here's what I'm getting at. It's been my goal in this chapter to convince you that Lou Dobbs has abandoned objectivity because he (and his bosses) have been pushed by two complementary forces that are altering the business of news: one, perceptual effects such as the hostile media phenomenon mean that audiences rarely consider news about controversial topics to be truly "objective"—they inevitably see such stories as being slanted *away* from their own views; and two, fragmentation in the media has allowed these aggrieved viewers to seek out news that is more to their liking and has consequently made a fortune for organizations (such as Regnery) that purposefully slant news *toward* certain partisan groups.

Dobbs either noticed or stumbled upon the fact that there was a large class of people with nativist, isolationist, protectionist, or anti-immigration notions, people who felt they weren't being served by traditional media. He decided to cater to them. Dobbs became a panderer. But there's a problem with this theory, and it has to do with the reporting you see on Dobbs's show: If I'm right—if Lou Dobbs has transformed himself into a populist just because objectivity doesn't pay as well as taking a strong, mad-as-hell stance—why is he bothering with facts at all? If Dobbs's viewers *care only about his pandering*, why doesn't the anchor just make things up or pander to an even greater degree than he does?

Matthew Gentzkow, a young economist at the University of Chicago Graduate School of Business who is an astute analyst of the media business, finds this puzzle intriguing. Gentzkow points out that most major news organizations devote substantial resources to reporting. Gathering news is an inherently expensive endeavor, and on some stories, such as the war in Iraq, its costs, in money as well as lives, can be astronomical. Yet outfits across the (perceived) ideological spectrum, from Fox News to CNN to NPR, bear these costs. Why? If Fox News were interested only in echoing its viewers' predetermined ideas, why would it spend any money maintaining a bureau in Iraq? Why not just report that things there are great? "It's really cheap to produce fiction," Gentzkow points out.

Moreover, news outlets pay a substantial price when they're found to have lied about what actually happened. The *New York Times*'s discovery that reporter Jayson Blair fabricated a string of stories in the paper led to a major internal shakeup, including the resignation of top editors and the institution of an independent ombudsman. Would the paper have done that much in response to the scandal if its readers didn't care about the truth?

This is Gentzkow's essential point, and it's an important thing to understand in any exploration of the Lou Dobbs phenomenon: *people consume news because they want the truth.* I've covered how psychological biases push you toward information that conforms to your beliefs. But remember, these forces aren't usually operating in the foreground; it's rare that you choose to watch, listen to, or read something called news because you're *consciously* looking for affirmation of your beliefs. Usually, you're just looking for the facts.* That's why people tell the Pew pollsters that they want their news to be objective, rather than to come with a point of view.

On the other hand, though, there's naive realism: we all harbor a different idea of what an objective news story should look like. And herein lies the basic problem faced by any news organization looking to get you as a customer: we all want objectivity, but we disagree about what objectivity is.

In 2006, Gentzkow and his colleague Jesse Shapiro published a technical outline of how these pressures operate on media companies. Their paper paints an elegant picture of the

---

* There are, of course, increasingly many "news-ish" outfits that try to cater specifically to our need for self-affirmation. These seek to entertain rather than inform— the entertainment being the fun of seeing the other side getting flogged to death in a brilliant, biting, cutting, clever, juvenile, simplistic, or self-gratifyingly rude way. *The Daily Show* and *The Colbert Report* are the most obvious examples. So, too, is right-wing talk radio more theater than truth, an effort to simply anger the audience into a paralysis so deep that listeners are unable to turn away. David Foster Wallace made this point best in his magisterial profile of the Southern California talk radio host John Ziegler, who Wallace said understands that it is not his job to be "responsible, or nuanced, or to think about whether his on-air comments are productive or dangerous, or cogent, or even defensible." A talk-radio host "has exactly one on-air job, and that is to be stimulating." He isn't a journalist—"he is an entertainer."

conditions that give rise to bias in the news. Gentzkow and Shapiro's first observation is that news organizations have an incentive to slant information toward their audiences' prior beliefs because doing so increases their chances of being seen as accurate.

For instance, as Gentzkow and Shapiro suggest, consider a newspaper—let's call it *The Inquirer*—that discovers that scientists have managed to sustain a cold fusion reaction. Should it report the cold fusion news? If the *Inquirer*'s readers are likely to find such a story very hard to believe, people at the newspaper will be reluctant to put it out; after all, cold fusion is so far-fetched that any story on it might prompt readers to conclude that the paper doesn't understand science, and thus that it shouldn't be trusted. The *Inquirer*, in other words, will have a strong incentive to hide the news—or to downplay it—to satisfy its audience's bias against believing in cold fusion.

But there is a corrective mechanism to this force, Gentzkow and Shapiro argue: news organizations that bend the news to satisfy their audiences run a risk that people will discover the truth some other way. If competing media outlets report the cold fusion news, the *Inquirer*'s readers might come to see the truth in the story—and then they'll blame the *Inquirer* for neglecting to print it. News organizations, then, must be careful about how they indulge their audiences' biases; if they go too far, people might start to regard their content as nothing more than worthless pandering.

These two observations give rise to several fascinating predictions about what kinds of stories news outlets are likely to slant to fit the audiences' tastes and which stories they'll deliver straight. Gentzkow and Shapiro say that news organizations will have little incentive to insert bias into "high-feedback" topics— subjects where the truth is easily verified, like sports or the

weather or the stock market. A media company would be foolish to pander to your preferences here because you're very likely
to easily see through the bias. In theory, Fox News could uplift
its viewers by reporting that as a result of Republican policies,
gasoline prices across the nation have fallen to unprecedented
lows. But because everyone can find the true price of gas, no
right-wing news network that cared for its reputation would lie
about gas prices; there's just too much feedback.

Gentzkow and Shapiro show, in a similar vein, that newspapers exhibit little slant toward local teams in their forecasts of
upcoming games. Between 1994 and 2000, the *New York Times*
made hundreds of football picks. But according to Gentzkow
and Shapiro's analysis, the paper showed no systematic bias in
favor of what its readers probably wanted to hear—that the
Giants and the Jets would win the next big game. This is understandable: if readers noticed that editors were continually
picking losing local teams, they'd dismiss all forecasts as bunk.

Bias is much easier, Gentzkow and Shapiro argue, for "low-
feedback" topics. These are the grand, sprawling subjects where
information is difficult to come by, hard to make sense of, and
given to competing explanations and interpretations. These are,
in other words, precisely the subjects along which the nation is
splitting into various versions of "reality." Think of things like tax
or health-care policy, global warming, or the wisdom of a foreign
war. For these, the truth is simply elusive, and a news organization can freely shoehorn the facts into a package that fits an
audience's views. It will take decades before we can assess with
any real clarity whether the various measures that George W.
Bush's administration undertook in response to the 9/11 attacks
were wise. In the meantime, in the absence of any definitive
truth, news outlets can spin the situation to please their viewers,
readers, and listeners. There are, after all, few risks to doing so.

To take a completely hypothetical example, say that a right-wing cable TV network consistently suggests that Bush's post-9/11 policies have been generally magnificent. What kind of evidence could conceivably come along to prove to its viewers that this isn't true? Failure to catch the terrorist ringleader? That simply shows how elusive the enemy is. An increase in terrorist attacks around the world? Only proves that the fight goes on. An attack in the United States? Everyone gets lucky now and then; what about all those attacks the administration prevented? It's the sort of spin that can't easily be unspun.

Gentzkow and Shapiro's model places a high value on competition in the news business. The more news organizations there are covering a certain topic, they argue, the more likely it is that the audience will be able to discover the actual truth of the matter—and thus, the less incentive a news organization will have to bend the news toward people's prior views. This idea constitutes, of course, the intellectual underpinning of freedom of the press, and, more generally, of democracy itself: truth and wisdom will emerge in a free marketplace of ideas. In recent years, many bloggers have picked up this thread as a rallying cry. The proliferation of voices online, they say, keeps big media honest—pushing newspapers and TV networks toward stories that deserve coverage or compelling them to reconsider the conventional wisdom or to correct errors in their reporting.

Gentzkow cites the now legendary controversy that forced the early retirement of the CBS anchor Dan Rather. A couple months before the 2004 presidential election, Rather reported that CBS had obtained documents showing that President Bush had been delinquent during his days in the Texas Air National Guard. Rather claimed that the documents came from the "personal files" of the late Lieutenant Colonel Jerry Killian, Bush's commander in the Guard. But within hours of Rather's broadcast, a handful of prominent conservative bloggers started to question the memos' authenticity, pointing to arcane problems in their typography and formatting. Eventually, many competing news outlets began to investigate the issue—and in a few weeks' time, CBS News and Rather relented, admitting that they could not prove that the documents were authentic.

The imbroglio perfectly fits Gentzkow's model. CBS's decision to run the story "is very much consistent with the view that this is what their viewers wanted to hear, so they were going to give it to them," he says. While there's no evidence that CBS News deliberately set out to lie to people, its reporting was unquestionably shoddy—a shoddiness prompted by its rush to put something out that it knew would attract a great many viewers sympathetic to the argument. People online played a crucial role in outing this bias; had the Bush-Guard story aired in the days before the Internet, the inaccuracies might never have come to light. "That's exactly what this model highlights," Gentzkow says. "There's no question that this profusion of new sources has played a disciplining role."

In some sense, though, the Rather story—what critics call "Memogate"—is sui generis; it's rare that a slanted news account can be so effectively, quickly collapsed by the discovery of a key piece of evidence. Usually, bias in the news is a much muddier affair. Usually, there can be no "gotcha" moment, because a single story is part of a larger drumbeat of biased accounts, and because the slant arises as much out of tone and style as out of factual inaccuracies. If you watch an evening of Fox News with a critical eye, you may be able to spot a few flubbed facts, but it will be like fixing your attention on the froth cresting at the top of a raging river—and what matters is the river itself, the torrent of one-sided interpretations of the news, the partial experts, the exaggerations, the omissions: the entire skewed manner in which Fox sees the news.

Such inchoate, amorphous bias is far harder to pin down than anything Dan Rather did. It's easy to catch a news anchor's phony memo, but all the bloggers in all the world cannot *prove* to the satisfaction of a dyed-in-the-wool Fox viewer that Fox is wrong about global warming, a classic "low-feedback" subject. Whatever competition it faces, Fox and its audience can live safely in the comfort of the lie—at least, until they personally begin to feel the planet starting to heat up.

All of this anticipates Lou Dobbs, who works in much the same manner: he covers a few epic topics, such as globalization and immigration, whose ultimate effects are hard to measure and easy to distort. The precise ways in which trade policy is affecting American workers and the American people is a topic worthy of several large books, books far more nuanced and serious than anything Dobbs offers his viewers. Economists tell us that free trade benefits the nation as a whole (through lower prices for goods), but that its negative effects are concentrated among certain populations—in recent years, among manufacturing workers. Immigration works similarly: the economy sees gains when labor markets are more flexible, but freer immigration increases competition for low-skilled jobs and thus hurts some native workers.

Many people might be harmed by these policies, and consequently, Dobbs doesn't have to put forward any Dan Rather–style lies in order to slant the news toward a specific ideology. Indeed, he can even send his correspondents out to dig up actual news, because he's sure to find many stories that corroborate his point of view, and the more of these that he can give his audience, the more likely they are to consider him a saint for giving them "real" news they want. And they'll keep watching.

Dobbs's bias is in what he won't say. Let's go back to North Carolina and the story of Apricot Textile. It's true that the state has lost more than a hundred thousand manufacturing jobs since NAFTA was passed. But North Carolina's economy has also grown substantially since the passage of Dobbs's hated trade bill, and the state has added many jobs to the rolls. Since NAFTA, more than six hundred thousand service-sector jobs were created in North Carolina. Its exports to foreign countries, especially to China and Mexico, two nations on Dobbs's most-wanted list, have recently taken off. In 2003, North Carolina saw a 77 percent increase in its exports to China. Between 1998 and 2006, the state's exports have grown by about 40 percent. Trade, in other words, is arguably benefiting North Carolina.

But by looking at the saga of one small textile plant in one small river town, Dobbs managed to hide all of this news. Instead of the full story, here is what he told his viewers at the conclusion of Sylvester's report on Apricot Textile: "Shipping containers arriving from China full, leaving the United States empty—how this country's failed and phony free trade policies have affected American workers and our future. That story is next. Stay with us."

6

"Truthiness" Everywhere

ate in the holiday shopping season of 2005, the technology columnist Robin Raskin began to worry about a hidden danger posed by a popular gadget that many American parents were then contemplating buying for their kids: pornography was popping up on the iPod. Apple had just released a version of the ubiquitous white-plastic-and-steel music player that was also capable of displaying video clips, and although the company marketed the device as a way for people to watch television shows, innovators online envisioned many less seemly possibilities. "There's scores of 'iPorn' everywhere," Raskin warned in one of several television appearances at the time. The iPod had become "a pedophile's playground," she said, and Apple was doing little to stem the smut.

Raskin's anti-iPod admonition grew out of what she calls an abiding interest in "digital kids." Children today use technology in ways that absolutely bewilders older people, and Raskin, a mother of three who has been writing about computers for more than two decades, has made it her mission to steer parents away from trouble. In the 1990s, she edited *Family PC* magazine, where her regular column, which was titled "Internet Mom," took as its refrain the dangers of the Web, instant messaging software, and other technologies that were spidering into American homes. *Family PC* folded in the tough advertising market that followed the September 11, 2001, terrorist attacks, but Raskin, who hoped to launch another lifestyle magazine one day, continued to go on TV to review certain gadgets. When she saw that the iPod might pose a menace to children, the Internet Mom was determined to sound the alarm.

That unseen dangers lurk in everyday objects is a cliché of local news—"Have you just eaten something that's going to kill you? Details at 11."— and Raskin's iPorn pitch piqued news directors everywhere. Raskin, a pert middle-aged woman with short brown hair and a deep, authoritative voice, also makes good TV. You might picture her as the Martha Stewart of consumer technology—direct but not rude, friendly but not perky.

And so it was that one morning in December 2005, Raskin found herself on Pittsburgh's Fox affiliate, WPGH Channel 53, calling the iPod one of the "scariest" gifts of the season. iPodporn, she said, was a scourge that parents needed to fight. On KGUN, an ABC station in Tucson, Raskin got similarly worked up, saying that iPorn "is free, it's on Apple's iTunes—it's not like they're hiding it anywhere." The ABC station in Columbus, Ohio, featured Raskin's warnings as part of a report by Kent Justice, a consumer correspondent who produces a regular segment called "On Your Side." Justice told viewers, "If you didn't know it, now prepare for it: hundreds of Web sites are selling iPorn."

A total of nine stations aired the Internet Mom's warning about the iPod. Most also featured an additional message from Raskin—and it's here that this story finds its legs. It's here that we begin to skip past the truth, past the conventional definition of factual, unbiased news and into a newer, murkier category of information.

Along with her warning concerning iPorn, Raskin used her time on TV to put forward recommendations for what she'd determined were a few "safe" holiday tech products. She touted a modern version of the old Coleco video game system—"$19.99 as a stocking stuffer!" she exclaimed in one interview—as well as an update of Pac-Man and a popular Japanese game called We Love Katamari. But these weren't unbiased reviews. Raskin was pushing the products because three companies—Panasonic, Namco, and Techno Source—had hired her to sell their wares during news appearances.

Raskin says that rather than acting as a "journalist," her true role on television during these segments was that of a "spokeswoman." Indeed, she'd approached the news stations with the iPorn story only as a way to hook them into running her demonstrations of sponsored products. "It was a great, grabbing headline," she says of the pornography angle. The TV stations were aware of Raskin's benefactors; she had disclosed the arrangement to them, and her solicitations had come through DS Simon, a public relations firm that commonly sends out marketing requests to local news outlets. Everyone on TV knew the game. Only the people at home were in the dark.

Robin Raskin secured her spot on local TV news through a couple of public-relations practices that are neither especially new nor uncommon but are still relatively unknown beyond the cloistered world of television news production. In the trade, they're called VNRs and SMTs: video news releases and satellite media tours. A VNR is a short clip of marketing propaganda produced in the language and style of real news. PR firms send TV news stations thousands of such videos every year, the most sophisticated of which are virtually indistinguishable from honest news, featuring interviews with (paid) experts and voiceovers by (fake) reporters who subtly pitch products during their narratives. Surprisingly often, news channels put these videos on the air.

A segment may appear to be an in-depth look at the travails of travelers during cold and flu season, but it quotes only experts who refer to Zicam nasal spray as a preferred treatment. A consumer safety piece warns viewers about scam artists who dress up flood-damaged cars and sell them as if they're perfect—an announcement drenched in irony, considering that the news segment is actually a dressed-up ad for CarFax.com, a commercial automobile research Web site. A Halloween report delves into the origins of the jack-o'-lantern, but the reporter—who's not actually a reporter but a PR man—ends the story by suggesting holiday recipes from Betty Crocker. Each of these segments was produced by marketing experts, rather than by journalists, and was funded by corporations looking to sell something, rather than by news agencies interested in the truth. Yet they were all presented as genuine news by channels across the country.*

---

* The Zicam segment aired on WMGM in southern New Jersey and KSFY in Sioux Falls, South Dakota, in the fall of 2006; neither station informed viewers that the video and the script for the story were provided by Zicam's manufacturer. In August 2006, WDTN in Dayton, Ohio, ran a version of the CarFax.com VNR, while two other stations—KGTV in San Diego and KUSA in Denver—used substantial portions of the sponsored video in their reports on flood-damaged cars. KGTV ran a brief on-screen message that the video was "courtesy of Carfax.com," but other stations ran no disclosure. The Betty Crocker piece was broadcast—again without any disclosure—by KHON in Honolulu and KFMB in San Diego late in 2006. KFMB's manager has since called the broadcast an error.

Public relations firms will sometimes arrange SMTs to accompany their VNRs. During a satellite media tour, an expert—a doctor, an author, or, like Robin Raskin, a journalist—holes up in a studio and fields questions from anchors at several stations, conducting what looks to the audience like an authentic news interview. What anchors don't often tell viewers is that the expert is working on behalf of a marketing firm, and that she's answering questions according to a PR script.

A typical SMT runs like one in which Raskin participated early in 2006, when she traveled from her home in New York to the floor of the Consumer Electronics Show in Las Vegas. From there, she spoke by satellite feed with anchors at three news stations—KEYT in Santa Barbara, California; WCYB in Bristol, Virginia; and WLTX in Columbia, South Carolina. Curt Wilson, the anchor in Columbia, told his audience that Raskin's appearance was "provided by vendors at the consumer trade show," but he didn't explain that she was pitching only products in which she had a financial interest. The two other stations offered no disclosure; Raskin was presented as if she were a reporter covering the convention.

"Let's talk about the trends—what are you seeing at this year's show?" Amy Lynn, the anchor in Santa Barbara, asked Raskin during the SMT.

"You're seeing things that *actually work*," said a beaming Raskin, her open palms drawing viewers to a half-dozen gadgets arrayed on a table before her. Raskin, who was identified as a "Technology Consumer Consultant" by an on-screen tag, then began a polished four-minute advertisement for her sponsors, Nokia, Motorola, Texas Instruments, and Swiffer (which was introducing a duster that was meant to clean up electronic gadgets). Looking at the segment, it's obvious why companies employed Raskin: the lady can *sell*. She demonstrated each firm's products with more enthusiasm than a barker on QVC, even at several points getting the station's anchor to join in the praise.

Slipping a Nokia wireless headset in her ear, Raskin told Lynn, "I can get you by saying 'Amy'—it has voice recognition, it'll just go ahead and dial you!"

"Oh, I love those!" Lynn said.

Between 2002 and 2006, Raskin participated in almost three dozen VNRs and SMTs—roughly eight a year, each of which was sponsored by three to five companies and was built around a holiday or news event. Raskin, who no longer does marketing work and now writes about technology on the Yahoo Web site, says she regrets her decision to promote products on TV. She did it only to make some extra money during a low period in her life, and she says that she didn't fully consider how the job would affect her journalistic credibility. But Raskin adds another line, partly in defense of her actions: public life is already so commercialized, so suffused with salesmanship, that it seemed nearly naive to recuse herself on mere ethical grounds. Fakery abounds. What's one more on the pile?

"I actually joked with my own colleagues that, 'Hey, I'm off to go do Whore TV,'" she says. "I was fully aware that that's what it was. And yet it's such a commonplace thing. I mean, there are people hawking drugs, guns, war. The worst that could happen to someone watching my segment is that you might buy a game you don't like."

On October 17, 2005, on the premiere of his late-night show, the comedian Stephen Colbert coined the term "truthiness," and it was good. For Colbert, who plays a blowhard TV pundit à la the Fox network's Bill O'Reilly, "truthiness" conveyed a neat précis of a strained worldview: Stephen Colbert believed America to be split between two camps whose philosophies could never reconcile—those who *"think* with their *head"* and those who *"know* with their *heart."* Colbert himself was a proud *know*er, and "truthiness," he explained, was the quality of a thing *feeling* true without any evidence suggesting it actually was. The archetypal example was George W. Bush's decision to invade Iraq. "If you *think* about it, maybe there are a few missing pieces to the rationale for war," Colbert conceded. "But doesn't taking Saddam out *feel* like the right thing, right here in the gut?"

Colbert planted "truthiness" in a fertile field, in soil full of it, you might say. At the time, combatants in Washington were battling over a vacancy on the Supreme Court, a situation bound to erupt in plumes of hot air. But the term really took off a month and a half after Colbert's debut, and it was popular culture rather than national politics that presented the key exhibit in building the case that the world had gone truthy.

The news concerned the author James Frey, whose memoir *A Million Little Pieces*, which told of Frey's harrowing trip through addiction, criminality, and a hard recovery, had just won the publishing industry's most lucrative prize—Oprah Winfrey had picked it for her televised book club. But early in 2006, the muckraking Web site the Smoking Gun, which began to look into Frey's story in order to find a mug shot of the writer to post online (the memoir told of several stints in jail), reported that it had found serious flaws in his tale. There was no evidence that Frey had lived through much of what he'd written. A *Million Little Pieces* was stacked on the nonfiction shelves, but Frey had invented large swaths of it.

Then came the moment of truthiness: Winfrey defended Frey. Even if his details couldn't stand up to scrutiny, she told CNN, the "underlying message of redemption in James Frey's memoir still resonates with me, and I know it resonates with millions of other people who have read this book." It wasn't that

Winfrey didn't believe the Smoking Gun's findings. Rather, she didn't think they mattered. The revelations were "much ado about nothing," she said, suggesting that what had really happened to Frey was less important than what one *believed* had happened to Frey. *A Million Little Pieces* felt real, and that was enough.

It's true that Oprah Winfrey later stepped back from the lie. After the *New York Times* columnist Frank Rich, a hardworking beat cop against the official sanctioning of lies, criticized her blasé attitude toward the truth, she invited Frey and his publisher to her show and sternly dressed them down. Winfrey also told her audience, "I made a mistake, and I left the impression that the truth does not matter." She added, "To everyone who has challenged me on this issue of truth, you are absolutely right."

Yet there was something in the air. There had been for some time. Oprah's jaunt into the dark side only proved that no one was safe from the fakery flooding the culture.

If there was a central font of fallacy, it was the war in Iraq, which, like the war in Vietnam, split wide the gulf between reality and perception, between what people wanted to be true and what was true. None of what had been said about Iraq—about its links to terrorism, about the deadly weapons it harbored, about the mission there having already been accomplished, and democracy having already taken root—none of it fit with reports describing the reality in Iraq.

But the White House's efforts to script the truth reached, as well, beyond the war. Early in 2005, for instance, *USA Today* reported that the Department of Education had covertly hired Armstrong Williams, a conservative commentator, to promote the Bush education plan, called No Child Left Behind, on TV and on the radio. Williams, who is black, was contracted to sell the plan to black audiences and to other minority journalists.

He did so enthusiastically, even persuading the comedian Steve Harvey to invite Secretary of Education Rod Paige twice to Harvey's morning radio show. Williams maintains that he genuinely supported the White House's education policies. But he didn't tell his audience that he'd been paid $240,000 for his efforts.

It soon emerged that Williams wasn't the only pundit on the dole. The *Washington Post* and *Salon* found that the Department of Health and Human Services employed two other commentators, Maggie Gallagher and Michael McManus, as consultants on another federal social project, the president's proposal for strengthening American marriages. While working for the government, each had praised the Bush marriage plan in their columns, but neither had revealed their conflicts of interest. Late in 2005, the *Los Angeles Times* reported that the Pentagon had hired the Lincoln Group, an upstart Washington PR firm, to run an elaborate pro-American propaganda operation in Iraq. At the same time that Bush officials were praising the independence and vibrancy of Iraq's newly liberated press, the Lincoln Group was translating stories produced by U.S. officials into Arabic and then bribing Iraqi journalists or hiring Arabs to pose as journalists in order to disseminate the phony news through the Iraqi media.

Thus by the time Colbert took to the airwaves, by the time James Frey landed in trouble, the rift between the actual and the artificial had already become a topic of wide discussion. For many on the left, it was Bush himself who stood as the clear cause of it. A born-again Christian who credits unquestioning faith with saving him from delinquency, Bush is notoriously, even proudly uncurious about the world. Online, many bloggers highlighted this detachment by branding themselves members of "the reality-based community." This was a reference to an infamous and revealing interview that an unnamed Bush aide had once given to the journalist Ron Suskind. According to the aide, opponents of Bush were part of "what we call the reality-based community"—a label not meant to be complimentary, because to the aide, "discernible reality" was a stock of faltering value. The United States was "an empire now, and when we act, we create our own reality," the official told Suskind. "And while you're studying that reality—judiciously, as you will—we'll act again, creating other new realities, which you can study too, and that's how things will sort out."

How could this happen? How did we land in a place where a political official feels comfortable publicly dismissing "discernible reality"?

Investigating the rise of carelessness toward "reality" is, of course, the headlong purpose of this book. But I've been driving at a theory more pervasive than the peculiar psychology of one president, the transgressions of a single dominant political machine, or the aims of certain powerful players. The truth about truthiness, I've argued, is cognitive: when we strung up the planet in fiber-optic cable, when we dissolved the mainstream media into prickly niches, and when each of us began to create and transmit our own pictures and sounds, we eased the path through which propaganda infects the culture.

Video news releases and satellite media tours suggest the ultimate cultural expression of these forces: they show us what might become of the world—or, indeed, what has become of the world—in an age of easy lying. Today, marketers, political operatives, and others who want to convince you of the virtue of some thing or idea—whether it is a Swiffer duster, a Nokia headset, a presidential candidate, a certain education policy, or the "truth" about global warming—can go about the business of persuasion covertly, without divulging their motives or even *the fact that they're engaged in persuasion*. Propagandists have become experts at mining the vulnerabilities of the many-media world (for instance, the dubious of ethics of bottom line–watching local news operations). They've adopted a range of methods to exploit the current conditions—some are as benign as the covert placement of products in films and TV shows, but others are more questionable, such as planting VNRs on the news, or buying up pundits, or spreading their messages anonymously and "virally" through blogs, videos, and photos on the Web.

Technically, what these operatives aim to do is capture one or many of the forces I've discussed so far: *selective exposure*, in which we indulge information that pleases us and cocoon ourselves among others who think as we do; *selective perception*, in which we interpret documentary proof according to our long-held beliefs; *peripheral processing*, which produces a swarm of phony experts; and the *hostile media phenomenon*, which pushes the news away from objectivity and toward the sort of drivel one sees on cable.

In practice, what propagandists are doing is simpler to describe: they've mastered a new way to lie.

Not long ago, I had a surprising conversation with Diane Farsetta, a researcher at the Center for Media and Democracy, or CMD, an organization based in Madison, Wisconsin, that monitors the public relations industry. Early in 2006, Farsetta's group published a pioneering report that documented the symbiotic relationship between local television stations across the country and PR firms that produce video news releases and satellite media tours.

VNRs first gained notoriety early in 2005, when the *New York Times* reported that many local stations aired prepackaged segments produced by federal agencies under the Bush administration. The TV stations ran spots that cheered the war

in Iraq, the Bush Medicare plan, and various small-time programs, from the administration's anti-obesity effort to its en-
deavors against holiday drunk-driving. But private VNRs far
outnumber federal videos, and during the last few years,
Farsetta's group has uncovered more than a hundred instances
of news programs incorporating promotional news into their
broadcasts without disclosing the source to viewers.

I'd previously heard about CMD's investigation—the work
led to an inquiry by the Federal Communications Commission
(FCC), one that has resulted in fines for some stations—but
when I dug into the report, Farsetta's findings faintly floored
me. TV stations, some in the largest cities in the nation, were
deceiving their viewers deliberately, blatantly, and in many cases
repeatedly. On CMD's Web site, you can see dozens of news segments lifted directly from VNRs. The effect would be comical—
four stations ran a piece on how to incorporate Bisquick into
your plans for National Pancake Week,* to take one example—
if the lying weren't so determined.

But the bigger surprise came when I spoke to Farsetta. I
had suspected that her discoveries must represent the excep-
tion on TV news, not the rule. When confronted by CMD, some
news directors excused their VNR broadcasts as oversights; in
the boiler room of a daily news operation, a hapless staffer can
sometimes unknowingly pull down corporate video from a digital feed and, before any higher-ups intervene, he might drop it
in to the five o'clock news. Mistakes happen.

"Isn't this a plausible scenario?" I asked Farsetta. "After all,
my local news isn't putting VNRs on the air every night, right?"

"Well, I don't know about that," she told me. Farsetta's group
tracked only a small number of the videos that marketers send

---

* Not an actual holiday.

to news stations, but even of those, CMD found many making it to the air. The largest PR firms put out more than a thousand VNRs every year; a typical local news station receives more than a dozen new VNRs every day. While the deception inherent in the practice confounds efforts to calculate how often VNRs end up on the news, the sheer volume of videos that PR companies produce suggests that stations are airing marketing videos far more often than viewers might suspect. Farsetta pointed out that in surveys, more than 90 percent of news directors have admitted using VNRs in their broadcasts.

Some stations edit the VNRs they put on the air—they'll often cut the prepackaged videos down for size, or they'll use small clips from VNRs as background footage in locally produced news. But Farsetta said that in the vast majority of cases that her group looked at, stations aired VNRs without significantly editing what marketers had given them. Indeed, sometimes the most dramatic alteration a news station makes to a VNR is to obscure where the video came from.

In 2006, DS Simon, one of the PR firms that Farsetta monitors, began to identify the sponsors of its VNRs with an on-screen tag and an audio label in the voiceover. "This was the one instance where a PR firm was trying to make sure to maximize the chance of disclosure," Farsetta said. Her group spotted fifteen broadcasts airing VNRs that had been produced with these added disclosures. But in twelve of them, TV news producers broadcast the videos after editing out the sponsor identifications. "It's in their interest not to disclose this," Farsetta said of news stations. "It's in their interest not to appear as though they're presenting you with ads instead of news."

Marketers began to create VNRs in the 1980s, but you couldn't guess, back then, that the videos would ever become a promotional vehicle of any practical value. Producing attractive video was expensive, so VNRs rarely looked slick enough to fit in with a broadcast program. Distribution was also a problem: PR firms sent out VNRs by mail on videotape, a system too clumsy for fast-paced newsrooms to work with. The digital revolution, of course, has changed all that. In the same way that hundreds of millions of us can create videos for YouTube or that Dylan Avery can make a 9/11 conspiracy film with wages from a part-time job, marketers can now produce and distribute video that looks just as good as anything a TV station can make, and for almost no money.

Technology has also upended how television stations produce news. Although it's subject to tremendous (and often justified) ridicule, local TV news has long been—and remains—America's first choice for information. Contrary to ABC News's slogan, more Americans actually get their news from local TV than from any other source. Local television's dominance took root in the late 1970s, with the advent of videotape. Before that—in the era of film—newsgathering was a slow, expensive endeavor. With video, producers could shoot and edit segments on trucks in the field, assembling news quickly and, more important, cheaply. The economics of videotape accounts for the parsimonious culture of local news. Video made newsgathering suddenly profitable, and station owners started looking to their news operations as a pot of gold. All news outlets try to make money, of course, but local news is particularly cognizant of the bottom line, and much of what critics decry about it—the emphasis on visually interesting stories, the dearth of investigative news—can be attributed to cost pressures.

Technological advances since the 1980s—smaller, more portable cameras; digital recording and editing; and the distribution of video through satellites and the Internet—allowed for further cost cutting in local news. In many U.S. TV newsrooms, you'll now find computer terminals belonging to a system called Pathfire, which hooks stations into a cloud of video coming in from all over the world—clips from syndicates such as the Associated Press, from other local stations, and from the large broadcast networks.

For producers, Pathfire is a palette from which to create full stories at extremely low cost; now images of overseas wars, out-of-state disasters, nearby sports victories, freakish weather events, adorable zoo animals, and gripping celebrity goings-on are quickly pulled down and cut up into digestible bits of news, with the producer never having to leave the studio. Stations increasingly lean on this third-party footage to pad their broadcasts. According to one study, more than a quarter of the video you see on a typical local newscast isn't at all local and was collected instead from video coming in on the cloud.

Many times, what you see isn't news, either. I've argued that advances in the production and distribution of media have quickened the pace of fakery entering the media. There are few better exhibits of this than the introduction of digital distribution in local news. When a producer logs into a system like Pathfire looking for footage to fill out the eleven o'clock broadcast, she is not only presented with videos from legitimate outfits such as the Associated Press. Pathfire also connects her to a smorgasbord of VNRs, which marketers upload into the system daily. PR companies don't pay television channels to air these sponsored segments—that would run afoul of the FCC's "payola" rules—but the footage is free, which, for the stations, is a very attractive offer. Marketing videos, in other words, are now mainlined into U.S. newsrooms, and producers everywhere are just a mouse-click away from hours of broadcast-quality promotional video

that they can put on the air at no charge. It's no wonder they
dip into the pool so frequently.

WMGM Channel 40, the New Jersey NBC affiliate that
serves Atlantic City and Philadelphia, offers a dismaying illus-
tration of the irresistibility of prepackaged promotional news
in some newsrooms. The station runs a regular feature called
Lifeline—"Your best source for South Jersey health news"—by
Robin Stoloff, a stylish young woman with a shock of blond hair,
whom WMGM identifies as a "health reporter." But it turns
out that "reporter" doesn't fully describe Stoloff's position at
WMGM. Her day job is in the station's ad sales department, far
removed from her on-camera duties. Once a week, Stoloff takes
to the screen to offer up a health story—often, though, Stoloff's'
dispatch contains not a single second of original reporting, and
it rarely focuses on "South Jersey health news."

Indeed, when I watched it during the spring of 2007, it was
difficult to find any stories by Stoloff that weren't lifted directly
from VNRs; many times, all she had done to the PR videos
was replace a publicist's narration with her own voice as she
read marketing copy. In addition to the Zicam story I mentioned earlier, Stoloff has reported that gargling with Listerine
is as effective as flossing for maintaining oral health; that bunion
surgery isn't very painless or difficult (a VNR provided by the
American College of Foot Ankle Surgeons); that many Americans are spending their tax refunds on cosmetic dental work (the
American Academy of Periodontology); and that low-carb diets
are better than low-fat diets for people trying to lose weight (a
promotion for *Annals of Internal Medicine*, the journal in which
the low-carb study was published).

Many of these stories offered no disclosure that they'd been
provided by PR firms. When I called Harvey Cox, WMGM's
news director, to ask why this was the case, he declined to

comment about his station's use of VNRs. Following my call, though, WMGM's reports by Stoloff began to consistently carry on-screen tags identifying their videos' PR sources.

Directors of local news stations are uneasy about disclosures that newscasts have routinely aired VNRs. The Radio and Television News Directors Association sharply criticized Farsetta's study, claiming that her findings did not represent typical practices at stations. The group also maintains that any effort by the FCC to require news stations to disclose VNR video would run afoul of the First Amendment.

In order to increase their appeal to news directors, marketers have lately been creating videos of artfully deceptive sophistication. Early VNRs appeared crudely commercial; they hawked products explicitly and rarely meshed with the quick-take, soundbitten style of TV news, a medium in which it's unusual for a talking head to say anything that lasts longer than ten seconds. Over the years, marketers have become adept at aping the vernacular of local broadcasts. Now they send out videos to coincide with news-making dates—tax day, the first anniversary of Hurricane Katrina, National Pancake Week. Many VNRs are also stuffed with content unrelated to the sale, information that news directors can point to as genuinely interesting and informative—the CarFax VNR, for instance, warns customers about the legitimate dangers of buying used cars. The latest breed of VNRs offers only quick glances at the sponsors' logos, to the point that some appear to be an exercise in subliminal persuasion.

In the fall of 2005, two stations in the Midwest, KTVI in St. Louis and WVTV in Milwaukee, ran a Halloween-themed VNR sponsored by Masterfoods (the manufacturer of M&Ms and Snickers) and 1-800-Flowers. "More than 93 percent of children go trick-or-treating every year," the announcer begins

as a troupe of delighted, costumed kids fills the screen. The
segment looks like every Halloween piece you've ever seen,
focusing mainly on sensible kid-safety guidelines offered by a
"parenting expert" named Julie Edelman. "Be sure that they
either have reflective strips on their costumes or a flashlight,"
suggests Edelman, the author of a book called *The Acciden-
tal Housewife*. And "don't put those masks on—'cause they
can't see so well where they're going, so try some make-up
instead."

Edelman also offers ideas to make the day more fun, like organizing a treasure hunt for candy and decorating your house
with flower arrangements set in ceramic vases shaped like jack-
o'-lanterns. At the mention of these, there are on-screen flashes
of the sponsors' products—there's a two-second shot of a package of glow-in-the-dark Snickers coming down the factory line
and the briefest glimpse of a flower arrangement by 1-800-
Flowers—but unless you were looking for it, the sell would have
skipped you by. In a two-minute spot, fewer than five seconds
are devoted to any marketing purposes.

You might question the efficacy of such surreptitious salesmanship, but for advertisers, a soft sale allows for the possibility
of sneaking past your defenses. The news makes a pitch credible; studies of how people react to VNRs show that we're much
more likely to believe and to remember a message if we see it
as part of a newscast than if we see essentially the same thing
in a commercial. Public relations mavens look at VNRs as an
opportunity to educate and acculturate customers, to plant imagery and ideas, rather than to inspire an immediate purchase.
Not a single viewer of the Halloween VNR may have been persuaded to run out to buy a basketful of candy, but this was not
the promotion's aim. Marketers, instead, want to lodge the pearl
of motivation at the seat of your soul—to solidify, in this case,

the image of Snickers and M&Ms as a quintessential Halloween snack, so necessary that even a parenting expert references them in her plans.

What is interesting about such VNRs, of course, is that they mark a larger cultural trend—the burrowing underground of propaganda, the transformation of salesmanship from a flashy, street-corner affair to a quiet, dressed-up sport of cunning and deceit. It's a shift that has been going on for at least a generation, although it is so profound that to describe it might be to tell a story of the obvious. Time was, those in the business of persuasion went about their efforts directly; when people sold to you, they made it plain. These were days when men traveled door-to-door convincing families of their need for vacuum cleaners or vegetable choppers or sets of well-bound Bibles. On radio and TV, the players pointed proudly to their sponsors, waxing rhapsodic on the virtues of all kinds of consumer products. Fred and Wilma Flintstone sang "Winston tastes good like a cigarette should," while Lucille Ball implored the housewives of America to "give your husband a carton of Philip Morris cigarettes."

Watch the famous 1971 debate between John Kerry and John O'Neill on *The Dick Cavett* show, and you're jarred by the host's frequent references to the numerous companies paying his salary. Just after O'Neill accuses Kerry of attempting "the murder of the reputations" of Vietnam war veterans, Cavett holds up a plastic bottle, smiles, and says, "Here is how a bath can smooth and soften your skin—leaving you radiant and refreshed with Calgon Bath Oil Beads." Later, he cuts to a break promising an ad that will offer "some important news about bathtub safety," and when the show returns, Cavett avers, "Lawry's Seasoned Salt is great on all kinds of meat, on salads, and on chicken, too."

Nothing is sold quite so explicitly anymore; such attempts would be considered uncouth or, more likely, taken for irony.

Today logos simply show up slyly in the movies and on TV, with no attempt at a sale. The movie *Cast Away* is awash in FedEx imagery, but the film's star, Tom Hanks, does not hawk overnight delivery. Still, without ever pitching its sponsor, *Cast Away* sets up a universe in which FedEx becomes, to the viewer, if not virtuous, at least ubiquitous. The example is most likely harmless, but it suggests, nevertheless, how heavily salesmanship has come to depend on a kind of deception.

What's replaced direct selling is a more subtle, though altogether more pervasive, form of promotion, one that rests on a seeming paradox: today marketers want to sell to you without appearing to sell. The rise of VNRs offers just a single example of what has become a trend. In countless other ways now, people looking to change your mind—whether on matters corporate or political—are digging underground. They're constantly cajoling, promoting, convincing, pitching, but they're doing so in a manner that's designed to fly below your conscious notice. To make the trick work, as in VNRs, they often have to lie.

I have argued that the particular way in which information now moves through society—on currents of loosely linked online groups and niche media outfits, pushed along by experts and journalists of dubious character, and bolstered by documents that are no longer considered proof of reality—amplifies deception. There is a dangerous marriage, then, between message and medium. Propagandists are playing a game that more than ever, manufactures lies, and they're routing it through a communications system that is exquisitely capable of maintaining the lie. Of course, they understand this better than the rest of us.

There is an interesting story about how we got to this point. It begins, as so many tales of deception do, in the tobacco industry—specifically in the early 1990s, within the assaulted confines of the second-largest cigarette company in the United States, R. J. Reynolds, better known as RJR, the makers of Winston, Salem, and Camel. These were difficult times for cigarette manufacturers. As Americans began to learn about the pervasive risks of tobacco, dangers the industry had long understood and suppressed, calls for regulating cigarettes attracted wide public support. Local, state, and even national politicians proposed a web of restrictions: raising cigarette sales taxes, banning smoking in public places, recognizing tobacco as a dangerous drug.

The industry had long maintained a legendary lobbying and public affairs apparatus, and it had succeeded, miraculously, for decades, in pushing back most antismoking efforts. But now the party was burning out. Americans were turning against cigarettes. The opposition was visceral, a matter of life and death. How could any marketing campaign reverse this reality?

For executives at RJR, the answer, initially, was to go after the base. Like long-shot politicians everywhere, RJR hoped to rouse a sleeping mass of like-minded combatants—a "smokers' rights" army, in this case—that could face down the coming advance. About a fifth of Americans smoked cigarettes, and occasionally some would contact RJR with tales of dispossession. Smokers' employers hassled them when they lit up at work, their towns contemplated doubling and tripling the cost of their habit, they were being kicked out of restaurants and bowling alleys and the layabout places they'd considered havens. In the mid-1980s, RJR, following the lead of its rival Philip Morris, launched a monthly magazine catering to America's smokers. *Choice*, it was called, and that's how its pages painted the issue: smoking was a fundamental freedom, and it was under attack.

Choice depicted the world as a place of woe for smokers. It urged them to act. Smokers needed to stand up, write letters, call their legislators, circulate petitions, and fight for what was theirs. To reinforce the message, RJR also began to organize "smokers' rights" chapters across the country, arranging for citizens to come together to discuss how to battle the growing legions of antismokers. "Field coordinators" working for the company rented local meeting spots and recruited smokers, and they instructed the groups according to a slick PR manual the firm had produced. The manual offered tips on the mechanics of activism and policy making—how to recruit others to the fight, how to get noticed by politicians and the media—and it urged smokers to think about their struggle in epic terms. Tobacco was "more deeply rooted in our nation's heritage than any other commodity," the manual declared, and those protecting its legacy were acting in the tradition of the American revolutionaries, the women who'd fought for suffrage, and those who'd campaigned for civil rights. "Successful movements like these are not just in the history books," RJR told smokers. "One of them is happening here and now, and you're part of it!"

You can think of RJR's fostering of smokers' rights as an attempt at the direct route of marketing. In organizing smokers, RJR was selling its message as plainly as Dick Cavett once sold Lawry's Seasoned Salt. The company didn't hide its own interests. Throughout the 1980s and early 1990s, in fact, RJR ran a number of advertisements in which it boasted of its courage to speak out for what it believed. "We know some of you may question what we say because we're a cigarette company," it said in one ad. "But we also know that by keeping silent, we've contributed to this climate of doubt and distrust."

The spots often pleaded with nonsmokers to consider the feelings of smokers. "We feel singled out. We're doing something perfectly legal, yet we're often segregated, discriminated against, even legislated against." The solution to the impasse, the company said, was painfully obvious: "common courtesy." If smokers and nonsmokers would only be civil to each other—the smoker asks whether others wouldn't mind if he lit up, the nonsmoker doesn't try to get cigarettes banned from every public place—tobacco would cease to be a contentious public issue. At the bottom of each of these spots, one image was given prominence: the firm's logo, "R.J. Reynolds Tobacco Company," stenciled out in a stylish serif font.

But smokers' rights never caught on. The problem was the smokers themselves. They had, as it turned out, little sympathy for their pushers. According to the industry's own research, many hated their addiction and wanted to quit. A large number even supported restrictions on smoking. RJR struggled to fill the smokers' rights meetings. The few die-hards who joined seemed to do so only for the free cigarettes and lighters the company handed out; they hardly looked like the Martin Luther King Jrs. of smoking.

Worse, RJR's direct appeals engendered tremendous opposition. Every time the company ran an ad, it got more feedback from critics than from supporters. Dozens of people would cut out the newspaper spots, scribble responses to each of the company's points, and mail back their thoughts. An advertisement would declare, "We're not criminals," and a critic would write back, "You are breaking one of the Ten Commandments—Thou shall not kill.'" There's a famous industry story, first reported by *Mother Jones* magazine, that describes one RJR field coordinator's encounter with a woman who came to a smokers' rights meeting holding a shoe box. When the company man introduced himself, the woman said, "I want you to know my mother got an invitation to this meeting." Holding out the box, she added, "She died of lung cancer. I brought my mother to your meeting."

In the summer of 1994, after the Food and Drug Administration and the Occupational Safety and Health Administration announced that they were looking into regulating tobacco, RJR signaled a shift in its strategy. The firm published a newspaper ad that differed in a subtle but telling way from its previous campaigns.

In this ad, the company's name was scaled down to small type; the protagonist here was not RJR, the money-loving industrial giant, but instead it was *you*—the typical American citizen. Indeed, right up at the top of the page was a big photograph of one such specimen. He was a middle-aged man in jeans and a work shirt, cuffs rolled up, a wide smile on his face. His baseball cap sported the word "Minnesota." You could tell by the way he leaned against his pickup truck that he was a man's man, no time to talk. And this fellow, let's call him Heartland Man, came to us with a plain-spoken complaint: "I'm one of America's 45 million smokers. I'm not a moaner or a whiner. But I'm getting fed up. I'd like to get the government off my back." He went on to make an expansive case. The move to restrict cigarettes, he warned, would harm everyone, not just smokers. Because once the government banned cigarettes, it'll "go for liquor and fast food and buttermilk and who knows what else. There's a line of dominoes a mile long."

A few months after the ad was published, Mongoven, Biscoe, and Duchin (MBD), a Washington PR firm that worked for RJR, proposed that the company sponsor an entire campaign inspired by the grievances of the Heartland Man. The effort would have little to do with new tobacco regulations or, really, with smoking or the rights of smokers; instead, the new campaign would take aim at a larger, more universal scourge, one whose dimensions every American, whatever his politics or preferred vice, could be expected to appreciate: the government was getting too damn powerful, too damn nagging, too damn invasive.

MBD asked hundreds of organizations that ordinarily didn't take a stand either way on smoking to join the effort. Soon, the campaign, which MBD called the Get Government Off Our Back project—referred to by insiders as GGOOB; "guh-goob," if you wanted to say it out loud—had attracted an impressive array of member groups. The U.S. Chamber of Commerce signed on, as did the Traditional Values Coalition, the National Rifle Association, Small Business of America, the Seniors Coalition, and the Home School Legal Defense Association, among many others. Perhaps GGOOB's most important member group was Americans for Tax Reform, whose founder, the influential conservative operative Grover Norquist—a man known for fighting taxes and government programs with the restraint that General Sherman brought on his march to Savannah—enthusiastically pressed GGOOB's case with reporters and Washington policy makers.

But one name was left out of the lengthy list of stars joining the new project. RJR, which sponsored GGOOB and had provided substantial donations to many of the groups that agreed to join, took no credit for the campaign. Nor did any other lobby with obvious ties to the tobacco industry. Indeed, to look at GGOOB's papers and press releases, you'd never guess a cigarette connection. In one position paper released by the group, a frequently-asked-questions section posed, "How did Get Government Off Our Back get started?" The true answer was that RJR's public relations company founded it. Instead, the document said that GGOOB was created at the "grassroots," by "loose networks of business groups, civic groups and other organizations" who'd come together more or less spontaneously. Why was GGOOB

necessary now? The paper didn't say it was because RJR wanted
to beat back new regulations on its business. Rather, GGOOB
was necessary because if nobody acted soon, "the American system could be in danger of collapsing under the weight of big
government." There was that line of dominoes a mile long.

GGOOB, plainly, was a front group. As Dorie Apollonio and
Lisa Bero, two researchers at the University of California, San
Francisco, who first uncovered the project's connections, explain, in starting up GGOOB, RJR found a way to push its own
agenda in a "politically palatable" manner. It's true that many of
the groups involved in GGOOB were deeply conservative; most
fit the mold of Americans for Tax Reform, ardent antitax cam-
paigners and small-government advocates who were not particularly representative of the country at large. Still, their motives
represented a vastly more powerful organizing force than the
narrow, unpopular aims of RJR.

Remember that RJR wasn't getting anywhere with the direct appeal. When the company tried to sell its ideas straight—
when it took out ads asking for some consideration, when it
sketched out the possibility of some middle ground on the issue
of smoking—people dismissed it. Polls showed antitobacco fervor rising around the country. Even smokers wouldn't join its
side. Now, by taking its propaganda underground—by turning
the battle into one about big government rather than big tobacco
and, crucially, by hiding its own association with the plan—RJR
could ride toward its goals upon a cresting wave of antiregula-
tory activism. And that's exactly how the plan played out.

In its first major action, GGOOB declared March 1995 national "Regulatory Revolt Month" and celebrated the invented
holiday with rallies in several states, some of which drew hundreds of supporters. The rallies were extensively covered in the
local media, but the press did not report—because the press

did not know—that these were tobacco-funded affairs. GGOOB also asked state lawmakers to pledge to oppose new government rules. Impressed by the project's apparent popularity, dozens of legislators, mainly Republicans, signed the promise. They, too, weren't told that they were joining a cigarette company's cause; presumably, many would have reconsidered had they been aware who was behind the GGOOB curtain.

In Washington, Republicans who'd recently taken over both houses of Congress pushed GGOOB's call to put a freeze on all new federal health and environmental regulations. Their bill didn't pass, but men like Norquist enforced a tough line against federal rules, and by the end of 1995, it was clear that GGOOB had succeeded in its effort to derail the harshest proposed restrictions on cigarettes. The FDA prohibited tobacco advertisements aimed at teenagers, but it did not impose any of the strict rules—including an outright ban on cigarettes—that the industry had long feared. A rule by the Labor Department to restrict smoking in the workplace, meanwhile, went nowhere. GGOOB succeeded. But the real victor, of course, was RJR.

A skeptic might point out that GGOOB merely won a battle but that tobacco still lost the war. In the years since RJR's tricky PR effort, after all, many of the restrictions it once fought have come to pass. Today the vast majority of Americans aren't allowed to smoke at work, and in many places it's illegal, not to mention uncouth, to wield a cigarette in public. The culture, more important, has shifted, so that the very thought of smoking as a "heartland" habit feels like a notion from the distant past. Yet it is precisely the tobacco industry's general failures that prove the importance—and the lasting appeal, to propagandists—of a deceptive PR plan like GGOOB.

By the 1990s, probably nothing could have saved cigarette companies from the fate they've suffered since; if you kill four hundred thousand people every year, and if the public comes to realize you're killing four hundred thousand people every year, no sort of PR campaign will win you permanent favor. But that's just what's so remarkable about GGOOB—the project helped to hold back a few big losses for the industry at a time of clear and growing antipathy toward cigarettes, and it worked only because, in the public mind, GGOOB had nothing to do with cigarettes. GGOOB showed that you can engineer a marketing win even if your position was ridiculous (a ban on cigarettes might lead to a prohibition on buttermilk!), even if your product was killing people, even if your own customers, people who were neurochemically addicted to what you sold, were on the fence about what you did. All you had to do was fight your battle from another front. All you had to do was don a disguise. You just had to lie.

The annals of tobacco burn bright with scams like GGOOB; at the risk of comically understating the case, it's fair to say that this was far from the only time a cigarette company came upon the utility of hiding the truth from the public.* But there was

---

* To name one other remarkable example: The health policy researchers Elisa Ong and Stanton Glantz, also at UCSF, found that around the same time that RJR was working on GGOOB, Philip Morris, the world's largest cigarette maker, directed its public relations firm to create a front group focused on the grand-sounding idea of "sound science." Philip Morris's PR firm sent letters to thousands of scientists asking them to join the new group, the Advancement for Sound Science Coalition, which called on the government to be cautious when using science in determining how to regulate businesses. Many of the people who signed on didn't know they were working for a cigarette company; Philip Morris documents show that the firm made sure to treat the scientists in a way that made them "feel" that they (the scientists) were dictating the front group's strategies. Steven Milloy, the Philip Morris employee who directed the effort, has since gone on to find much success in the business of sound science. He now runs a Web site called JunkScience.com and is a frequent commentator on Fox News, where he regularly dismisses findings—on global warming, secondhand smoke, and other health and environmental threats—that threaten industry. Journalists Chris Mooney and

still something noteworthy about GGOOB, something seminal in its design and constituency that can be traced, over the years, to the bog of truthiness we find ourselves navigating now, more than a decade afterward.

If you look through the many PR pros and consultants working with RJR of the early 1990s, you find a clutch of players who turn up, with surprising frequency, at the sites of several of the major scuffles over truth we've witnessed since the millennium. Among these RJR all-stars are three men who merit special mention: Thomas Synhorst, who worked for years as an aide to Republican senators Charles Grassley and Bob Dole, was a part-time field coordinator for RJR and was responsible for conducting the company's smokers' rights operations in the Midwest. Douglas Goodyear was an executive at Walt Klein and Associates, a public relations and marketing company in Denver that worked closely with RJR on many projects, including GGOOB. And Timothy Hyde was RJR's in-house public affairs chief, involved in virtually all of its campaigns, including GGOOB.

In 1997, these three men got together to create a lobbying and public relations firm of their own. They called the partnership the DCI Group. If the name sounds forgettably generic, that's in keeping with DCI's ethos. On behalf of some of the largest companies in the world, DCI pulls strings in the shadows, fostering positive outcomes by creating the appearance of a groundswell of public support. Its entire business is creating projects like GGOOB.

Paul Thacker, among others, have reported that Milloy regularly receives money from cigarette and oil companies.

Tales of DCI's sneaky coalition-creation efforts are legion. In the late 1990s, when the federal government was trying to break up Microsoft over antitrust charges, the software company hired DCI—among several other lobbying firms—to cook up ways to enhance its standing in the capital. DCI appears to have helped the company found at least one pro-Microsoft industry group, Americans for Technology Leadership, whose president, an amiable fellow named Jonathan Zuck, was frequently quoted in the press as offering sensible-sounding reasons why Microsoft should be left alone.

I say that DCI's role in the creation of ATL is only *apparent* because the story has never been definitively unraveled, and one rarely knows for sure what has happened in cases involving DCI. When ATL officials lobbied members of Congress, state officials, and reporters on behalf of Microsoft, they purported to be completely independent from the company and from DCI. But ATL's executive director was also an employee of DCI, and Microsoft and several groups funded by Microsoft were listed as its founding members. ATL's murky role so agitated Oracle, one of Microsoft's main rivals, that it hired a private investigation firm to look into the group. But Oracle's P.I.s couldn't get very close to the truth, either: the gumshoes were discovered when they tried to pay the janitors at ATL's Washington office for bags of trash belonging to the advocacy group.

In 2003, Nicholas Confessore, a writer for *Washington Monthly* magazine, discovered that DCI had branched out into an even more creative propaganda venture, one that Confessore labeled "journa-lobbying." At the time, a magazine named *Tech Central Station* was gaining some notice on the Web, especially among conservative bloggers, who appreciated its wonky but engaging discussions of controversies in science, technology, and economics. *TCS*, which the journalist James Glassman founded at the height of the Internet boom, often espoused the pseudo-libertarian point of view that has long attracted certain geekier sects online. *TCS*'s writers, for instance, did not look favorably on regulations to curb greenhouse gases or the government's move to break up Microsoft or federal efforts to control drug prices. Though the magazine's style wasn't for everyone, even critics of *TCS* didn't doubt its writers' authenticity. Glassman had previously worked at the *New Republic* and the *Atlantic Monthly*, and he'd edited the Capitol Hill newspaper *Roll Call*. He was a real journalist.

Except maybe not anymore. As Confessore discovered, *Tech Central Station*, unbeknownst to its readers, was covertly published by the DCI Group, and DCI and *TCS* shared owners, employees, and office space. Moreover, many of the DCI Group's corporate clients were also "sponsors" of *TCS*, and *TCS*'s editorial positions, seen in this light, made a lot more sense. Among the benefactors were ExxonMobil, Microsoft, and PhRMA, the trade group that represents the pharmaceutical industry.

Glassman denied that the DCI connection affected his site's content.* He may have genuinely believed that, just as the scientists working for cigarette company front groups believed they'd independently arrived at the positions that favored their bosses. But that *TCS*'s punditry closely orbited the positions of its sponsors was evident on a host of issues, even beyond global warming, telecom policy, prescription drugs, and Microsoft.

In the spring of 2006, the writers Charles Wilson and Eric Schlosser published *Chew on This*, a version of Schlosser's earlier book *Fast Food Nation*, this one meant to educate

---

* Late in 2006, DCI sold the site to its editor, Nick Schultz, and Glassman left the company to found a magazine called *The American*. *Tech Central Station* is now called *TCS Daily*.

schoolchildren on the dangers of eating junk food. In response to the book and to the coming *Fast Food Nation* movie, Mc-Donald's, according to internal documents obtained by the *Wall Street Journal*, launched a vigorous campaign to "discredit the message and the messenger"—the messenger here being Schlosser.

McDonald's was one of DCI's sponsors, and soon its strategy came to life on Glassman's *TCS* in a feature called "Fast Talk Nation." The *TCS* site attacked *Chew on This* and included a form letter for parents to print out and send to schools where Schlosser and Wilson were speaking. The letter alleged that Schlosser favored legalizing marijuana—this was a reference to *Reefer Madness*, Schlosser's book examining the cost of the black market in drugs—and that he wasn't fit to lecture to kids. In an afterward to *Chew on This*, the authors wrote that "headmasters and principals received e-mails, letters, and phone calls urging them to cancel our visits."

No schools did. And when the press found the McDonald's/DCI/*TCS* connection, "Fast Talk Nation" was taken down. Still, you can see in this example the efficacy of the secret attack, of stealth PR. What DCI built, in *TCS*, was a system to "launder" ideas, as Confessore called the practice. By filtering the positions of corporations through creative and highly readable pundits, DCI could apply a sheen of respectability, of legitimacy, to naked business agendas. McDonald's, by itself, could not criticize Schlosser; it couldn't risk its image, for one, and people would have dismissed what it said anyway, just as they'd ignored what tobacco companies had said about cigarettes. Why would you believe anything *McDonald's* told you about junk food and kids?

But when the idea is separated from the company, when doubts about Schlosser are raised by all sorts of groups that sound well-meaning, and when blogs and discussion forums you're reading keep alerting you to the *TCS* page on Schlosser's sketchy past, well, then, don't you have to wonder? You don't know that McDonald's is part of this campaign. You don't even know there *is* a campaign. So if you're a parent, maybe you pause before picking up *Chew on This*. Or maybe you write a letter to a school. Many did, getting roped in to a machine built by DCI, *TCS*, and McDonald's, without even knowing it.

I can't provide you with anything near an exhaustive catalog of DCI's machinations; to do so would turn this book into a directory of mendacity, and, more to the point, it'd be impossible. Much of what the firm does we do not know. That's the essence of DCI: we hear about its actions only when it slips up in some way, or when canny reporters start nosing around in areas usually left unexplored.

It seems safe to say that DCI created front groups for Microsoft. But what about the fake groups we haven't uncovered? Lobbying firms have become skilled at the tactic, known as "astroturfing,"* and it's unclear how many phony coalitions representing other clients have littered the discourse and altered public policy over the last couple of decades.

Similarly, stories of DCI's political push-polling operations occasionally find a way into the papers. In these schemes, operators call up voters and pretend they're pollsters conducting a survey, but instead of soliciting information, they attack an opponent. DCI seems to have carried out some of the infamous push-polls against John McCain that Bush operatives designed during the 2000 Republican primary in South Carolina. In one poll, operators called McCain "a liar, a cheat, and

---

* The term was coined in 1986 by that font of political quippery, the late Texas senator Lloyd Bentsen.

a fraud." But nobody has ever proved DCI's involvement, and it's likely that nobody ever will. It seems plausible that DCI has conducted other push-polls in other elections. But we don't know of them.

Meanwhile, there's evidence that DCI is slinking further into the digital shadows. Around the time that the film *An Inconvenient Truth* was released in theaters, a short animated video criticizing the Al Gore global warming documentary began to make the rounds on online video-sharing sites. The cartoon was something like a spoof of Gore's famous touring slideshow on climate change, with the former vice president lecturing a bunch of bored penguins on the dangers of carbon emissions—although really the spot was so unfocused and underproduced that it was difficult to know what it was getting at. There seemed to be nothing more sophisticated to it than the joke that Al Gore is wooden and boring (which is not to downplay its rhetorical potential; the joke that Gore is boring has certainly attained a cloying permanence, if late-night TV is a guide).

The video was posted on YouTube by someone going by the handle "toutsmith." He identified himself as a twenty-nine-year-old in California, apparently an ordinary YouTuber, and there was no reason to suspect that he wasn't; anyone of more nefarious connections would probably have offered a more substantive response to Gore's polemic.

But there was something—something very small—that set the penguin video apart from the millions of other amateur political productions vying for attention on the Web. As a *Wall Street Journal* reporter discovered, someone had bought up ads on Google pointing to the penguin movie. Why would a homebrew political agitator take out ads? Because, of course, this wasn't home brew. The *Journal* reporter had a brief e-mail discussion with "toutsmith," and he examined the fellow's messages to see how they'd been routed through the Internet. It turned out that toutsmith's e-mail was coming from a computer belonging to—wait for it—the DCI Group. To this day, though, that's about all we know of the plan. DCI has refused to comment on its role in criticizing the Gore movie (the firm refuses to comment on all of its work). Was the penguin video part of some larger campaign? Are there other DCI-sponsored videos online criticizing Gore? Or are some blogs or MySpace profiles, or video games possibly supported by the firm? And if there were, would we ever know it? How would we ever find out?

The point is not that the DCI Group doesn't tell the truth. What is important is the design and the nature of its lies, and how difficult they are, now, to dig up. Only recently have investigators begun to unearth the awesome reach of the tobacco industry's propaganda operation during the 1980s and 1990s, and the successes have mainly come about because millions of cigarette documents are now public and searchable, a result of government lawsuits against manufacturers. But the players who touted tobacco are now free agents, and they're working in a system that is vastly more sympathetic to their game.

In fact, all we know about any of this is fragmentary. There is a story about how these things work, but we can only guess it. In a suite in Redmond or San Antonio or Dallas or Detroit or Mountain View or Washington, a CEO or a candidate muses on the necessity of confronting a certain public danger.* Here the message gleams; it's simple and direct, maybe as plain as, *We need to get the government off our backs*, or *This movie will be trouble*.

---

* Google, whose motto is "Don't be evil," is among the firms recently known to have hired the DCI Group.

Later, down in Government Affairs, company men versed in minutiae turn musing into strategy, as they outline aims and aspirations, identifying necessary goals: guaranteeing that there are three commissioners supporting the company in the FCC's examination of unbundling obligations of incumbent local exchange carriers, for example, or holding up the effort in Congress on corporate average fuel economy standards. From there, the thing is shipped to a shop like DCI, where the work begins. Eager old hands mold strategy into a full-bore campaign, the effort getting dirty now, coalitions rising out of the swamp. Americans for Economic Progress, People Against Environmental Radicalism, the Committee for Common Sense—each of them is given a staff of experts and prognosticators, souls who clamor for news attention and earnestly press their reps on behalf of the many they say they represent.

There are mailings and newspaper ads, experts are corralled, and, depending on the scope, there might be a phone bank operation, online videos, video news releases, a letter-writing campaign, or manufactured rallies in several cities. The message is sent, too, to the journalistic operation down the hall and to others known to be friendly, and here writers and anchors take to the project with aplomb, making the sponsors' case so elegantly, so convincingly, that people don't even think to ask about connections.

There must be a few lies along the way, certainly. Americans for Economic Progress is really one American, a man in a cubicle in an office on K Street. Coincidentally, it's the same cubicle that houses the Committee for Common Sense. The experts are on the take, and aren't quite experts besides. The videos picture events that are not replicable in reality. The phone bankers are phony. The journalists, well, they've got problems; they'll say anything, those guys.

But these things can be excused, they're not going to matter because all along the way, the connections have been severed: as the message slips away from the company or the candidate, the sponsor recedes from responsibility, and by the time the bloggers get to it, the lie has spread blamelessly throughout. Real people are invested in the message now, actually fighting on its behalf. This is the key, really, to the enterprise. By now, so many have participated so enthusiastically that the message has become a thing of the culture. And when that happens—if you've set up a whole reality that says something false is true, and if so many people have bought into that reality and are even defending it—one has to ask, Is it really even a lie anymore?

Living in a World without Trust

I n 1954, a political scientist named Edward Banfield, his wife, and his two children moved to a poor, underdeveloped village in Southern Italy to live among the peasants. This was a missionary's endeavor, but Banfield, a clear-eyed, rational fellow not known for altruism, was no missionary. His goal instead was to figure out what was wrong with the place—or, to be more precise, what was wrong with its people. Why, when the villagers in the North of Italy were succeeding, had Southern peasants remained peasants, mired in deprivation unseen in most of the Western world?

In nine months of observation, Banfield traced their difficulties to a severe cultural flaw. In Montegrano—the name was fictitious—people simply did not trust each other and therefore could not "act together for their common good or, indeed, for any end transcending the immediate, material interest of the

nuclear family." Life here was brutal and senseless, and to get
ahead, every villager looked out for number one. Banfield saw
these attitudes in every daily interaction. Fathers in Montegrano
taught their sons, "If someone asks you how many goats your
father has, the answer is, you don't know." When women went to
the doctor, they lied about their symptoms, so suspicious were
they of someone else discovering a weakness. A schoolteacher,
asked whether he would report a public official who he found
had taken bribes, told Banfield that he would not, because "there
are so many more dishonest people than honest ones that they
can gang up on you . . . twist the facts so that *you* appear to be
the guilty one."

In *The Moral Basis of a Backward Society*, Banfield's short
book describing his field work there, Montegrano comes to us as
if out of a nightmare. As his title suggests, read today, Banfield's
work smacks of a quaint ethnocentrism; in his introduction, he
wrote that "there is some reason to doubt that non-Western cul-
tures of the world will prove capable of creating and maintaining
the high degree of organization" necessary to create a modern
economy and democratic order. Still, Banfield was clearly on
to something in Montegrano, an idea that sociologists, in the
decades since, have demonstrated through a host of studies and
experiments. Society works better when people trust one another.

This may sound obvious. Clearly, a society ceases to look very
social when people are as suspicious of each other as they are in
Banfield's Montegrano. But even beyond the Hobbesian landscape that Banfield saw in Southern Italy, trust plays a large—a
surprisingly large—role in the well-being of a culture. Countries
where people trust one another typically see higher economic
output than do places where trust is low; this happens because
trust lowers what economists call transactional costs (you've got

to pay fewer bribes, for instance, in a trusting place than in one without trust) and fosters economic cooperation. People are even healthier in trusting societies. In U.S. states where people say they trust each other, death rates are lower than in states where people say they don't. Trust is also a key ingredient in what the political scientist Robert Putnam calls "social capital," which describes the range of interpersonal connections that he says make for vibrant societies.

In a famous 1995 academic article called "Bowling Alone" (and later in a best-selling book), Putnam argued that Americans are pulling out from voluntary civic interaction with each other—since the 1960s, declining numbers participate in associations such as the Elks, the PTA, church groups, and sports groups like bowling leagues; Americans no longer visit one another or go to restaurants together, they play cards less frequently, they give blood in lower numbers, they shun volunteering. And one of the main causes of declining civic participation in the United States—but also one of the symptoms, because the two forces feed into each other—is falling trust.

The United States was once among the most trusting countries in the world, but people no longer feel the same way about their fellow citizens. For decades, pollsters have been gathering data on what sociologists call "generalized trust," which describes, broadly, how likely it is that two strangers from a given community will be willing to trust each other. In 1960, when Americans were asked, "Do you believe that most people can be trusted or can't you be too careful in dealing with people?" nearly 60 percent said they trust most people. The number has plummeted since. By the early 1970s, it dipped below 50 percent. In 1990, it was just below 40 percent. And in 2006, the portion of Americans who said that most people can be trusted was 32 percent, the lowest ever.

Pinning down why Americans don't trust one another anymore has been a matter of considerable and sometimes contentious academic debate. Eric Uslaner, a political scientist at the University of Maryland, says that people are less trusting because they're less optimistic; prior to the 1960s, most Americans thought that their children's lives would be better than their own, but since then, confidence in the future has fallen. And if you're optimistic, you've simply got more reasons to trust people than if you believe the future is bleak.

Putnam, meanwhile, argues that declining social capital has more to do with that perennial hobgoblin of culture, television. People are associating with one another less because they're spending a lot of time watching TV, and they trust each other less because TV distorts their worldview. Other researchers find a host of other causes: that young people are more distrustful because they're abundantly materialistic, or that people don't trust one another because institutions—the government, the media, churches, businesses—have proved, again and again, undeserving of it.

In this book I've explored how modern communications technology has shifted our understanding of the truth. I argue that new information tools haven't merely given us faster and easier access to news, but that they've altered our very grasp on reality. The pulsing medium fosters divergent perceptions about what's actually happening in the world—that is, it lets each of us hold on to different versions of reality.

I've also spent some effort arguing that deception is on the rise—that there are more and better liars today because lying is simply easier. Now, it's true that social trust in the United States has been falling since long before the advent of the Internet, since before even cable TV, so these new things certainly didn't set the slide in motion. But they'll make the picture worse; a medium that makes lying easier, of course, won't foster trust. And although there are examples of trust flourishing online— eBay, for instance—the broad measures of American social trust (plummeting through the 1990s) bear out the idea that new communications tools at least haven't revitalized trust (an idea that, in the early days of the Internet, held many adherents).

My theory that the new medium will contribute to an even greater fall in trust depends on a factor that people who study social capital call *particularized trust*. Whereas generalized trust has to do with what we think of strangers, particularized trust describes how we feel about people who are like us—in our families, in our ethnic groups, in people at our company, or in other groups we may belong to. In terms of civic vibrancy, you can think of particularized trust and generalized trust as "good" and "bad" forms of trust, in the same way that high-density lipoproteins, or HDL, form the "good" cholesterol and LDL is the bad cholesterol. The virtues of trust I mentioned previously—better economic outcomes, and so on—flow from generalized trust.

Particularized trust can't be captured well by surveys, so there is little data on whether it's advancing in the United States. But researchers do know where particularized trust pops up often: small towns, for instance. You might think of the classic American small town as a quintessentially trusting and trustworthy place, a carefree haven where people don't lock their doors, where they watch out for one another, where no one would harm a soul. But that doesn't mean folks there are generally trusting people, says Eric Uslaner. They simply trust *one another*. "Do you remember *The Andy Griffith Show*?" Uslaner asked me. "The small town where everyone was nice and friendly. I was talking to a colleague once who happened to be an Andy Griffith fanatic. He'd watched every episode that ever existed. And he told me about this episode where someone came in from *out* of town. Well—people looked at him as if he had horns. That's the problem with small towns."

Particularized trust destroys generalized trust. The more that people trust those who are like themselves—the more they trust people in their own town, say—the more they distrust strangers. And when particularized trust far outweighs generalized trust, loathsome things happen. For an even starker example than the time a stranger visited Andy Griffith's town of Mayberry, think of the Ku Klux Klan or street gangs or any criminal conspiracy. Uslaner points out that these groups rely on very high levels of trust; as soon as members of a band of thieves stop trusting one another, the jig is up. But their trust is particularized—it's within the group and comes at the expense of trust in strangers. The Klan is, after all, a *secret* conspiracy; people in the Klan don't even trust outsiders enough to allow them to know who's in and who's out.

The people of Montegrano, too, had very high particularized trust. The villagers worried so much for their own families that they couldn't care for anyone in the community. "The world being what it is, all those who stand outside the small circle of the family are at least potential competitors and therefore also potential enemies," Banfield wrote of the villagers' mindset. "Toward those who are not of the family the reasonable attitude is suspicion."

I've cemented this book in a set of case studies—narratives of modern deception, each one, from the story of the Swift Boaters to the saga of the DCI Group, highlighting a particular flaw in the way we talk to one another today. But the problems I've described apply to dozens of stories I haven't covered. Selective exposure, selective perception, the cult of fake experts, and the end of objectivity in the news: these are merely pistons in what has become, today, a powerful engine of propaganda, one that drives nearly all the recent examples of our society's unfettered departure from "the reality-based world."

You can see this engine at the heart of the leading instance of fallacy in our time—the news that dominated the run-up to the Iraq war, a propagandistic effort so thoroughly effective that it subsumes, even today and probably for years to come, nearly every national policy. Begin with the idea that Saddam Hussein was involved in the September 11, 2001, attacks. Then, that he harbored terrorists; that Iraq posed a threat to the nation with weapons of mass destruction; that the threat was imminent; that war would be easy; that war would be cheap; that Iraqis would greet our soldiers as liberators; that Western-style democracy represented the likely postwar path of that country; that war commanders had a plan for instituting such a government; that the fight there had been quickly won; that the *ongoing* fight there was effective; that any insurgents were "foreign fighters," "dead-enders," in their "last throes," and on and on and on, all of the lies folding into one another and forming, for many people, new truths, new realities in which to invest one's soul.

Certainly, the United States and other nations have entered into war on false premises before, but the lies of Iraq spread faster and wider and stuck better than the lies of the past, and it happened for all the reasons I've talked about here. Think of all the "experts" who populated cable news, peddling the idea—based, we learned later, on completely faulty intelligence—that Iraq was dangerous. The press chose to believe them. Meanwhile, credible experts on the other side were pushed out, nowhere to be seen.

In chapter 5, I told you about how news organizations have an incentive to pander to their audiences when the actual truth is hard to discover—and here, in their credulousness toward prowar experts, we saw that mechanism at work. Selective perception, too, took hold. When weapons inspectors reported finding nothing that pointed to WMD in Iraq, we—large numbers of Americans—took that to mean that Saddam was hiding his contraband. We did so, of course, because of our prior conceptions; based on his past behavior, based on our worst fears, rather than on our clearest thoughts. Is that interpretation of reality any more strained than looking at the scene at the Pentagon on the morning of 9/11 and deciding, against all evidence pointing otherwise, that an airliner did not crash there?

But the misperceptions involve not only war. We frequently see myths superseding truth in questions over the validity of science. Reality is splitting over global warming; as the science proving a human cause of climate change grows stronger, conservatives have lately been burrowing deeper into their conviction that it's wrong. In such areas as stem cell science and evolution, religious belief has pushed a minority to sever its ties with empirical fact. It is perfectly okay now for presidential candidates to admit that they do not believe in the scientific theory of evolution—even if you aim for the highest office in the land, you can divorce yourself from truth.

And it's not only us Americans, either. The first 9/11 conspiracy theories took hold in the Arab world, where niche broadcasters transformed latent anti-Western sentiment into far-flung alternative histories of catastrophe. What's ironic is that these media are freer of government control than were the government-run channels that dominated the region in the past, but in this marketplace of information, the satellite Arab channels have seen that the best way to cultivate an audience is to play to home-field cheering squads—no different, really, from what Fox News does.

The underlying story here is this: new communications technology breeds particularized trust. We saw this in chapter 2, when I discussed how people chose information according to their biases; the fans of the Swift Boat Veterans, you could say, had very high particularized trust in those who were offering a view of the Kerry-Vietnam story that was consistent with their own, and their particularized trust worked against their generalized trust in others who pointed out flaws in the Swift Boat allegations.

But really, you can see the same idea in everything I've discussed so far. What's new about today's world is that we've got a choice about which reality to believe. When you look at a picture of a plane slamming into a building, are you going to choose to see the missile that some people say they see in it, or will you choose to see another reality? When you listen to people expound on what happened in the 2004 presidential election, will you trust the authority of those experts who say it was clean or of those who say it wasn't? If nothing on TV news is really objective, will you choose the Bill O'Reilly view of the world or the Lou Dobbs view or the Keith Olbermann view? If every video on YouTube might represent the paid-for ideas of some propagandist trying to sway you, do you choose to believe that the pro-Obama spot your friend just sent you represents a genuine strain of grassroots support for the senator? Or is it just a cookup?

What arises from all this, finally, is the condition Stephen Colbert diagnosed as "truthiness." Truthiness means you choose. But you're not just deciding a reality; you're also deciding to trust that reality—which means deciding to distrust the others. Whenever you choose, you're making a decision to form a particularized trust. This is the essence of the new medium.

Navigating it requires forming bonds with those who are going the same way you are and rejecting those who've decided to see things differently.

Choosing means trusting some people and distrusting the rest. Choose wisely.

Acknowledgments

In the spring of 1987, my family moved from our native South Africa to Southern California, and that has made all the difference. My sister and I were kids then, but I remember still how suddenly transformational the whole thing was; it was as if the change in scenery had jogged some deep-set neuronal assembly, because afterward, following the cliche of America, I began to see everything as newly possible. Writing this book—the very idea of writing as a career—has only been an option for me because my family, those many years ago, took that leap into the unknown. That they did it despite numerous hardships means the world to me. It's why this book is for them.

True Enough began more recently in the summer of 2004, when I received an e-mail from a literary agent asking me if I'd like to write a book. I politely declined, citing a lack of ideas and an attenuated attention span. Fortunately that agent, Larry Weissman, has a knack for persuasion. Larry had read some of my previous magazine articles and thought one of them—about the fragility of photographic truth in the digital age—might be the tip of a much bigger idea. I'm enormously grateful to Larry for helping me develop it, and after having done the thing, I'm glad I listened to him.

Eric Nelson, at Wiley, has been an astute and patient editor—astute in quickly getting the essence of my idea, and patient during the many silent months in which I set about putting it to paper.

True Enough benefited from many generous people willing to spend long hours with me discussing the campaigns they took part in, the research they've produced, and their unconventional beliefs. Given my premise, some of my sources were understandably wary of participating; I'm grateful that they decided to talk to me despite their reservations. The San Francisco Public Library and the U.C. Berkeley library have my enduring appreciation for the train of books they allowed me to divert to my apartment; Google, meanwhile, should be medaled for finding a way to grease the wheels of that train with its ingenious Books and Scholar search engines.

There are loads of others without whom this book could never have come about, especially David Talbot, Joan Walsh, Andrew Leonard, Scott Rosenberg, and Kevin Berger, the *Salon* editors who hired me, trusted and defended me as a writer, and, later, allowed me the time to work on this. I am indebted also to Erin O'Connell for, in addition to so much else, helping me to pursue the plan at all. Several friends read drafts and offered comments as the book unfolded. For their thoughts and ideas, I thank Katharine Mieszkowski, Page Rockwell, Cary Tennis, as well as, again, Andrew and Scott.

Finally, Helen Bailey deserves accolades enough to fill another book entirely. My first reader, my closest editor, my keenest taskmaster, Helen was the wonderbug I kept in mind during much of the writing. She helped me through some of the toughest spots and made the easy parts even easier, and I can't imagine the slog it would have been without her. Thank you, Helen.

Notes

Introduction

2 *Late in April 2005*   For more on Christine Maggiore, see Charles Ornstein and Daniel Costello, "A Mother's Denial, a Daughter's Death," *Los Angeles Times*, September 24, 2005; "Did HIV-Positive Mom's Beliefs Put Her Children at Risk?" *ABC News*, December 8, 2005. Eliza Jane Scovill's autopsy report is available online at www.aidstruth.org/ejs-coroner-report.pdf.

5 *The "controversy" over*   See T. C. Smith and S. P. Novella (2007), "HIV Denial in the Internet Era." PLoS Med 4(8): e256; Angela Hutchinson, Elin Begley, Patrick Sullivan, Hollie Clark, Brian Boyett, Scott Kellerman, "Conspiracy Beliefs and Trust in Information about HIV/AIDS Among Minority Men Who Have Sex with Men," *Journal of Acquired Immune Deficiency Syndromes*, August 2007, 45(5)15:603–605; Laura Bogart, Sheryl Thorburn, "Are HIV/AIDS Conspiracy Beliefs a Barrier to HIV Prevention Among African Americans?" *Journal of Acquired Immune Deficiency Syndromes*, February 2005, 38(2)1: 213–218.

1. "Reality" Is Splitting

9 *In April 2004*   My narrative of the Swift Boat Veterans' early days is informed chiefly by interviews with Merrie Spaeth. John O'Neill, one of the leaders of the group, declined to talk to me. Also very helpful was Pamela Colloff's oral history of the group. See Pamela Colloff, "Sunk," *Texas Monthly* (January 2005): 100.

A law review article by Arthur May, a professor of media studies at George Washington University, led me to the fact that the mainstream press ignored the group in its early months. See Arthur L. May, "Swift

Boat Vets in 2004: Press Coverage of an Independent Campaign,"
First Amendment Law Review, University of North Carolina School
of Law 4 (2006): 66–106.

15 *Like many on the right*   In September 1981, shortly after the *Wash-*
ington Star closed down, the *Washington Post's* daily circulation stood
at 725,000. As of April 2007, its average weekday circulation was
699,000, according to the Audit Bureau of Circulation—down about
4 percent. For more, see Associated Press, "Papers Increase Capital Coverage," September 16, 1981; and Burrelles Luce, "Top 100
U.S. Daily Newspapers," available online at www.burrellesluce.com/
top100/2007_Top_100List.pdf, last accessed September 25, 2007.

16 *This trend toward niches*   The first and best book to explore the
potential negative effect of personalized niche media on culture is
by the law professor Cass Sunstein. See Cass Sunstein, *Republic.com*
(Princeton, NJ: Princeton University Press, 2001).

   For more adulatory coverage of niche culture, see Chris Anderson, *The Long Tail: Why the Future of Business Is Selling Less of More*
(New York: Hyperion, 2006).

18 *To understand what I mean*   For more on how news logos affect
news perception, see Shanto Iyengar and Richard Morin, "Red Media,
Blue Media: Evidence for a Political Litmus Test in Online News
Readership," *Washington Post*, May 3, 2006.

20 *My guess about how*   See the National Annenberg Election Survey
press release "Cable and Talk Radio Boost Public Awareness of Swift
Boat Ad, National Annenberg Election Survey Shows," August 20,
2004.

22 *Shared truth are absent*   For more on Americans' beliefs about Sad-
dam Hussein's involvement in 9/11, see Dana Milbank and Claudia
Deane, "Hussein Link to 9/11 Lingers in Many Minds," *Washing-*
ton Post, September 6, 2003; Steven Lee Myers and Megan Thee,
"Americans Feel Military Is Best at Ending the War," *New York Times*,
September 10, 2007.

   The Harris survey on Americans' beliefs about weapons of
mass destruction is available online at www.harrisinteractive.com/
harris_poll/index.asp?PID=684, last accessed September 25, 2007.

   For more on global warming, see Naomi Oreskes, "Beyond the
Ivory Tower: The Scientific Consensus on Climate Change," *Science*
306, no. 5702: 1686. Pew's poll on global warming is available online at
http://people-press.org/reports/display.php3?ReportID=280, last accessed September 25, 2007.

The Pew Center's analysis of Americans' fracturing views on the economy is available online at http://people-press.org/reports/display .php3?ReportID=268, last accessed September 25, 2007.

2. The New Tribalism: Swift Boats and the Power of Choosing

29 *Brock and Balloun's experiment*:   Selective exposure has had a controversial history; after Leon Festinger proposed the idea, some experiments failed to support its existence. The best survey of the many studies—the failures as well as the successes—can be found in John L. Cotton, "Cognitive Dissonance in Selective Exposure," in Dolf Zillmann and Jennings Bryant, eds., *Selective Exposure to Communication* (Hillsdale, NJ: L. Erlbaum Associates, 1985).

For the cigarette study, see Timothy Brock and Joe Balloun, "Behavioral Receptivity to Dissonant Information," *Journal of Personality and Social Psychology* 6 (August 1964): 413–428.

Also see Lauren Slater, Opening Skinner's Box: Great Psychological Experiments of the Twentieth Century (New York: W. W. Norton, 2004).

33 *But the normal rules*:   For John O'Neill's "tap code" comment, see John J. Miller, "What the Swifties wrought: the power of an ad campaign," *National Review*, November 29, 2004.

41 *To understand this difference*   See Aaron Lowin, "Approach and Avoidance: Alternate Modes of Selective Exposure to Information," *Journal of Personality and Social Psychology* 6 (May 1967): 1–9; and Aaron Lowin, "Further Evidence for an Approach-Avoidance Interpretation of Selective Exposure," *Journal of Experimental Social Psychology* 5 (July 1969): 265–271.

46 *In the 2000 election*   See Shanto Iyengar, Kyu Hahn, and Markus Prior, "Has Technology Made Attention to Political Campaigns More Selective? An Experimental Study of the 2000 Presidential Campaign," prepared for presentation at the Annual Meeting of the American Political Science Association, San Francisco, September 2, 2001.

For more on bloggers' networks, see Lada Adamic and Natalie Glance, "The Political Blogosphere and the 2004 U.S. Election: Divided They Blog," Annual Workshop on the Weblogging Ecosystem, www.blogpulse.com/papers/2005/AdamicGlanceBlogWWW .pdf, Japan.

49 *To look into the question*   For more on wartime efforts to change American food habits, see Brian Wansink, "Changing Eating Habits

on the Home Front: Lost Lessons from World War II Research," *Journal of Public Policy and Marketing* 21, no. 1 (2002): 90–99. Kurt Lewin's paper on his efforts to convince housewives to serve organ meat is available online at http://print.nap.edu/pdf/ARC000024/pdf_image/35.pdf, last accessed on September 25, 2007.

52 *Numerous experiments with small groups*:   For more on green soldiers adjusting to the "social reality" see, Samuel Andrew Stouffer, "The American Soldier: Combat and Its Aftermath," (Princeton: Princeton University Press, 1949). For more on Kurt Lewin's ideas on social reality as well as the propinquity effect, see Elihu Katz and Paul Lazarsfeld, *Personal Influence: The Part Played by People in the Flow of Mass Communications* (Glencoe, Ill.: Free Press, 1955).

3. Trusting Your Senses: Selective Perception and 9/11

59 *"Boom!"*   Philip Jayhan's "Boom!" quotes come from an interview he did with Jack Stratia on August 11, 2005. Audio for the interview can be found online at www.harmonymindbodyspirit.com/stratia.shtml, last accessed September 24, 2007.

65 *Psychologists call these*   For more on flashbulb memories, see Yadin Dudai's *Memory from A to Z: Keywords, Concepts, and Beyond* (Oxford: Oxford University Press, 2004).

The Zogby poll was paid for by 911Truth.org, an organization that questions the official story of the attacks. Survey questions can be found on the Web here: www.911truth.org/page.php?page=zogby_2006, last accessed September 24, 2007. Further details on the Ohio University 9/11 poll are available at www.newspolls.org/question.php?question_id=716, last accessed September 24, 2007.

68 *The results were remarkable*:   For more on selective perception, see Albert Hastorf and Hadley Cantril, "They Saw a Game," *Journal of Abnormal and Social Psychology* 49, 1 (1954); and Neil Vidmar and Milton Rokeach, "Archie Bunker's Bigotry: A Study in Selective Perception and Exposure," *Journal of Communication* 24, no. 1 (March 1974): 36–47.

76 *The most powerful proof*   The most-detailed refutation of Jayhan's missile-on-the-plane 9/11 theory can be found in Eric and Brian Salter's article "Analysis of Flight 175 'Pod' and Related Claims," on the Web at www.questionsquestions.net/WTC/pod.html, last accessed September 24, 2007. The online discussion group feting Jayhan's theory is found at www.democraticunderground.com/

discuss/duboard.php?az=view_all&address=125x8515, last accessed September 24, 2007.

84 *Otherwise, you can guiltlessly*:   For more on the Ted Boudreaux picture, Ken Light, and the malleability of photos, see my article (which, incidentally, sparked the idea for this book) "A Picture Is No Longer Worth a Thousand Words," April 22, 2004, published on Salon.com and available at http://archive.salon.com/tech/feature/2004/04/22/doctored_photos/index. html, last accessed September 24, 2007. Also, see Steve Casimiro, "Can Digital Photos Be Trusted?" published in *Popular Science* and available at www.popsci.com/popsci/technology/generaltechnology/d6002684e4646010vgnvcm1000004eecbccdrcrd. html, last accessed September 24. 2007.

88 *Both versions of* Loose Change   For more on *Loose Change*, see my article "The 9/11 Deniers," published in Salon.com on June 22, 2006, available at www.salon.com/ent/feature/2006/06/27/911_conspiracies/index.html, last accessed September 24, 2007. Also see Nancy Jo Sales, "Click Here for Conspiracy," *Vanity Fair* (August 2006).

  The best analysis of the film is "Sifting through *Loose Change*," put together by Jim Hoffman, who questions the official story of 9/11 but believes *Loose Change* does a disservice to the "truth movement." See the analysis at http://911research.wtc7.net/reviews/loose_change/index.html, last accessed September 24, 2007.

94 *The Warren Commission's*   For an analysis of the Warren Commission's use of classified documents, see Kermit L. Hall, "The Kennedy Assassination in the Age of Open Secrets," *Organization of American Historians Newsletter* 25 (February 1997).

4. Questionable Expertise: The Stolen Election and the Men Who Push It

99 *They dug for evidence*:   See Robert F. Kennedy Jr., "Was the 2004 Election Stolen?" *Rolling Stone* (June 2006). Other claims that the GOP stole the 2004 election can be found in Mark Crispin Miller, *Fooled Again: How the Right Stole the 2004 Election and Why They'll Steal the Next One Too (Unless We Stop Them)* (New York: Basic Books, 2005).

  I investigated many of these claims. See my articles "Don't Get 'Fooled Again,'" November 14, 2005, Salon.com, http://dir.salon.com/story/books/review/2005/11/14/miller/index.html, last accessed September 24, 2007; "Was the 2004 Election Stolen? No." June 3,

2006, Salon.com, www.salon.com/news/feature/2006/06/03/kennedy, last accessed September 24, 2007. A colloquy between me and Kennedy, "Was the 2004 Election Stolen?" June 6, 2006, www.salon.com/opinion/feature/2006/06/06/rfk_responds/, last accessed September 24, 2007.

See Mark Crispin Miller's criticism of me and of Salon, "Some Might Call It Treason: An Open Letter to *Salon*," June 16, 2006, *Huffington Post*, www.huffingtonpost.com/mark-crispin-miller/some-might-call-it-treaso_b_23187.html, last accessed September 24, 2007.

Also on this topic, see Mark Hertsgaard, "Was Ohio Stolen in 2004 or Wasn't It?" *Mother Jones* (November/December 2005).

103 *The pattern, indeed*:   See Benjamin I. Page, Robert Y. Shapiro, and Glenn R. Dempsey, "What Moves Public Opinion?" *American Political Science Review* 81, no. 1 (March 1987): 23–44. For more on expertise and public opinion, see Page and Shapiro, *The Rational Public: Fifty Years of Trends in Americans' Policy Preferences* (Chicago: University of Chicago Press, 1992), 347–348, 358–359.

107 *Surveys suggest that*   A Zogby survey—sponsored by those who question the 2004 election—found 32.4 percent of respondents "not at all confident that [Bush] won fair and square." See more at www.scoop.co.nz/stories/HL0609/S00346.htm, last accessed September 24, 2007.

112 *"This was a case"*   For more on Kathy Dopp's op-scan county theories, see Thom Hartmann, "Evidence Mounts That the Vote May Have Been Hacked," *Common Dreams*, November 6, 2004, www.commondreams.org/headlines04/1106-30.htm, last accessed September 24, 2007. See also Walter Mebane, Jasjeet Sekhon, and Jonathan Wand's rebuttal, published online at http://www-personal.umich.edu/~wmebane/commondreams/commondreams.html, last accessed September 24, 2007.

115 *John Ware became deeply*:   For more on the Doctor Fox effect, see Donald H. Naftulin, John E. Ware Jr., and Frank A. Donnelly, "The Doctor Fox Lecture: A Paradigm of Educational Seduction," *Journal of Medical Education* 48 (July 1973): 630–635; John E. Ware and Reed G. Williams, "The Doctor Fox Effect: A Study of Lecturer Effectiveness and Ratings of Instruction," *Journal of Medical Education* (February 1975): 149–156; and John E. Ware and Reed

G. Williams, "An Extended Visit with Dr. Fox: Validity of Student Satisfaction with Instruction Ratings after Repeated Exposures to a Lecturer," *American Educational Research Journal* 14, no. 4 (Autumn 1977): 449–457.

For more on peripheral and central processing, see John Cacioppo and Richard Petty, "Effects of Message Repetition and Position on Cognitive Response, Recall, and Persuasion," *Journal of Personality and Social Psychology* 37 (1979): 97–109.

For more on the recognition heuristic, see Daniel G. Goldstein and Gerd Gigerenzer, "Models of Ecological Rationality: The Recognition Heuristic," *Psychological Review* 109, no. 1 (2002): 75–90.

For more on how comprehensibility affects how we look at experts, see S. Ratneshwar and Shelly Chaiken, "Comprehension's Role in Persuasion: The Case of Its Moderating Effect on the Persuasive Impact of Source Cues," *Journal of Consumer Research* 18, no. 1 (June 1991): 52–62.

136 *Here, then, is your decision*   See Steve Freeman and Joel Bleifuss, *Was The 2004 Presidential Election Stolen? Exit Polls, Election Fraud, and the Official Count* (New York: Seven Stories Press, 2006).

For the Election Science Institute's study of the 2004 Ohio exit polls, see Susan Kyle, Douglas A. Samuelson, Fritz Scheuren, and Nicole Vicinanza with Scott Dingman and Warren Mitofsky, "Ohio 2004 Exit Polls: Explaining the Discrepancy," June 6, 2005, http://electionscience.org/Members/stevenhertzberg/report.2005–07–19.7420722886/view, last accessed September 24, 2007.

Warren Mitofsky's official explanation of what went wrong in the 2004 exit poll can be found at www.vote.caltech.edu/media/documents/EvaluationJan192005.pdf, last accessed September 24, 2007. His analysis of exit poll failures in previous elections is in "Voter News Service after the Fall," *Public Opinion Quarterly* 67 (2003): 45–58.

For more on the effects of media logos and exit polling, see Murray Edelman and Daniel M. Merkle, "The Impact of Interviewer Characteristics and Election Day Factors on Exit Poll Data Quality," paper presented at the annual conference of the American Association for Public Opinion Research, Fort Lauderdale, Florida, 1995.

For the Election Science Institute's study of the 2004 Ohio exit polls, see Susan Kyle, Douglas A. Samuelson, Fritz Scheuren, and Nicole Vicinanza with Scott Dingman and Warren Mitofsky, "Ohio 2004 Exit Polls: Explaining the Discrepancy," June 6, 2005, http://electionscience.org/Members/stevenhertzberg/report.2005–07–19.7420722886/view, last accessed September 24, 2007.

Mark Lindeman's response to Freeman et. al, "Beyond Exit Poll Fundamentalism," is available online at http://inside.bard.edu/ ~lindeman/beyond-epf.pdf, last accessed September 25, 2007. The pollster Mark Blumenthal's exhaustive analysis of Kennedy's theories, "Is RFK, Jr. Right about Exit Polls?" is published online at www.mysterypollster.com/main/2006/06/is_rfk_jr_right.html, last accessed September 24, 2007.

Charles Stewart's analysis of the differences between exit polls in the Ukraine versus the United States, "Addendum to Voting Machines and the Underestimate of the Bush Vote," December 5, 2004, can be found at www.vote.caltech.edu/media/documents/ Addendum_Voting_Machines_Bush_Vote.pdf, last accessed September 24, 2007.

All of the papers I mention by Walter Mebane are available at his Web site, www-personal.umich.edu/~wmebane/, last accessed September 24, 2007. I focus on research published in the following: "Election Forensics: The Second-Digit Benford's Law Test and Recent American Presidential Elections," delivered at the Election Fraud Conference, Salt Lake City, Utah, September 29–30, 2006; "Voting Machine Allocation in Franklin County, Ohio, 2004: Response to U.S. Department of Justice Letter of June 29, 2005"; Walter R. Mebane Jr. and Michael C. Herron, "Ohio 2004 Election: Turnout, Residual Votes and Votes in Precincts and Wards." Included in Section VI of Democratic National Committee Voting Rights Institute Report, "Democracy at Risk: The 2004 Election in Ohio"; "The Wrong Man Is President! Overvotes in the 2000 Presidential Election in Florida," *Perspectives on Politics* (September 2004); Jonathan N. Wand, Kenneth W. Shotts, Jasjeet S. Sekhon, Walter R. Mebane Jr., Michael C. Herron, and Henry E. Brady, "The Butterfly Did It: The Aberrant Vote for Buchanan in Palm Beach County, Florida," *American Political Science Review* (December 2001).

5. The Twilight of Objectivity, or What's the Matter with Lou Dobbs?

146 *Now, many of CNN's*   For more on the changes at CNN, see Ken Auletta, "Mad as Hell," *New Yorker*, December 4, 2006.

148 *But Pew's statistics*   See Pew Research Center for the People and the Press, "2006 Pew Research Center for the People and

the Press News Consumption and Believability Study," available online at http://people-press.org/reports/pdf/282.pdf, last accessed September 24, 2007.

149 *In order to understand*   The relevant research by Lee Ross and Mark Lepper is as follows: Charles Lord, Lee Ross, and Mark Lepper, "Biased Assimilation and Attitude Polarization: The Effects of Prior Theories on Subsequently Considered Evidence," *Journal of Personality and Social Psychology* 37, no. 11 (1979): 2098–2109; Robert Vallone, Lee Ross and Mark Lepper, "The Hostile Media Phenomenon: Biased Perception and Perceptions of Media Bias in Coverage of the Beirut Massacre," *Journal of Personality and Social Psychology* 49, no. 3 (1985): 577–585.

For more on naive realism, see Lee Ross and Andrew Ward, *Naive Realism: Implications for Social Conflict and Misunderstanding* (Stanford Center on Conflict and Negotiation, 1994).

156 *Alterman called his book*   See Eric Alterman, What Liberal Media? The Truth about Bias and the News (New York: Basic Books, 2003).

160 *"The Mac people . . . "*   See David Pogue's review of Windows Vista, "Vista Wins on Looks. As for Lacks . . . ," *New York Times*, December 14, 2006. His review of the iPod Nano is "IPod's Law: The Impossible Is Possible," *New York Times*, September 15, 2005.

165 *In his 1985 autobiography*   See Henry Regnery, *Memoirs of a Dissident Publisher* (Washington, DC: Regnery Publishing, 1985). Among Regnery's seminal publications are Freda Utley, *The High Cost of Vengeance* (Chicago: Henry Regnery Company, 1949); William F. Buckley, *God and Man at Yale: The Superstitions of "Academic Freedom"* (Chicago: Regnery Publishing, 1951); Russell Kirk, *The Conservative Mind: From Burke to Eliot* (Chicago: Regnery Publishing, 1953); Gary Aldrich, *Unlimited Access: An FBI Agent Inside the Clinton White House* (Washington, DC: Regnery Publishing, 1996); Mark Fuhrman, *Murder in Brentwood* (Washington, DC: Regnery Publishing, 1997); Bernard Goldberg, *Bias: A CBS Insider Exposes How the Media Distort the News* (Washington, DC: Regnery Publishing, 2001); John O'Neill and Jerome Corsi, *Unfit for Command: Swift Boat Veterans Speak Out against John Kerry* (Washington, DC: Regnery Publishing, 2004).

Also see David Brock, *Blinded by the Right: The Conscience of an Ex-Conservative* (New York: Crown, 2002); and Deborah E.

Lipstadt, *Denying the Holocaust: The Growing Assault on Truth and Memory* (New York: Free Press, 1993).

172 *Dobbs, in his book* See Lou Dobbs, War on the Middle Class: How the Government, Big Business, and Special Interest Groups Are Waging War on the American Dream and How to Fight Back (New York: Viking Adult, 2006).

174 *Gentzkow points out* See Matthew Gentzkow and Jesse Shapiro, "Media Bias and Reputation," *Journal of Political Economy* 114, no. 2 (2006).

6. "Truthiness" Everywhere

185 *Only the people at home* Robin Raskin's promotional videos can be found on the Web site of the Center for Media and Democracy, which gathered the majority of the VNRs and the SMTs I cite in this chapter. The center's two reports on these practices are available online at www.prwatch.org/fakenews/execsummary and www.prwatch.org/fakenews2/execsummary, last accessed September 24, 2007.

189 *But early in 2006* See www.thesmokinggun.com, "A Million Little Lies: Exposing James Frey's Fiction Addiction," January 8, 2006.

191 *This was a reference* See Ron Suskind, "Faith, Certainty and the Presidency of George W. Bush," *New York Times Magazine*, October 17, 2004.

199 *The Radio and Television* See the Radio and Television News Directors Association's response to the CMD study at www.rtnda.org/foi/vnr_study.pdf, last accessed May 10, 2007.

201 *The news makes a pitch* For more on how viewers react to VNRs, see Anne R. Owen and James A. Karrh, "Video News Releases: Effects on Viewer Recall and Attitudes," *Public Relations Review* 22 (1996): 369–378.

207 *MBD asked hundreds* See Dorie E. Apollonio and Lisa A. Bero, "The Creation of Industry Front Groups: The Tobacco Industry and Get Government Off Our Back," *American Journal of Public Health*, 97, no. 3 (1997): 419–427. For more on Philip Morris's "sound science" campaign, see Elisa Ong and Stanton Glantz, "Constructing 'Sound Science' and 'Good Epidemiology': Tobacco, Lawyers, and Public Relations Firms," *American Journal of Public Health* 91, no. 11 (2001): 1749–1757.

Epilogue: Living in a World without Trust

222 *In* The Moral Basis   For more on the people of Montegrano, see Edward Banfield, *The Moral Basis of a Backward Society* (Chicago: Research Center in Economic Development and Cultural Change, University of Chicago, 1958).

See also Robert Putnam, *Bowling Alone: The Collapse and Revival of American Community* (New York: Simon & Schuster, 2006).

Index

CPSIA information can be obtained
at www.ICGtesting.com
Printed in the USA
JSHW040847300820
7499JS00001B/12